The
TRUMPETER SWAN

Frontispiece: A pair of trumpeters in flight over their breeding grounds on the Red Rock Lakes Refuge, southwestern Montana.

The
TRUMPETER SWAN

ITS HISTORY, HABITS, AND
POPULATION IN THE UNITED STATES

By

Winston E. Banko

UNIVERSITY OF NEBRASKA PRESS / LINCOLN AND LONDON

First printed by the
United States Department of the Interior,
Fish and Wildlife Service,
April 30, 1960

First Bison Book Printing: 1980

Most recent printing indicated by first digit below:

1   2   3   4   5   6   7   8   9   10

Library of Congress Cataloging in Publication Data
Banko, Winston E
  The trumpeter swan.

  "A Bison book."
  Reprint of the 1960 ed. published by U.S. Fish and
Wildlife Service, Washington, which was issued as no.
63 of North American fauna.
  Bibliography: p. 189
  Includes index.
  1. Trumpeter swan. 2. Birds—United States. I.
Title. II. Series: North American fauna ; no. 63.
[QL155.A4 no. 63, 1980] [QL696.A52] 591.97s
ISBN 0–8032–6057–1 (pbk.) [598.4'1] 80–12533

Manufactured in the United States of America

CONTENTS

ILLUSTRATIONS

Page

TABLES

ILLUSTRATION CREDITS

Credits for illustrations are as follows: Frontispiece and figures 7–14, 18–20, 24–37, 42, 45–47, Winston E. Banko; figures 2 and 44, Cecil Wetmore; figures 4 and 17, Mel Monson; figure 16, David de Lancey Condon; figures 23 and 43, W. Verde Watson; figure 38, U. S. Fish and Wildlife Service; drawings in figures 21 and 22, Mrs. P. W. Parmalee; maps and other illustrations, Shirley A. Briggs.

FOREWORD

The appeal of swans to man throughout history has come down to us in legend, custom and in many forms of art. That the world's largest species of this storied bird should have become nearly extinct in its native North America was thus especially tragic. The continuing recovery in numbers of this beautiful and graceful symbol of American wilderness is a major accomplishment in wildlife preservation.

The establishment of the Red Rock Lakes Migratory Waterfowl Refuge was the climax of this effort in the United States, and any study of the trumpeter swan necessarily focuses on the Refuge and the adjoining country. In this magnificent mountainous setting a few of the swans had survived, and the remoteness of the country has made it possible to maintain the wilderness environment favored by the birds.

The present United States population of trumpeters is found mainly in a 60-mile radius encompassing parts of southwestern Montana where the Refuge is found, eastern Idaho, and northwestern Wyoming, including Yellowstone National Park.

This report on the trumpeter evolved from studies made from 1948 to 1957 when I served first as an assistant and later as manager, of the Red Rock Lakes Refuge. I have also drawn extensively on the records of the National Park Service, the U. S. Fish and Wildlife Service, and the National Museum in Washington, D. C. Other pertinent information bearing on the life history of the trumpeter swan in the United States has been extracted from published articles, unpublished reports and records, firsthand accounts and correspondence. This account includes a historical record of this bird in the United States and Alaska, an outline of its habits and characteristics in its native Rocky Mountain environment, and furnishes information necessary to guide its future.

A comparable study of the trumpeter by the Canadian Wildlife Service has also been underway since about 1950. These investigations are being conducted chiefly in British Columbia and Alberta by Mr. Ronald H. Mackay, Wildlife Biologist, who made available some preliminary results of swan banding studies in Alberta, and was helpful in many other ways. For the most part, I have dealt with the trumpeter in Canada only in a general way since the Canadian findings will probably be published later.

I wish to express my appreciation for the cooperation received over the years from the many individuals and agencies who furnished information useful in preparing this report. Generally, acknowledgment for this has been handled directly in the text, but special thanks and credit are due to several individuals.

Edmund B. Rogers, former Superintendent, and David de Lancey Condon, Chief Naturalist, Yellowstone National Park, generously opened the Park files to me and furnished every help possible. Condon and Walter H. Kittams, Park Biologist, reviewed the manuscript in its final stages.

James Rooney of Yakima, Washington, supplied valuable bibliographic assistance. Lowell Adams, U. S. Fish and Wildlife Service, also gave an early review and critique of the MS.

The information regarding the geological background of Red Rock Lakes, Montana, was supplied by Dr. George Kennedy, Geophysicist,

University of California, who has an intimate knowledge of this region.

Dr. Herbert K. Friedmann, U. S. National Museum, provided the technical physical descriptions of both species `of swans native to North America from an unpublished manuscript.

Joseph Flakne, Programming Director, and Marie Tremaine, Chief Bibliographer, Arctic Institute of North America, provided for an inquiry into the possible role of the swans in the economic life of Alaska before acquisition by the United States, and made available interesting and scattered notes regarding Old World swans in arctic Russia.

H. Albert Hochbaum, Director, and Dr. Frank McKinney, Assistant Director, Delta Waterfowl Research Station, reviewed the manuscript and were generous with helpful comments and suggestions. Dr. McKinney, and indirectly, Paul Johnsgard of Cornell University, supplied me with the English translation (Johnsgard) of O. Heinroth's (1911) classic German work on the ethology and psychology of the Anatidae.

I am grateful to several residents of the Red Rock Lakes region who contributed to the historical aspect of this work. Credit and thanks are due the following residents of Monida, Montana: Cecil Wetmore, James F. and Alta Hanson, and A. Blaine Fordyce. Sam A. Trude of Island Park, Idaho, furnished information on that area in the early 1900's.

In the Branch of Wildlife Research, Earl L. Atwood, Chief Biometrician, Patuxent Research Refuge, assisted in determining the significance of the population statistics.

In the Branch of Wildlife Refuges, special recognition is due Richard E. Griffith for his particular interest in the manuscript work which extended over a period of many years. In a large measure his patient and unflagging support made this report possible. The final draft was typed under the direction of Miss Winifred G. Baum, who deserves mention for positive action when time counted most. I am also greatly indebted to Dr. Ray Erickson and Miss Shirley A. Briggs for their tireless efforts in checking and editing the final draft, work made especially difficult under the prevailing deadline.

It is impossible to mention everyone who has been helpful in preparing this report.

WINSTON E. BANKO.

MAY 1, 1958.

INTRODUCTION

LEGEND AND TRADITION

Of all the earth's varied avian forms, the swans have been woven into the cultural expressions of previous civilizations to a greater extent than any other group of birds, with the exception perhaps of the birds of prey. With their great size, migratory habits, graceful manner, and distinctive voice, the majestic swans have apparently inspired all the peoples who knew them.

No doubt our more primitive ancestors were most interested in swans because of their value for food. Although wild swans were apparently never preferred, their availability and size caused them to be taken when other sources of meat were short. As man gradually developed a regard for spiritual values, swans were employed as an important symbolic element in the myths and religious ceremonies of many of the early cultures. This was true not only among the early peoples of northern Slavic or Nordic origin, but also in the regions along the Mediterranean where the long migrations of some of the northern-reared swans terminated.

Although there is frequent mention of swans in Greek mythology, they were apparently not included among the many varieties of birds and animals commonly kept by the Romans. Swans were known to the ancient Egyptians and to the early Christian prophets. In early canons, the latter listed swans among the birds and animals which were not to be eaten.

The use of swans as common subjects in story, myth, and ceremony was most prominent in the culture of the more northern races of mankind, where these birds entered into the ceremonies of the shamans of the East, the wizard men of Lapland, and the medicine men of our

4

own native Indians (Beebe, 1906: 159). The notable interest of the ancients in these distinctive fowl grew with the passing of centuries. This later expressed itself in the widely prevalent Eurasian "swan-maiden" legend, and more tangibly in such items as some of the early coins of Germany and the badge of Henry IV of England.

Many of the legends which slowly evolved out of early European swan mythology are perpetuated in the fairy tales, customs, and traditions of certain countries, being now for the most part only relics of a forgotten age. "Swan upping" (the taking up of swans for the purpose of pinioning and marking) is still practiced annually upon the Thames River. Records of the English interest in swans date back over 800 years to the 12th century A. D. during which the complications of swan ownership resulted in the enactment of special laws and regulations. After 40 years of study, Norman F. Ticehurst (1957) has thoroughly documented the long and interesting history of the mute swans in England.

Swans have been accorded a special place in the folklore, history, literature, drama, arts, and musical expressions of contemporary peoples as well. In fact, it is difficult to name a medium of man's expression that does not owe a modicum of debt to these birds. In this respect the swans as a group are unique in the bird world.

It is evident therefore that much of the present interest in these noble birds stems in part from the traditions of many previous civilizations and peoples, extending far back into history. With this heritage in mind, we have a responsibility for the welfare of this group of birds, and must perpetuate such living symbols of beauty and grace for the enjoyment and inspiration of generations yet to follow.

DESCRIPTION AND SYSTEMATICS

The swans are similarly specialized waterfowl of the diverse and prolific family of the Anatidae, and as such they have been given status as a subfamily, the Cygninae. This group of waterfowl is characterized by necks as long as, or longer than, the large heavy body, and short strong legs and feet equipped with large webs and prominent nails. This combination of characteristics adapts them well for a specialized shallow-water existence, in which they consume large quantities of leafy aquatic plants, and dig and root out succulent rootstocks and tubers.

With the exception of the black swan of Australia (*Chenopis atratus*) and the black-necked swan of South America (*Cygnus melancoriphus*), the adult plumage of all species of swans is entirely white. With the further exception of the common mute swan of Europe (*Cygnus olor*), which possesses a prominent knob at the base of the upper mandible in common with the black-necked swan, the remaining four species are all smooth-billed (that is without a basal knob), white-plumaged, distinctive-voiced swans with an exclusively circumpolar distribution. A general account of the characteristics, distribution, and habits of all species of swans, with emphasis on their traits and requirements in captivity is given by Jean Delacour (1954: 57–90). In this work, the plumage and appearance of both adults and cygnets have been accurately portrayed in full color by Peter Scott.

The division of the swans of the world into 3 genera, 2 subgenera, and 7 species is generally accepted as most nearly logical and correct (Wetmore, 1951: 338). The systematics of the swans will not be treated here. (See appendix 1.)

Using Wetmore's classification of the swans, which has been adopted by the American Ornithologists' Union, the classification and current principal distribution of the swans is outlined in table 1. The status, distribution, migration and habits of mute, Bewick's, and whooping swan populations in Eurasia are treated by Alfred Hilprecht (1956: 8–17), Witherby et al. (1939: 168–179), and G. P. Dementiev and N. A. Gladkov (1952).

Table 1.—Classification of the subfamily Cygninae

Scientific name	Common name	Principal distribution	
		Breeding	Wintering
Olor cygnus (Linnaeus)_____	Whooper Swan_____	Northern and middle Eurasia.	Southern and middle Eurasia.
Olor bewickii Yarrell_____	Bewick's Swan_____	Northern Eurasia_____	Southern and middle Eurasia.
Olor columbianus (Ord)_____	Whistling Swan_____	Northern North America.	Southern and middle North America.
Olor buccinator (Richardson)_	Trumpeter Swan_____	Northern and middle North America.	Middle North America.
Cygnus olor (Gmelin)_____	Mute Swan_____	Northern and Middle Eurasia.	Southern and middle Eurasia.
Cygnus melancoriphus (Molina).	Black-necked Swan___	Southern South America.	Southern South America.
Chenopis atratus (Latham)__	Black Swan_____	Australia and New Zealand.	Australia and New Zealand.

The significant specific differences among the swans in the genus *Olor* are primarily of an anatomical nature, principally in variations of the tracheal route through the furculum and along the sternum. The variations of the trachea are also responsible for voice differences which, with other external differences, are of definite value to the field worker in making positive identifications wherever the ranges of the various species overlap, as they do to a limited extent over the circumpolar range of this genus.

Since wild populations of the Bewick's swan (*Olor bewickii*) have never been observed in North American waters, and the whooper swan (*Olor cygnus*), though formerly breeding in Greenland, has only three recent Continental records (St. Paul Island: Wilke, 1944: 655; Karl Kenyon, 1949 (letter); Amchitka: Kenyon, 1957 (letter)), the American field ornithologist need be concerned mainly with distinguishing the trumpeter (*Olor buccinator*) from the whistling swan (*Olor columbianus*). Although field identification of trumpeters vs. whistlers may be fairly certain in those cases where the bird in question gives voice, or where a distinct yellow spot is visible on the lores, it may be difficult or impossible to determine the species with certainty without a postmortem examination if these characteristics are not evident. (The subtle superficial differences between these two species will be treated later under the topic Life Cycle.)

In considering the circumpolar distribution of the genus *Olor*, another point should be mentioned here. The two largest species of this group, the trumpeter and the whooper, according to the authorities (Delacour, 1954: 72–73, 84–85; Witherby, et al., 1939: 171, 174) range during their breeding season principally over the interior of the continents with which they are associated, while the breeding ranges of the two smaller species, whistling and Bewick's swans, are primarily along the continental fringes and the islands of the Arctic Ocean.

The numerical status of the trumpeters in North America is only partially understood at this time owing to the difficulty of censusing completely the wintering trumpeters in Alaska and British Columbia. The best recent estimates of this rather obscure population place it between 600 and 1,000 birds (Munro, 1949: 710), while the 1957 trumpeter-swan census in the United States found 488 individuals in this country. Thus, the total continental population of trumpeters probably numbers 1,500 or more.

The status of whistling swans in North America is much different. The midwinter inventory by the U. S. Fish and Wildlife Service in January 1958 found 78,425. Wintering populations fluctuate and are about equally divided between the Pacific and Atlantic flyways (Stewart and Manning, 1958: 205–207).

DISTRIBUTION AND STATUS

GEOLOGICAL OCCURRENCE

At one time or another in the distant past, before man appeared on the North American Continent, trumpeter swans must have occurred commonly within nearly every region of what is now the United States. The advance and retreat of a succession of ice ages in the northern hemisphere determined the distribution and status of this species as it did those of the other faunal elements. The climatic changes may also have been responsible for the passing of one North American species of swan from the scene. This extinct species has been tentatively designated *Cygnus paloregonus*, the remains of which were discovered at Fossil Lake, Oregon. (In addition one Eurasian species has also become extinct at some time in the distant past. This is the giant swan of Malta, *Palaeocycnus*, which was larger than any of the swans in existence today.)

Remains of the progenitors of both trumpeters and whistlers have been identified from widely separated geologic formations in the United States. Alexander Wetmore (1956: 25) lists trumpeter occurrences in such deposits as follows, "Modern form reported from Pleistocene: Aurora, Illinois; Itchtucknee River, Florida. Late Pleistocene: Fossil Lake, Oregon." In Illinois the trumpeter remains were associated with bones of the giant beaver and mastodon (Wetmore, 1935: 237), while in Florida remains of the trumpeter were found in Pleistocene material together with the bones of such birds as the California condor (*Gymnogyps californianus*), whooping crane (*Grus americana*), and jabiru stork (*Jabiru mycteria*) (Wetmore, 1931: 19), all of which are of course now unknown in that whole region. An unusual Pleistocenic associate of the trumpeter

8

identified from Fossil Lake, Oregon, deposits was a flamingo (*Phoenicopterus copei*). Dr. Herbert Friedmann (1935:23) has also recorded the presence of trumpeter bones from Kodiak Island, Alaska. So through the centuries the ancestors of the trumpeters existed under far different circumstances and in regions which today might no longer be considered suitable.

PRIMITIVE HISTORY

Long before Caucasian man made his appearance in North America, swans were used in various ways by many of the indigenous Indian tribes. The swans were undoubtedly sought principally for food, and today their remains are occasionally exhumed in archeological excavations. The bones of the trumpeter can be specifically identified in many such instances.

H. K. Coale (1915:89), in his valuable early treatise on the status of this species, quotes a reliable source from Ohio as stating:

We have in our collection a great many bones of the trumpeter swan. It seems that this bird, although a very rare migrant at the present time, was here in great numbers in pre-historic time, and we find their bones in the villages of the old Indians, who always used the leg bone for making implements, while the wing bones were seldom used. I found specimens in the Baum, Bartner, and Madisonville village sites.

In bibliographical material furnished by E. S. Thomas, Curator of Natural History of the Ohio Historical Society, various other authors have also reported unearthing bones of the trumpeter swan among kitchen-midden material from at least four ancient Indian village sites in that State. The remains of the trumpeters found in these excavations varied greatly in age, from early historic, in the case of the Fairport Harbor Village site, to from 2,377 to 2,750 years ago for the Kettle Hill Cave and Toepfner Mound sites, as estimated by Thomas using carbon-14 datings.

Trumpeter bones have also been exhumed in ancient kitchen-midden material in Illinois. P. W. Parmalee, Curator of Zoology at Illinois State Museum, wrote (correspondence) that findings in six sites covered a time range of at least 1,500 years. Most of the swans seem to have been used for food, though some bones were cut into beads. At the Cahokia village site, near East St. Louis, about 375 trumpeter bones have been identified. This village is thought to have been vacated just before the coming of the white man. (See also Parmalee, 1958, in Bibliography.)

Swans also entered the lives of the early peoples by contributing to their dress, ceremony, and legend. The journals of a number of early American explorers and travelers, gathered and edited by R. G.

Thwaites (1906), contain many firsthand references to the roles played by these great white birds in the lives of the Indians. Like the plumage of the eagle, feathers of the swans were valued for their decorative and symbolic value.

Although little pertinent life-history information can be learned from the accounts of our native swans during pre-Caucasian times, we do find that the swans were present and taken frequently enough to have entered the lives of the natives as a recognizable part of their culture.

EARLY HISTORICAL NOTES (1632–1832)

Early accounts of our native swans, and of trumpeters in particular, are brief and scattered in the literature over a long period of time. A New Englander, Thomas Morton, wrote of the native swans in 1632 (Force's Historical Tracts, vol. 2 : 46):

> And first of the Swanne, because she is the biggest of all the fowles of that Country. There are of them in Merrimack River, and other parts of the Country, greate Store at the seasons of the yeare. The flesh is not much desired of the inhabitants, but the skinnes may be accompted a commodity, fitt for divers uses, both for fethers, and quiles.

Although Morton gives no clue to the species identity of the swans which seasonally visited that part of New England in the early days, later accounts by other observers indicate that both trumpeters and whistlers probably were represented. Jeremy Belknap (1784) listed a New Hampshire swan with a "sound resembling that of a trumpet", C. Hart Merriam (1877) thought that both were in Connecticut in early times, with one trumpeter reported in his day, and J. A. Allen (1878) stated that the trumpeter doubtless was common in Massachusetts 200 years earlier, and "may still be looked for as a straggler."

The next early report appears to have been in a history written by John Lawson, Surveyor-General of North Carolina, and first published in 1709. It is the first to separate the trumpeter as a bird distinct from the lesser species and positively record its occurrence on the eastern seaboard. This record is as follows (Lawson, 1714: 86):

> Of the Swans we have two sorts: the one we call trompeters because of a sort of Trompeting Noise they make. These are the largest sort we have; which come in great Flocks in the Winter, and stay, commonly in the fresh Rivers, until February, when the Spring comes on, when they go to the Lakes to breed. A Cygnet, that is a last year's Swan, is accounted a delicate dish, as indeed it is. They are known by their Head and Feathers, which are not so white as Old ones.

Lawson's account is pertinent for several other reasons. First, we learn that the early settlers were familiar enough with *Olor buc-*

cinator to give it the common name of "trumpeter"; second, the presence of this species in "large flocks" on the "fresh Rivers" gives us the first and only clues to its original status and winter habitat along the east coast; and third, the positive remark calling attention to the time of departure (February) when "they go to the Lakes to breed" suggests the nesting of this species somewhere to the east of the accepted eastern limits of the breeding range of this species which was documented later. Lawson's specific use of the term "Lakes" is especially interesting, inasmuch as he does not hint of the breeding grounds of the whistling swan in his notes on the lesser species, and trumpeters are indeed wholly pond or lake breeders, never known to nest along the banks of rivers. The trumpeter is not mentioned again in United States ornithological literature for another century, and so the possible breeding status of this species east of the Ohio River before settlement by the white man remains obscure.

More than half a century was to elapse before the next pertinent record of swans was left by Samuel Hearne, an employee of the Hudson's Bay Company. Hearne's diary contains several brief remarks on the swans made on his epic journey from Hudson Bay to the Arctic Ocean during the period 1769–72. One of his statements (Hearne, 1795: 371) not only initially documents the entry of the plumage of the swans into the world of commerce but records that great numbers of swans were taken for food by the Hudson Bay Indians. He states:

In fact, the skinning of a Bear spoils the meat thereof, as much as it would do to skin a young porker or roasting pig. The same may be said of swans (the skins of which the Company have lately made an article of trade); otherwise thousands of their skins might be brought to market annually, by the Indians that trade with the Hudson's Bay Company's servants at the different settlements about the Bay.

In the accounts which follow, the plumage of these great birds, first valued by the earliest colonists, gradually became and remained an article of frontier commerce for over a hundred years, eventually reaching the London fur market by the thousands of skins. This fact, perhaps more than any other now apparent, caused the gradual reduction of numbers and range of both the North American swans, and particularly the near extinction of the trumpeter.

Lewis and Clark appear to be the next explorers who mention the swans to any extent. Observations of these birds were made several times during the course of their transcontinental journey during the period 1804–6. The following brief note is found in Elliot Coues' edited account of this expedition (1893: 1284). The notation was made in northwestern Missouri on July 4, 1804, during the beginning of their ascent of the Missouri River and while nearly opposite the present town of Atchison, Kansas, and records, "A great number of young swans and geese on a lake opposite Fourth of July Creek." This strengthens the brief note by Widmann (1907) and Blines (1888) that swans once bred in north Missouri. In the Lewis and Clark account (Coues, 1893: 743–915) the two North American swans are correctly separated on the basis of size and voice for the second time. The first of these observations was penned while Lewis and Clark were in winter quarters at Fort Clatsop near the mouth of the Columbia River. This note suggests for the first time the name "whistling swan" for the lesser swans observed. The last paragraph was written on March 28–29, 1806, while the expedition was ascending the Columbia River on their return journey home. (In quotations from this source, interpolations in brackets are by Dr. Coues):

The birds which most strike our attention are the large [Cygnus buccinator], as well as the small, or whistling swan [C. columbianus].

*   *   *   *   *   *   *

The small differs only [mainly] from the large in size and note; it is about one-fourth less, and its note is entirely different. It cannot be justly imitated by the sound of letters; it begins with a kind of whistling sound, and terminates in a round full note, louder at the end; this note is [not] as loud as that of the large species; whence it [this small swan] might be denominated the whistling swan; its habits, color, and contour appear to be precisely those of the larger species. These birds were first found below the great narrows of the Columbia, near the Chilluckittequaw nation; that were very abundant in this neighborhood, and remained with the party all winter; in number they exceeded those of the larger species in the proportion of five to one.

*   *   *   *   *   *   *

Deer Island is surrounded by an abundant growth of cottonwood, ash, and willow, while the interior consists chiefly of prairies interspersed with ponds. These afford refuge to great numbers of geese, ducks, large swan [Cygnus buccinator], . . . In the course of the day we saw great numbers of geese, ducks, and large and small swans [Cygnus buccinator and C. columbianus], which last are very abundant in the ponds where the wappatoo grows, as they feed much on that root.

Hans Pilder (1914: 170) furnished some information on the trade in swan skins by the Hudson's Bay Company and the Canadian Company during the years 1806–22. According to his data the numbers of swan skins which were exported by these companies were as follows: 1806, 396 skins (Hudson's Bay Company); 1807, 1,192 (Hudson's Bay Company); 1818, 2,463 (Hudson's Bay Company) plus 600 (Canadian Company); 1820, 800 (Canadian Company); 1822, 1,800 (Hudson's Bay Company). Since the companies merged in 1822, the last figure is apparently that of the combined export.

Apparently the first record of trumpeters breeding in the United States is found in Dr. T. S. Roberts' (1936: 205) account of a journal entry by Count G. E. Beltrami on July 13, 1823. Count Beltrami accompanied Major Stephen H. Long's expedition into the Minnesota and Red River Valleys, encamping at that date near what is now called Swan Lake (Nicollet County) where Beltrami noted, "In the evening we halted near a little wood which lies along the banks of the Lake of Swans. It was the season at which these beautiful birds cannot fly—the old ones, because they are changing their feathers; the young, because they have yet only a soft down."

William Keating (1825, vol. 1: 446), geologist with the Long expedition, recorded that at the Lake Traverse fur post, on the border of Minnesota and South Dakota, 2 packs of 60 swan skins were worth 120 Spanish dollars. This is the first reference to swans being taken in the United States for commercial purposes.

Uses made of these swan skins are not itemized by these early writers. Delacour (1954: 76) says they were used for the manufacture of powder puffs. E. H. Forbush (1929: 306) says that "the trade in swansdown offered further incentive for the destruction of the species." The feathers were certainly used for adornment in many ways, and the quills made excellent pens. John James Audubon, America's noted early ornithologist and artist, preferred trumpeter quills for drawing fine detail, as in the feet and claws of small birds, saying (1838: 538) that they were "so hard, and yet so elastic, that the best steel pen of the present day might have blushed, if it could, to be compared with them."

During the late 1820's the traffic in swan skins apparently increased. C. P. Wilson, editor of the Hudson's Bay Company publication, *The Beaver*, furnished additional notes regarding that Company's trade in swan skins. He wrote (correspondence):

In regard to the old sale lists . . . 5,072 skins were sold in London on 16th April, 1828, and on the following 10th. December 347,298 goose, swan and eagle quills and wings were sold. On the 29th. October that year the Company imported 4,263 swan skins from York Factory and Mackenzie River districts; 18 from Moose River and East Main in the southern part of James Bay; and 26 from the Columbia region, but no distinction is made between Trumpeters and Whistlers.

In 1828, Audubon set down a significant account of an Indian swan hunt. These notes record for the second time the taking of swans specifically for their plumage in the United States proper.[1] All other instances of this sort have a Canadian origin. Audubon's account (McDermott 1942: 154) describes the deliberate slaughter of "at least

---

[1] The calendar of the American Fur Company's papers of 1834–47 (Nute, 1945) gives no information. The records of the North-West Company, the only other big fur company in North America exclusive of the Hudson's Bay Company, were either amalgamated with those of the Hudson's Bay Company in the merger of the two concerns in 1821 or have been lost. Thus, there seems little likelihood that further information on this subject will ever come to light.

50" swans by Indians near the confluence of the Mississippi and Ohio Rivers (in Kentucky), the skins of which were "all intended for the ladies of Europe."

A year or so after the noted English ornithologist William Yarrell had demonstrated a systematically reliable difference between the anatomy of the whooper swan and that of its smaller relative, the Bewick's swan, Sir John Richardson was successful in discovering similar constant differences between the two closely related North American species (Swainson and Richardson, 1832, vol. 32: 438, 464). Although these two species had previously been separated on the basis of both size and note, and indeed the common names of trumpeter and whistling swan were already in use among the ornithologists of that day, it remained for Richardson to describe a positive method of identifying these two closely related species which would invariably serve when more superficial characteristics were either absent or in doubt. The differing point of anatomy discovered by Richardson, the form and route of the trachea through the sternum, is the only reliable characteristic allowing positive speciation today.

Richardson's notes are also helpful in outlining the former range and distribution of this species and in stressing its importance in the fur trade. Richardson contributed:

This is the most common Swan in the interior of the fur-counties. It breeds as far north as latitude 61°, but principally within the Arctic Circle. . . . It is to the trumpeter that the bulk of the Swan-skins imported by the Hudson's Bay Company belong.

Elsewhere in his treatise on the northern zoology of the Continent, Richardson noted that the trumpeter was established across the Continent and north to a latitude of 68°, breeding "in the interior between the sixtieth and sixty-eighth parallels."

Richardson apparently was ignorant of Count Beltrami's account of swans breeding in Minnesota in 1823, and he apparently discounted Lawson's brief note that in North Carolina "they [trumpeters] go to the Lakes to breed" by omitting this remark in his 1831 description of this species, though he does mention some of Lawson's remarks regarding the trumpeter. We may conclude that Richardson believed the breeding range of this species to be confined mainly to the interior of Arctic Canada.

LATER HISTORICAL NOTES (1833–1925)

For two decades following Richardson's published description of the trumpeter and its range in North America, only a rather extensive account of the trumpeter by Audubon and a remark by Pierre Jean De Smet shed further light on the status of this species in the United

States. By this time the trumpeters of the eastern seaboard appear to have been exterminated, as Audubon (1838: 536–537) relates:

the larger Swan, the subject of this article, is rarely if ever seen to the eastward of the mouths of the Mississippi.

*   *   *   *   *   *   *

This species is unknown to my friend, the Rev. John Bachman, who, during a residence of twenty years in South Carolina, never saw or heard of one there; whereas in hard winters the *Cygnus Americanus* is not uncommon, although it does not often proceed further southward than that State.

Audubon (1838: 537–538) does outline the occurrence of the trumpeter in the Ohio and Mississippi River valleys rather completely, furnishing at the same time a note on its abundance there, stating:

The Trumpeter Swans make their appearance on the lower portions of the waters of the Ohio about the end of October. They throw themselves at once into the larger ponds or lakes at no great distance from the river, giving a marked preference to those which are closely surrounded by dense and tall canebrakes, and there remain until the water is closed by ice, when they are forced to proceed southward. During mild winters I have seen Swans of this species in the ponds about Henderson [Kentucky] until the beginning of March, but only a few individuals, which may have stayed there to recover from their wounds. When the cold became intense, most of those which visited the Ohio would remove to the Mississippi, and proceed down that stream as the severity of the weather increased, or return if it diminished. . . . I have traced the winter migrations of this species as far southward as the Texas, where it is abundant at times, . . . At New Orleans . . . the Trumpeters are frequently exposed for sale in the markets, being procured on the ponds of the interior, and on the great lakes leading to the waters of the Gulf of Mexico. . . . The waters of the Arkansas and its tributaries are annually supplied with Trumpeter Swans, and the largest individual which I have examined was shot on a lake near the junction of that river with the Mississippi. It measured nearly ten feet in alar extent, and weighed above thirty-eight pounds.

Whilst encamped in the Tawapatee Bottom when on a fur trading voyage, our keel boat was hauled close under the eastern shore of the Mississippi. . . . The great stream was itself so firmly frozen that we were daily in the habit of crossing it from shore to shore. No sooner did the gloom of night become discernible through the gray twilight, than the loud-sounding notes of hundreds of Trumpeters would burst on the ear; and as I gazed over the icebound river, flocks after flocks would be seen coming from afar and in various directions, and alighting about the middle of the stream opposite to our encampment.

Although Audubon apparently became familiar with migrating or wintering trumpeters during his widespread travels, and even kept a male in captivity for about 2 years when living at Henderson, Kentucky (1838: 541), he never was privileged to see a nest or young of this species.

A noteworthy breeding record is contained in the writings of Pierre Jean De Smet, who was a noted early Jesuit missionary of the Pacific Northwest. On April 15, 1842, De Smet was traveling with a band of Flathead Indian warriors and was encamped near Flathead Lake in western Montana when he wrote, according to Thwaites (1906, vol. 27 : 359) :

The warriors had gone on ahead and dispersed in every direction, some to hunt and others to fish. . . . The warriors returned in the evening with a bear, goose, and six swan's eggs.

Since western Montana, and especially the Flathead Valley, was later the source of many trumpeter breeding reports, this record is believed valid. De Smet, in 1845, reported seeing swans during the summer on the marshy lakes in southeastern British Columbia which form the source of the Columbia River (Thwaites, 1906, vol. 29 : 206). This suggests that the adjacent region of the Kootenays at one time may have been included in the ancestral breeding range of this species.

The brief notes on the native swans made by the naturalists who accompanied the various expeditions sent out by the Secretary of War during the period of 1853–55 furnish some pertinent data on the occurrence of the trumpeter, chiefly in the Far West. Dr. George Suckley accompanied one of these surveys as naturalist westward from the Mississippi River to the Pacific coast, and though he records the trumpeter near the beginning of his journey in Minnesota and at the end on the Columbia River, no mention is made of this species between these two localities. Dr. Suckley (1859 : 248–249) recorded :

It [trumpeter] is, like the preceding species [whistler], more abundant on the Columbia river than at Puget Sound. In the winter of 1853–54 I noticed immense flocks of swans, apparently of this species, collected along the shores of the river mentioned, and spread out along the margin of the water for a distance varying from an eighth to a quarter of a mile. I obtained a fine trumpeter swan on Pike lake [near Fort Snelling] Minnesota, in June 1853. They are quite common on the lakes in that vicinity in summer, breeding and raising their young.

Supplementing Dr. Suckley's notes, J. G. Cooper, another naturalist on this expedition added (1869 : 249) :

The trumpeter swan associates with the preceding species [whistler] at the same season and in the same places. Both arrive from the north in the beginning of December, but I have not had an opportunity of noticing their departure.

Earlier, the naturalist of another similar survey, Dr. J. S. Newberry, noted that farther south the swans were not as abundant as they were on the Columbia River, writing (1857 : 100) :

The trumpeter swan visits California and Oregon with its congeners, the ducks and geese, in their annual migrations, but, compared with the myriads of other water birds which congregate at that season in the bays and rivers of the west, it is always rare. Before we left the Columbia, early in November, the swans had begun to arrive from the north, and frequently while at Ft. Vancouver their trumpeting call drew our attention to the long converging lines of these magnificent birds, so large and so snowy white, as they came from their northern nesting places, and screaming their delight at the appearance of the broad expanse of water, perhaps their winter home, descended into the Columbia.

This bird [whistler], considerably smaller than the last, is perhaps more common at the west. In California swans are much less common than on the Columbia, where during the winter season at least, they are exceedingly abundant.

Dr. A. L. Heerman (1859: 68) recorded the occurrence of the trumpeter in the Suisun and Sacramento Valleys of California, and in the San Francisco market. Since he made no mention of whistling swans, there may be some doubt about the accuracy of his identification.

George Barnston, an official of the Hudson's Bay Company, verifies the general impression left by these observers as he relates (1862: 7831–7832):

In the winter months all the northern regions are deserted by the swans, and from November to April large flocks are to be seen on the expanses of the large rivers of the Oregon territory and California, between the Cascade Range and the Pacific where the climate is particularly mild, and their favourite food abounds in the lakes and placid waters. Collected sometimes in great numbers, their silvery strings embellish the landscape, and form a part of the life and majesty of the scene.

Roderick MacFarlane was the next observer who made a significant contribution to our knowledge of the trumpeter as it existed in the days of long ago. MacFarlane was an experienced northern fur-trader, employed by the Hudson's Bay Company as a post and district manager for 22 years, from 1852–74, finally being appointed a Chief Factor of that firm in 1875. He was apparently one of the most qualified naturalists of "The Honorable Company" being an enthusiastic and astute wildlife observer, collaborating with such other famous early naturalists as Spencer F. Baird, Robert Kennicot, and Edward Preble, who were also keenly interested in the fauna of the Arctic.

During the period 1862–66 MacFarlane was especially active in collecting mammals, birds, and eggs. He was then stationed at Fort Anderson, located at latitude 68°30′ N., longitude 128° W., which served a portion of the lower Great Mackenzie Basin fur trade. He collected representative fauna in the approximate area bounded to the north by the Arctic Ocean, to the east by the coast of Franklin Bay, to the south by the 67° of latitude, and to the west by the lower Mackenzie River—roughly a radius of about 125 miles, all within the Arctic Circle (66°33′ N. Lat.).

With MacFarlane's background in mind it is interesting to review his notes (1891: 425):

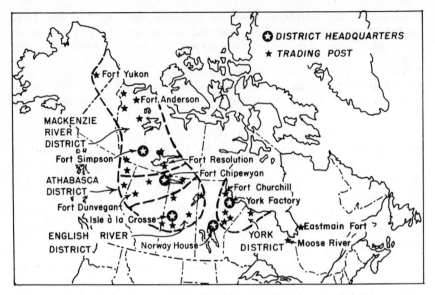

FIGURE 1.—Locations of some Hudson's Bay Company posts which engaged in swan-skin trade, 1828–1884.

Several nests of this species [trumpeter] were met with in the Barren Grounds [east of the Fort], on islands in Franklin Bay, and one containing six eggs was situated near the beach on a sloping knoll. . . . It usually lays from four to six eggs, judging from the noted contents of a received total of twenty-four nests.

MacFarlane was apparently able to distinguish between the nests of the trumpeter and those of the whistler, as he reported the following information under the heading *Whistling Swan:*

The maximum number of eggs taken in the twenty nests of this swan which I find recorded, was five, while the nest itself was always placed on the ground, and several were also found on the coast and islands of Liverpool and Franklin Bays in the Arctic Ocean.

Later MacFarlane added (Mair and MacFarlane, 1908 : 324), "For some time back swans seem to be annually dwindling in numbers."

With Richardson's earlier statements in mind, the following summary by MacFarlane is particularly pertinent. Speaking of the Hudson's Bay Company's London sales, MacFarlane wrote (1905 : 754) :

We find 57 swan skins in the above summary [of London fur sale-offerings 1888–1897], and they no doubt belonged to the Hudson's Bay Company. Although no skins of *Olor columbianus* or *Olor buccinator* appear in the fur catalogues for 1897, 1900, 1902, or 1903 yet for many years they never failed in having quite a number of swan skins for sale in London. From 1853 to 1877 they sold a total of 17,671, or an average of nearly 707 a year. There were seven good years (1853 to 1856, 1861, 1862, and 1867), with sales ranging between 985 and 1,312 in 1854 (maximum), and seven poor years (1870 to 1877), with returns varying between 338 and the minimum (122) in 1877.

Continuing, MacFarlane throws further light on the origin of some of the swan skins in the fur trade:

From 1858 to 1884, inclusive, Athabasca District turned out 2,705 swan skins, nearly all of them from Fort Chipewyan. Mackenzie River District, according to a statement in my possession, supplied 2,500 skins from 1863 to 1883. From 1862 to 1877 Fort Resolution, Great Slave Lake, contributed 798 thereof. For 1889 Athabasca traded but 33, as against 251 skins in 1853. In 1889 and 1890 Isle a la Crosse, headquarters of the English River District, sent out two skins for each outfit [post?].

Unfortunately, MacFarlane makes no attempt to distinguish between the two species of swans, so that Richardson's original range statement cannot be compared with this record. A statement by Thomas Nuttall (1834: 371) that the trumpeter furnished the bulk of these skins is quoted by H. K. Coale (1915: 83), but as this statement is in the exact wording used by Richardson the latter was no doubt the original source.

From this information it is possible to trace in a rough way the decline of the trade in swan skins by the Hudson's Bay Company over a period of nearly 100 years, from 1806 to 1903. Since this trade by the Hudson's Bay Company began before 1772 and (as John Richardson said in 1832) was principally at the expense of the trumpeter, the effect of such exploitation on the far-flung breeding populations of this species for more than 125 years must have been devastating and largely responsible for its extermination over vast regions, particularly in the heart of its Canadian breeding range.

The relatively high price asked for trumpeter swans' eggs during the last decade of the 19th century also indicates the scarcity of the birds during this period. "The Standard Catalogue of North American Birds Eggs" (Lattin, 1892) lists the cost of a single egg at $4, compared with a whistling swan egg price of $2.50, heath hen—$3, and whooping crane—$3.

Another brief note by George Barnston (1862: 7831) gives a definite swan breeding record for Eastmain Fort on James Bay. He states that swans are generally scarce in the Hudson Bay region, but a considerable number hatch in this area.

Since whistling swans have never been reported nesting as far south as 52° N. (the latitude of Eastmain Fort), this is presumably a valid trumpeter breeding record, and the easternmost to come to my attention.

There were three ecologically distinct regions in the United States in which trumpeters could be said to have once been a more or less common breeding species in areas of suitable habitat. These regions were—

(1) the Red Rock Lakes–Yellowstone–Jackson Hole region of southwestern Montana, northeastern Idaho, and northwestern Wyoming, (2) the Flathead Valley in western Montana, and (3) southern Minnesota and northern Iowa. Elsewhere in the United States, the trumpeter was recorded as a breeding species only occasionally or from widely separated locations. The prairie pothole country in the provinces of southern Canada and the Great Plains marshes of the United States were of small importance in supporting the total continental breeding population. Thus, little of the original prime breeding range of this species extended to the United States.

During the period 1850–1900 a great many observations of the trumpeter swan in the United States were recorded. It was during this time that the work of the scientific field naturalist began to show up prominently in the literature. This in turn awakened scores of other interested observers to the value of ornithological factfinding, and the number of reports increased correspondingly. Except for notes on the breeding range, there seems little point in listing the scores of single occurrence records, since the trumpeter can be so easily confused with the whistler, and apparently often was. State ornithological works cover these occurrence records adequately.

Several records of false or questionable nature have appeared in the literature of the past. The note by D. E. Merrill (1932: 460) reporting a trumpeter shot near Mesilla Park, New Mexico, is apparently a case of mistaken identity (J. Stokely Ligon, correspondence), and no skin is now available for confirmation (W. A. Dick-Peddie, correspondence). According to J. Van Tyne (correspondence), B. H. Swales, a qualified critical judge, does not believe the J. C. Wood "record" in the *Auk* (1908: 326), stating, "This record is worthless—based entirely on memory. Wood did not know the swans or appreciate the value of accurate identification." Alfred M. Bailey (correspondence) reports that there is only one definite trumpeter record for the State of Colorado, that which Burnett reported (1916: 199) as being shot near Fort Collins on November 18, 1897, other reports notwithstanding.

Enough acceptable records are available from the states of Washington, Oregon, and California in the Pacific flyway; Montana, Wyoming, North Dakota, Nebraska, Kansas, and Texas in the Central flyway; Minnesota, Wisconsin, Iowa, Illinois, Missouri, and Louisiana in the Mississippi flyway; and Maryland, Virginia, and North Carolina in the Atlantic flyway to demonstrate that the trumpeter still appeared as a migrant or winter resident in those states during the last half of the 19th century. Forbush (1912) cites a report from A. S: Eldridge of Lampasas, Texas, that flocks of 75–1000 trumpeters were seen there in the 1890's but none had been seen since 1909.

The continuity of the occurrence of trumpeters in the Yellowstone Park region can be traced from statements made, or specimens secured, by Elliot Coues (1874: 544), Dr. C. Hart Merriam (1891: 91), and W. C. Knight (1902: 40), to establish this general region as ancestral breeding range, even though their status in the Park during these early days is not evident.

After the early observations cited, M. P. Skinner's random sight record data from 1915 to 1921 sheds some light on the number of swans in the Park during this period.   Skinner (1925: 154) records:

My records of Trumpeter Swans seen in Yellowstone Park are as follows:

May 29, 1915	4	Aug. 14, 1919	2
May 31, 1915	4	Sept. 6, 1919	5
Aug. 16, 1917	1	July 4, 1920	2
June, 1919	1	May 29, 1921	1

Skinner found a swan's nest near Lewis Lake in 1919.   This established that trumpeters bred within the Park—a fact previously unknown.   During the same summer, Dr. H. M. Smith, an early fisheries worker in the Park, reported 6 cygnets on a lake near Delusion Lake.

A report for March 1920 from Acting Superintendent Lindsley of Yellowstone Park stated, "There are 20 to 30 trumpeter swans wintering in the outlet of Yellowstone Lake where there is constantly open water; also two wintering on Lewis River near the bridge, and two on Bechler River."

Although the original status of the early swan populations inhabiting the Red Rock Lakes area is obscure, their occurrence in these marshes can also be traced from early times.   From the 1880's (Bent, 1925: 298) to 1896 (Brower, 1897: 138) and 1910 (French, letter) the early existence of these birds in that area is outlined.   Information from older residents of the Centennial Valley confirms and amplifies these records establishing successive seasonal residence of swans on the Red Rock Lakes marshes since the early 1890's.   This also agrees with information collected by Wright and Thompson (1935: 104), though again the actual level of any of these early populations was never recorded.   A. C. Bent's source did report that he saw "quantities" of swans and killed "many" young birds for food in the Centennial Valley, so they were by no means rare there.

A later note regarding actual swan numbers in the Red Rock Lakes area is that left by C. S. Sperry when he surveyed these marshes as a waterfowl food-habits biologist for the U. S. Biological Survey in 1922. Sperry noted "about 15 swans" were reported on the Lakes during that nesting season. He further remarks that this species was

Figure 2.—A day's bag of waterfowl in 1895 at Red Rock Lakes included a
trumpeter swan.

"frequently" encountered during his week's work on these marshes in
September of that year.

The published notes concerning the early history of the trumpeter
in Alaska before 1925 are both limited and brief. This is of course
partly due to the fact that the United States did not acquire this vast
region from Russia until 1867, but a search of the Russian records revealed little additional information. Swans do not seem to have been
important in early Alaskan fur trade, although the taking of swans in
arctic Russia for economic uses has apparently been practiced for
years.

The initial comment on the trumpeter in Alaska seems to be that left
by Dr. Edward Adams, a competent English ornithologist, who made
the following observation during the period 1850–51 (1878: 430) :

> *Cygnus buccinator.* This was the only species of Swan I met with at Michalaski
> [St. Michael]. The first appeared on the 30th. of May; but they were at no time
> numerous, from two to eight or ten keeping together. A few of them are said
> to breed here; but most of them go further north.

Although this note was subsequently credited by Baird, Brewer, and
Ridgway (1884: 433), this has not been the case since that time, other

writers apparently overlooking this account or believing that Dr. Adams confused the trumpeter with the whistler. Subsequent egg records of trumpeters in the Norton Sound area strengthen Dr. Adams' original statement.

Later, Dall and Bannister (1869: 294) stated that eggs of the trumpeter were obtained by a Mr. Lockhart at Fort Yukon, thus establishing the first definite breeding record for this species in Alaska. One of these eggs, on deposit in the U.S. National Museum, was received in April or May of 1863.

E. W. Nelson (1887: 93) refers to Dall's note and remarks that both trumpeters and whistlers are to be found on the southeastern Alaskan coast during the migrations, and attributes the lack of knowledge regarding this species in the Territory to the unexplored interior.

In addition to these notes, there are two egg records, one in the Chicago Natural History Museum and another in the U. S. National Museum, both credited to trumpeters in Alaska and apparently unpublished. The R. M. Barnes collection at the Chicago Natural History Museum contains four eggs of this species which were collected June 28, 1902, 38 miles northeast of Cape Nome by Walter E. Bryant.[2] The U. S. National Museum also contains an egg (one of two) collected by J. B. Chappel in Norton Bay (near Cape Denbigh) in 1867.

There is also a clutch of 5 swan eggs in the National Museum attributed to the whistler but whose measurements, shape, and texture leave little doubt that they belong to the trumpeter. This collection is credited to A. H. Twitchell and was made June 4, 1915, at Bethel, Alaska.

Table 2 outlines the former breeding range of the trumpeter on the continent, particularly in the United States and Alaska. The breeding range in Canada is shown in a general sense on the map, figure 3, based upon the preceding testimony of Richardson, MacFarlane, and Barnston as well as more recent information written later by J. A. Munro (1949: 49), Brooks and Swarth (1925: 38), J. D. Soper (1949: 240), and others.

These records vary a great deal in value, but the fact that most questionable records apply to the same general region as records of higher caliber, or have been accepted by earlier qualified observers, would appear to upgrade their value. The sparse and localized nesting population of trumpeters in the United States no doubt accounts for the comparative paucity of U. S. breeding records.

---

[2] U. S. Fish and Wildlife Service files refer to a set of four eggs in the R. M. Barnes collection with a date of June 15, 1905, but otherwise with the same data as these. Only one such set is in the collection, so the Service files must be in error on the date. Measurements of these eggs provided by Melvin A. Traylor (letter) are average for the trumpeter, and there seems no reason to doubt the record.

Table 2.—Trumpeter swan breeding records in the United States and Alaska to 1925

State and locality	Date	Authority	Reference
Washington: Cherry Lake (Whitman Co.).	Until 1918	Old settler	C. F. Yocom (1951: 17).
Montana:			
Near Flathead Lake (w. Montana).	Apr. 15, 1842	Pierre Jean De Smet	R. G. Thwaites (1906).
Thompson River (w. Montana).	1871	E. S. Cameron	A. C. Bent (1951: 296).
Clearwater drainage (Missoula Co.).	1881	E. S. Cameron	H. K. Coale (1915: 87).
Lake Rodgers (Flathead Co.)	1881	E. S. Cameron	H. K. Coale (1915: 87).
Swan Lake (Lake Co.)	1881	E. S. Cameron	H. K. Coale (1915: 87).
Flathead Lake (w. Montana)	1881	E. S. Cameron	H. K. Coale (1915: 87).
Centennial Valley (Beaverhead Co.).	1883–1888	Ed Forbes	A. C. Bent (1951: 298).
Flathead Valley (w. Montana).	Until 1886	E. S. Cameron	H. K. Coale (1915: 87).
Headwaters of South Fork of Flathead River.	1889	E. S. Cameron	A. C. Bent (1925: 297).
Swan Lake (Beaverhead Co.)	June 10, 1896		J. V. Brower (1897: 138).
Red Rock Lakes (Beaverhead Co.).	1910	Cecil French	U. S. Fish and Wildlife Service files.
Big Lake (Stillwater Co.)	1917	Rancher's report	A. A. Saunders (1921: 42).
Big Lake (Yellowstone Co.) 35 mi. northwest of Billings, Mont.	1920	G. B. Thomas	U. S. Fish and Wildlife Service files.
Red Rock Lakes (Beaverhead Co.).	1922	C. C. Sperry	U. S. Fish and Wildlife Service files.
Highland Lakes (Fergus Co.)	None	P. M. Silloway (1903: 15).	A. A. Saunders (1921: 41).
Idaho:			
Henrys Lake (Fremont Co.)	August 1877	C. E. Bendire	C. Hart Merriam (1891: 91)
Grays Lake (Bonneville Co.).	1923, 1924	B. Fordyce (MS.)	U. S. Fish and Wildlife Service files.
Icehouse Creek Reservoir (Fremont Co.).	Early 1920's	S. A. Trude (MS.)	U. S. Fish and Wildlife Service files.
Wyoming:			
Jackson's Hole	None		W. C. Knight (1902: 40).
Lakes near head Green River.	None		W. C. Knight (1902: 40).
Near Lewis Lake (Yellowstone Park).	1919		M. P. Skinner (1920).
South of Delusion Lake in Yellowstone Park.	July 19, 1919	M. P. Skinner	A. C. Bent (1925: 297).
Yellowstone (Valley) Region	None	F. V. Hayden	E. Coues (1874: 544).
North Dakota:			
Island Lake (Barnes Co.)	Mid 1880's	Newspaper report	R. Reid (correspondence).
Rock Lake (Towner Co.)	1895	Alfred Eastgate	N. A. Wood (1923: 23).
Along Red River of The North.	None		W. W. Cooke (1887).
Nebraska:			
Watt's Lake (Cherry Co.)	None		J. M. Bates (1900: 16).
Swan Lake (head of the Little Blue; Adams Co.).	None		J. M. Bates (1900: 16).
Minnesota:			
Swan Lake (Nicollet Co.)	July 13, 1823	G. E. Beltrami	T. S. Roberts (1936: 204).
Pike Lake (near Old Fort Snelling).	June 1853		G. Suckley (1859: 249).
Heron Lake (Jackson Co.)	1883	Thomas Miller	T. S. Roberts (1936: 205).
Everson Lake (Meeker Co.)	1884 or 1885	L. O. Dart	T. S. Roberts (1936: 205).
Along Red River of The North.	None		W. W. Cooke (1887).
Iowa:			
Near Sac City (Sac Co.)	1859	J. A. Spurrell	U. S. Fish and Wildlife Service files.
	1870	J. A. Spurrell	U. S. Fish and Wildlife Service files.
Oakland Valley (Pottawattamie Co.).	1871	W. C. Rice	Baird, Brewer, Ridgway (1884: 432).
Near Hdwtrs. Des Moines River (Emmet Co.).	As late as 1875	J. W. Preston	R. M. Anderson (1907: 192).
Little Twin Lakes (Hancock Co.).	As late as 1883	J. W. Preston	R. M. Anderson (1907: 191).
Near Newton (Jasper Co.)	None		W. W. Cooke (1887).
Spirit Lake (Dickinson Co.)	None		A. A. Mosher (1889: 66).
Missouri:			
Lowland lakes near Alexandria (Clark Co.).	None		J. Blines (1888: 343).
Northeastern Missouri	None	Old hunters	Otto Widman (1907).
Opposite Atchison, Kans. (Buchanan Co.).	July 4, 1804	Lewis and Clark	R. G. Thwaites (1906).

State and locality	Date	Authority	Reference
Wisconsin:			
Northwest Wisconsin	None		Grundtvig (1895: 99).
Southern Wisconsin	"Early forties"		Kumlien and Hollister (1903: 31).
Jefferson County	1842–1845		Kumlien and Hollister (1903: 31).
Indiana: Kanakee marshes (Lake Co.).	None	T. H. Ball	A. W. Butler (1897: 642).
Alaska:			
Norton Sound	1850–51		Dr. E. Adams (1878: 430).
Fort Yukon	Before 1863	Mr. Lockhart	U.S. Natl. Mus. (egg collection).
Norton Sound, near Cape Denbigh.	1867	J. B. Chappel	U. S. Natl. Mus. (egg collection).
Norton Sound, 38 mi. NE of Cape Nome.	June 28, 1902 [1]	R. M. Barnes (egg collection).	Chicago Natural History Museum.

[1] See footnote, page 233.

From all of the foregoing information it is evident that trumpeter swans were once an abundant and widespread species on the continent. Although both of the native swans were killed by the early colonists for food and plumage, the first substantial inroads into trumpeter populations occurred when the fur trade exploited this species over wide regions for more than a hundred years. The surge of western settlement during the latter part of the 19th century was also partly responsible. The white settlers not only killed and dispossessed these birds in the southern portions of their breeding range, but further reduced or extirpated populations breeding farther north as the increased hunting pressure to the south took its toll among migrating flocks.

EARLY MIGRATION NOTES

It is believed worthwhile to present here a number of brief statements by the early observers in order to document the migration habits of the trumpeter when many of the original flocks were more or less intact.

SPRING MIGRATION (departure)

In regard to departure times, John Lawson (1714) noted that the "trumpeters" along the coast of North Carolina in 1700–1701 "stay . . . until February . . . when they go to the Lakes to breed." Also, Major Long corroborated this early movement of swans generally, reporting (James 1823: 191) under date of February 22, 1820, "swans, geese, and ducks flying up the river" while on the Missouri River in the northwest corner of Iowa. Lewis and Clark (Coues, 1893: 915) noted great numbers of both swan species still on the lower Columbia River on the 29th of March, though whether these were the original winter residents or spring migrants enroute from points farther south is not mentioned.

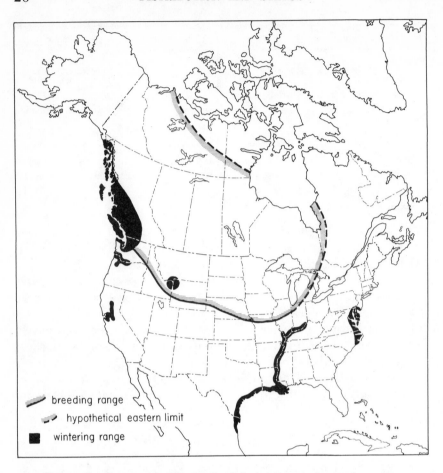

FIGURE 3.—Former breeding and wintering range, trumpeter swan.

In the Mississippi River drainage, John J. Audubon (1838: 537) corroborated the Lawson and Long testimony implying that the normal movement north commenced in February. Observations made at Red Rock Lakes confirm a statement of Audubon's that trumpeters move back towards their breeding grounds during the late winter upon the advent of moderating weather.

A. C. Bent (1925: 301) supplies a couple of late departure dates as follows, "Arkansas, Helena, April 29, 1891; British Columbia, Osoyoos, April 25."

SPRING MIGRATION (arrival)

Several early observations agree that the trumpeter arrives on its northern nesting grounds among the earliest of any of the Arctic avifauna. The journal of Samuel Hearne (1795: 285, 435) under date of April 12, 1772, and latitude of about 60° when just south of the Great Slave Lake bears this entry:

On the twelfth we saw several swans flying to the Northward; they were the first birds of passage we had seen that Spring except a few snowbirds.

         *   *   *   *   *   *   *

In the interior parts of the country the larger Swan [trumpeter] precedes every other species of water-fowl, and in some years arrive so early as the month of March, long before the ice of the rivers is broken up. At those times they always frequent the open waters of falls and rapids, where they are frequently shot by the Indians in considerable numbers.

Richardson (Swainson and Richardson, 1832: 464) noted the early arrival of the trumpeter on its far northern breeding grounds, "It breeds . . . principally within the Arctic Circle, and in its migration generally precedes the Geese a few days."

Although both Barnston (1862: 7831) and Dr. Adams (1878: 430) agree that the trumpeter arrives on its breeding grounds in small flocks, the coastal arrival of trumpeters in the Norton Sound area of Alaska noted by Adams was preceded by both geese and ducks.

A. C. Bent (1925: 301) lists some average dates of arrival for this species as follows, "Nebraska, March 16; South Dakota, April 2; Minnesota, Heron Lake, April 4; Saskatchewan, April 16; British Columbia, April 20." In the light of previous testimony, however, these would appear to be later than average arrivals.

FALL MIGRATION (departure)

Richardson (Swainson and Richardson, 1832: 438) furnishes the sole remark regarding this topic, writing, "*Cygnus buccinator* . . . remains later in the season [than the Geese]." This agrees with my observations at Red Rock Lakes where the trumpeters are consistently the last to leave the remaining patches of open water before the final freezeup.

FALL MIGRATION (arrival)

R. G. Thwaites (1906, vol. 21: 336) presents a note from Townsend's narrative written at Fort Vancouver on the lower Columbia River, December 1, 1835, "The duck and geese, which have swarmed throughout the country during the latter part of the autumn, are leaving us, and the swans are arriving in great numbers." This agrees well with the observation by Dr. Suckley (1859: 249) in the Puget Sound and/or Columbia River regions, where both swans arrived from the north at the beginning of December.

Dr. J. G. Cooper (1869: 83), writing of unidentified swans about the same period, stated, "Swans were seen in large flocks on the Columbia River, in the Cascade Canyon, as early as October 29th, this year (1860), and their migration southward seemed generally early. I saw them, however, on lakes of the Columbia Plain about the same time in 1853." Dr. Newberry (1857:100) mentions an early November arrival on the Columbia. In the Mississippi flyway, Audubon (1838:537) reports late October arrivals usual on the lower Ohio River.

A. C. Bent (1925:301) lists some fall occurrence dates as follows, "Minnesota, Spicer, October 8, 1913; Michigan, St. Clair Flats, November 20, 1875; Washington, Douglas County, November 9, 1912; Colorado, Fort Collins, November 18, 1897, and November 15, 1915."

Dr. Grinnell found trumpeter swans in October and November of 1887 abundant at the extreme upper end of Lower St. Mary Lake near Glacier National Park (Bailey, 1918).

RECENT OCCURRENCE, BREEDING, AND MIGRATION REPORTS, TO 1957

Positive identification as to species, trumpeter vs. whistler, was not possible in most of the following reports, but they do constitute the opinion of trained or reliable wildlife observers and as such probably represent valid trumpeter records.

Since the Red Rock Lakes Refuge was established in 1935, the information from Montana, Idaho, and Wyoming is believed to be especially pertinent. As might be expected from the resultant increase in the swan population following establishment of the Refuge, these birds may be moving about in this tri-State region more than is generally realized and in some instances appear to be nesting in areas previously unoccupied. It is necessary to depend upon sight and/or sound observations in all these cases since, although over 300 trumpeters have been banded on the Refuge and stations of their introduction, no band recoveries have yet been made outside the generally recognized area of known use. (The banding data which have been gathered will be treated later under Management). The known sightings of trumpeters since 1925, as well as the last previous occurrence report, are presented below by flyway for each State, Province, or Territory considered.

PACIFIC FLYWAY

California. Donald D. McLean (1937: 228), California Division of Fish and Game, gives a convincing description of a trumpeter which was seen in Lassen County and identified from its call, on November 8, 1935. The bird was seen between Grasshopper Valley and Termo, by Bailey Creek.

The next previous California report seems to be that of A. L. Brown, who stated that the trumpeter was formerly a regular winter visitant to Lassen County (Honey Lake Valley) up to about 1910 (McLean, correspondence).

Nevada. Frank W. Groves, present Director of the Nevada State Fish and Game Department, who was familiar with the trumpeter from his previous experience at the Malheur National Wildlife Refuge, reported by letter dated December 2, 1952, to the Fish and Wildlife Service that he found a swan while driving east from Carson City. The bird was larger than a whistling swan, and lacked the yellow spot at the base of the bill. Groves was convinced that its call, while not completely typical, was that of a trumpeter.

This lone trumpeter, if such it was, must have been a stray from the groups which had been transferred to the Ruby Lake Refuge in Nevada or the Malheur Refuge in Oregon from the Red Rock Lakes Refuge. There is no earlier report of the trumpeter in Nevada.

Oregon. The only report of trumpeters within the boundaries of Oregon since 1925 seems to be that of Gabrielson and Jewett (1940) who state, "On September 7, 1929, Oberholser, Gabrielson, and Jewett saw a single swan at Davis Lake that, judging from its huge size, might have been this species. This is the only recent record of even its hypothetical occurrence within the State." Earlier reports and records of this species in Oregon precede 1900.

Washington. Allan Brooks (1926: 129) states that a small number of trumpeters cross the International Boundary from British Columbia into Washington State each year (18 in 1924). Whether this is still true is not known, although J. A. Munro and Ian McT. Cowan (1947: 55) write, "In addition to the numerous wintering bands, that are widely distributed [in British Columbia], a smaller number is transient and apparently winters south of the Canadian–United States boundary. Migrating birds are met with both spring and fall in various localities in the extreme southern part of the Province."

J. B. Lauckhart, Chief of the Division of Game Management, Washington Department of Game, advised (correspondence), "We do have some swan killed each year during the hunting season, but we have never identified one as a trumpeter." The occurrence of the trumpeter in a wintering status in Washington is thus obscure.

On April 7, 1939, W. C. Ralston saw and heard 20–25 trumpeters at Othello, Washington.

The next earlier reports are mentioned by Stanley Jewett et al. (1953: 102) of a specimen taken at Moses Lake, Washington, in 1912, and the skin received by Edson in 1913 from a hunter who took the specimen at the mouth of Nooksack River, Bellingham Bay (Whatcom County).

Idaho. In addition to counts made in the winter range of the trumpeter in the Island Park area of Fremont County, Idaho, these great birds are occasionally noted farther down the Snake River drainage and more frequently elsewhere in eastern Idaho. David de Lancey Condon (MS), Chief Naturalist for Yellowstone National Park, noted:

> On April 17, 1937, I observed five swan on a slough on Marsh Creek which is a tributary to the Portneuf River, 30 miles south of Pocatello, Idaho, which, after careful examination with field glasses were felt to be trumpeter swan. On April 18, 1937, a pair of trumpeter swan were watched for some time on an oxbow lake in the Snake River bottoms near Roberts.

Robert Salter (1954), Game Bird Supervisor of the Idaho State Fish and Game Department, also set down several occurrence records well outside the Island Park area in eastern Idaho:

> They normally do not go further downstream along the North Fork of the Snake River than St. Anthony which is approximately 30 air line miles south of the Island Park area. We have three records in recent years of trumpeter swan being found in Idaho outside Fremont county. In the fall of 1943 Mr. Hawley Hill, District Supervisor, positively identified by dissection a trumpeter swan which had been illegally killed on the Snake River near Burley in Cassia County. On March 30, 1951, Mr. E. L. Keppner, Conservation Officer, made a sight and "sound" record of five trumpeter swan on Elk Horn reservoir in Oneida County. On January 9, during the 1952 winter inventory, 11 swans were seen from the air on Spring Creek, which runs into American Falls reservoir in Bannock County. Mr. Winston E. Banko, Refuge Manager of Red Rock Lakes Refuge, was in Idaho Falls and went out the next day to observe these birds. We were able to approach within 75 yards of three birds which then flushed. Banko identified them as trumpeters [from their voice].

Swans, apparently trumpeters from the wintering flock at the National Elk Refuge in Jackson Hole, Wyoming, only rarely take a cruise downstream as far as Swan Valley on the South Fork of the Snake River in Bonneville County, Idaho. My field notes, under date of December 12, 1956, read:

> Arno Winterfield was contacted in Swan Valley [Bonneville County, Idaho] regarding the former and present status of trumpeter in that area. He advised that he came to Swan Valley in 1915 and had never seen swans there until the winter of 1954 or 1955 when he saw 8 or 9 flying low downstream alongside the Snake River south of the community of Swan Valley. As he watched, the birds turned and headed back upstream. He did not recall that old-time residents of Swan Valley had ever mentioned wintering or breeding swans in that area.

U. S. Fish and Wildlife Service files hold an earlier trumpeter breeding record for Idaho. R. F. James, in a game warden report dated November 23, 1932, reports a nest on an island in the Pend Oreille River just below the Idaho-Washington line.

The next previous records for Idaho are breeding accounts given for Grays Lake, Idaho, in 1923 and 1924 (A. B. Fordyce, MS) as well as on Icehouse Creek Reservoir, Fremont County in 1920 (S. A. Trude, MS), both brief manuscripts in Service files.

In addition to these reports, R. H. Mackay (1957: 339) documents both sight record and band-recovery data establishing the presence of Alberta trumpeters among flocks of Montana birds in 1955 and 1956 during the wintering period in the Island Park country of Idaho.

British Columbia. Although reports of breeding trumpeters in British Columbia are rare, and for the most part unsubstantiated, hundreds of birds winter along the coast as well as in the interior. J. A. Munro (1949: 709) states:

It is not an exaggeration to say that trumpeter swans, at one time or another during the winter, visit most of the many lakes on Vancouver Island and along the mainland coast. The number fluctuates from year to year but probably exceeds 600 individuals. Thus, the winter population is believed to approximate 1,000. . . . wintering populations of trumpeter swans are distributed over the western half of the province of British Columbia between north latitudes 49° and 55°. . . . Some of these frequent lakes and rivers at points distant from the sea; others inhabit the lower reaches of coast streams; and still others resort to the shallows and mud flats of sheltered estuaries. There are also interior populations, of which some winter on rapid stretches of river that remain open even in the coldest weather.

Segments of the population wintering in British Columbia have been counted from time to time by Munro and others, but it is difficult to secure anything like a true census due to the widely separated locations of wintering flocks and the relatively poor weather for operating aircraft which prevails over the entire region at this season. Also, the possible presence of whistling swans further complicates the matter. R. H. Mackay (correspondence, March 19, 1958) writes:

Whistling swans winter in British Columbia to some extent. The largest group is a flock varying annually from 150–225 birds that winter regularly on the South Thompson River near Kamloops in the interior of the Province. Other irregular occurrences have been noted in the Lower Mainland region of the Fraser, on the Queen Charlotte Islands, and at Lonesome Lake where two or three whistlers have been recorded with the trumpeters on occasion.

Although the breeding grounds of the trumpeters wintering in this Province are in the main still undiscovered, it is seen that easily half of the total North American population winters here.

Alaska. For over 50 years following E. W. Nelson's (1887) statement that both species of swans were noted to occur "in migration" in southeastern Alaska, little was written to clarify the status of the trumpeter in that Territory, though collection of several clutches of eggs in the Norton Sound region confirmed Dall and Bannister's (1869) breeding record.

A report by E. L. Kepner found in U. S. Fish and Wildlife Service files, and dated March 8, 1924, states:

Camp Kora Kora; Lake Minchumina, Kantishna District. This low lying section of the interior is especially adapted to the waterfowl. . . . the great white Trumpeter Swan is the least plentiful of all the species, but he is also in evidence in goodly numbers, and I have also noticed the hunters after it. . . . I believe the Treaty regulations between the U. S. and the Dominion of Canada afford them all the protection required. Lake Minchumina appears to be a favored spot for them to stop over and feed and rest on their northern and southern migration.

This report implies that a remnant of the arctic breeding population still remained 35 years ago. Lake Minchumina is located in central Alaska at about latitude 64° N. If still in existence, this population may form a portion of those currently wintering in British Columbia.

Ira N. Gabrielson's (1946: 102) note was the next pertinent occurrence record. This confirmed E. W. Nelson's earlier remark that the trumpeter was to be found in southeastern Alaska at certain seasons including wintering populations, in common with British Columbia.

Subsequent swan census work in Alaska, accomplished during the annual January waterfowl inventory since that time, indicates that the number of swans which actually winter in southeastern Alaska varies greatly, but generally is fewer than indicated in Gabrielson's report, whose count of March (1945) probably included at least some northward-bound birds actually in transit. The swan census data gathered by the U. S. Fish and Wildlife Service in coastal Alaska during the period 1949–57 are presented in table 3.

Table 3.—Swans censused, Alaskan waterfowl inventory, January, 1949 to 1957

[U. S. Fish and Wildlife Service records]

Year and location	Number of swans	Year and location	Number of swans
1949: [1]		1954:	
Ketchikan area	35	Ketchikan area	[2] 127(+50)
Petersburg area	4	Petersburg area	34
Sitka area	2	Craig area	[2] 56(+25)
Total	41	Total	[2] 217(+75)
1950:		1955: [3]	
Ketchikan area	124	Ketchikan area	32
Craig area	2	Petersburg area	16
Total	126	Craig area	59
		Sitka area	2
1951: [1] All areas	0	Total	109
1952: Ketchikan area	37		
1953:		1956: Ketchikan and Petersburg areas combined (reduced coverage)	15
Ketchikan area	[2] 49(+30)	1957: Ketchikan area	82
Craig area	12		
Total	[2] 61(+30)		

[1] Widespread and prolonged freezing of fresh-water lakes and protected bays.
[2] Figures in parentheses are estimated numbers in addition to swans counted.
[3] Mild winter noted, many inland lakes open, vessel survey.

In addition to the southeastern Alaskan areas listed, swans have been reported from time to time wintering on the Alaska Peninsula, Kodiak–Afognak Islands, and Prince William Sound (W. A. Elkins, correspondence). Although the species of these birds has not been determined, it is believed that they represent trumpeters also.

The census figures presented in table 3 are not directly comparable for many reasons. The exact habitat covered may not be the same from year to year even within a designated district, census observers and techniques (aerial, vessel, etc.) vary frequently, the weather no doubt affects distribution greatly and in unknown ways, and swans may not return to the same district each year. Also, the possible occurrence of wintering whistlers in southeastern Alaska cannot be entirely dismissed at this time.

Since small numbers of whistling swans have been known to pass the winter as far north as Washington, Idaho, and British Columbia, the data in table 3 may include some of the lesser species also, although there appears to be little doubt that the trumpeters are substantially represented here.

Alda Orton's (1951:10) article reporting the presence of a small number of breeding trumpeters on the lakes of the Naha River Valley north of Ketchikan appears to be the first breeding record for this species in that area. In this instance it is interesting to note that the breeding and wintering range overlap as they do in the Red Rock Lakes and the Yellowstone Park areas to some extent.

The first indications of a substantial breeding flock of trumpeters in Alaska was brought to light as a result of field work in the lower Copper River Basin by Melvin A. Monson (1956: 444–445). Flying the area comprising the convergence of the Tasnuna and Bremner River Valleys with that of the Copper River on August 11, 1955, Monson censused 69 adult swans and 5 broods totaling 15 cygnets. Identification of several of this group as trumpeters had previously been made on the ground from voice calls, bill characteristics, and egg specimens obtained.

Trumpeter swan investigations are currently underway by U. S. Fish and Wildlife personnel at the Kenai National Moose Range on the Kenai Peninsula, Alaska. The following information was gathered in the preliminary studies by David Spencer (Refuge Supervisor), Jim Johnson (Refuge Manager), and Jim Branson (Game Management Agent), and furnished by Spencer (correspondence, August 30, 1957). I have summarized it as follows:

Swans have been known to nest on the northern part of the Kenai Peninsula over a long period of years. From time to time a few birds have been shot by waterfowl hunters. Two of these which were recovered in 1951 and 1956 were identified as trumpeter swans. It appeared likely these were Kenai nesting

FIGURE 4.—Aerial view of trumpeter breeding grounds in lower Copper River
Basin, Alaska, at confluence of Tasnuna, Bremner, and Copper Rivers.

birds. Investigations in 1957 were aimed at determining the identification of
the Kenai nesting swans and to estimate the nesting population.

The first birds, one pair and one juvenile, were noted on the east fork of
Moose River on April 2. The main group of swans arrived on the nesting ground
about the third week in April. A flock of 48 adult swans observed April 30 were
believed to be migrating birds as there was no evidence that this flock remained in the area.

Approximately 20 pairs of swans nested on the Kenai Moose Range this year.
An additional 10 nonbreeding birds appeared to be in the area. Three clutches

of eggs had measurements within the trumpeter size range.   The male of a nesting pair which was collected was identified as a trumpeter.

The fact that only a single juvenile bird was observed to return in the spring suggests considerable loss among the first-year birds.   The single swan (specimen) collected had been previously shot.   Banding is indicated as an initial step in management, since it will be necessary first to determine the wintering area of the Kenai population before steps are taken to analyze losses.

CENTRAL FLYWAY

Utah.   At least two sight records of swans believed to be trumpeters have been made by well-qualified wildlife observers in Utah during the period 1925–57.   While positive identification was not made in either of these cases, it is not believed likely that both are in error.   Dr. Clarence Cottam (correspondence) reported that A. V. Hull, formerly a Service employee at the Bear River Refuge, observed a trumpeter on that area on June 14, 1932; also that in July 1940 Dr. D. I. Rasmussen and Leo K. Couch reported an immature trumpeter on Strawberry Reservoir.

There is apparently no record that the trumpeter has ever bred within the State of Utah, although several early occurrence records do exist before 1925 (1 in 1923, 1 in 1907 or 1908, and 6 specimens captured in 1901—Cottam, correspondence).

Wyoming.   Vernon Bailey (1930: 188) mentions a few early random Park trumpeter occurrence records, among them 2 breeding pairs seen in 1926, 1 pair on Bridger Lake and the other near Yellowstone Lake. George Wright and Ben Thompson (1935: 104) add, "prior to 1929 a pair of trumpeters had been known to make unsuccessful nesting attempts at Trumpeter Lake in Lamar Valley."   Wright and Thompson sum up the early situation:

Early superintendents' reports have mentioned the presence of swans in the Park. . . . but we have not been able to ascertain whether there was a period of interruption when the birds did not breed in the Park at all, or whether they simply became so scarce as to be generally overlooked.   The latter is probably the case.

It is a fact that in recent years there has been an increase in the number of trumpeter swans breeding in the Park.   To a degree this increase may be more apparent than real, inasmuch as more attention has been focused on the swans than before and nesting stations recently reported may have been previously overlooked.

Other recent records are given under Annual Swan Census, 1929–57.

Two recent Wyoming reports of the trumpeter's occurrence outside the Yellowstone–Jackson Hole area have been made.   The first is especially interesting.   Robert L. Patterson (correspondence) furnished this as follows:

Of . . . interest is a report of a pair of wild swans and five cygnets seen in September, 1953, on a small lake in the vicinity of Pathfinder Migratory Bird

Refuge in central Wyoming. We rather assume that this observation was of trumpeter swans although, of course, it is not verified. The observation was made by George Wrakestraw, one of our wildlife biologists.

The second record is that of 2 trumpeter cygnets, banded on Lowe Lake in the Grande Prairie region of northwestern Alberta in the summer of 1956 by Canadian Wildlife personnel. The birds were found dead, apparently shot, near Cody, Wyoming, on or before October 27, 1956 (R. H. Mackay, 1957 : 339).

Montana. In this state no reports of trumpeters occurring outside their known range during the early part of the 1925–57 period are known. There are several interesting reports since 1950.

K. F. Roahen (correspondence), U. S. Game Management Agent, reported a trumpeter found dead in poor flesh (weight 27 pounds) at Freeze-out Lake, Fairfield, Montana (35 miles west of Great Falls), on October 10, 1950.

Henry Lentfer, taxidermist in Livingston, Montana, furnished this note (correspondence, January 1, 1956) :

A Mr. Hansen who works for the Montana Power Company told me about a pair [of swans] that evidently were about to nest on a small lake near Mystic Lake on the Rosebud last spring or early summer as he saw them for quite a while and then one flew into the powerline and was killed . . . (weight 22½ pounds).

Ralph L. Hand, retired U. S. Forest Service official, also furnished an interesting note of a flight of about 30 swans believed to be trumpeters seen over Missoula, Montana, on October 31, 1953.

Besides the winter movements of the trumpeters in the Madison Valley northwest of Yellowstone Park, birds occur there as far north as Ennis, Montana, during the spring, summer, and fall months. A pair or two are usually found nesting on Ennis Lake.

Trumpeters have been reported at various places along the Beaverhead Valley as far north as Twin Bridges, Montana, over 100 airline miles northwest of the Red Rock Lakes Refuge. A pair of breeding swans have occasionally been reported near Twin Bridges; however, this report has never been verified. A number of late fall and early spring occurrences of trumpeters near Dillon, Montana,, have been reported in recent years by Joseph H. Buck, former Red Rock Lakes Refuge employee.

During the winter months the occurrence of a trumpeter or two along the Yellowstone River outside the Park between Gardiner and Livingston is also occasionally observed by Park Service personnel; however, such sightings indicate only sporadic use of that area.

More recent records are given under Annual Swan Census, 1929–57.

Nebraska. During the 1956 fall hunting season a trumpeter family of 5, which included 3 cygnets banded in the Grande Prairie region of northwestern Alberta (Lowe Lake), were all shot in western Nebraska. Two of the cygnets were killed on October 27—one at Schoolhouse Lake and one at Shoup Lake near Valentine (Cherry County)—while the third was found dead November 2 on the Loup River 12 miles west of Fullerton (Nance County), having previously been shot. One of the adults was shot and crippled October 30 near Fullerton while the other adult was captured wounded near Shelton (Buffalo County) on November 2. The crippled adults were taken to Grand Island where they could be cared for. No other reports for this species in Nebraska appear to have been made since the November 11, 1929, Holt County record (Haecker, Moser, and Swenk, 1945: 5).

North Dakota. Information received from J. F. Cassel, Chairman, Department of Zoology, North Dakota Agricultural College, indicates that a pair of trumpeters in company with 125 whistling swans were observed on Slade Lake near Dawson, North Dakota, by Lee Pettibone on April 25, 1928.

Russell Reid, Superintendent of the Historical Society of North Dakota, wrote (correspondence), "During October 1930, I observed two swans flying over Lake Isabel south of Dawson, North Dakota. These swans appeared to be exceptionally large but . . . identification could not be positive."

There do not appear to be any reports from this State in the last 25 years.

Alberta. The presence of a breeding group of trumpeters in northwestern Alberta in the Grande Prairie district has been known for some time. J. D. Soper (1949: 240) reported 64 adults and 14 cygnets in this area. These birds have been under seasonal observation by the Canadian Wildlife Service since that time.

A breeding pair of trumpeter swans was reported in the Cypress Hills region of southeastern Alberta by Robert Lister (1951: 157). These were observed without young in 1948 but were accompanied by cygnets in 1949 and 1950. These presumably winter somewhere in the United States.

MISSISSIPPI AND ATLANTIC FLYWAYS

A field report (U. S. Fish and Wildlife Service files, Patuxent Refuge) by B. J. Shaver dated August 31, 1937 noted two trumpeter swans on a small marsh lake in Beltrami County, Minnesota. These birds were reported to have been there all summer, but no young birds were seen. No other records show trumpeter occurrence east of Alberta or North Dakota.

HABITAT

BREEDING HABITAT

LIFE ZONE CHARACTERISTICS

The trumpeter swan originally nested over a wide latitudinal range, roughly 1,700 miles at the greatest distance. Although the principal breeding grounds were reported to be mainly within the northern portions of the continent, it is apparent that this fowl formerly nested from at least as far east as the eastern shore of James Bay west to coastal Alaska. This species thus once occupied a variety of different ecological environments.

Established breeding records of the trumpeter document nesting in the following life zones of North America:[1]

1. Arctic-Alpine Zone (Mackenzie Bay, Norton Sound).
2. Open Boreal Forest Zone (lower Mackenzie Basin, Kenai Peninsula).
3. Closed Boreal Forest Zone (upper Mackenzie Basin, Grande Prairie region, Yellowstone region [including Red Rock Lakes]).
4. Aspen Parklands Zone (Cypress Hills, Alberta).
5. Montane Pine Zone (Yellowstone region).
6. Pacific Rainforest Zone (Naha Valley, Alaska).
7. Eastern Deciduous Forest Zone (northeastern and northwestern Missouri, south central Minnesota, southern Wisconsin).
8. Short Grass Prairie Zone (Flathead Valley, Montana; northwestern Nebraska).
9. Tall Grass Prairie Zone (northern Iowa, southern Minnesota).

---

[1] Life zone names based on unpublished information in U. S. Fish and Wildlife Service files.

While the range of life zones occupied by various groups of breeding trumpeters in the past has been great, the fur-trade records would seem to confirm that the trumpeter has been found breeding more typically in the Open Boreal Forest than in any other life zone. As the species existed near the southern limits of its breeding range in the United States, it was to be found nesting chiefly in the Closed Boreal Forest, Montane Pine, Eastern Deciduous Forest, Short Grass Prairie and Tall Grass Prairie Life Zones.

PHYSICAL CHARACTERISTICS

Although trumpeters originally lived in many different major groups of environments, as embraced by the life-zone concept, there is much evidence that this species is far more limited in the variety of habitat it will accept as actual breeding grounds. Its ecological niche may therefore be said to be as confined as its life zone range was generous. This characteristic would be expected in such a specialized waterfowl.

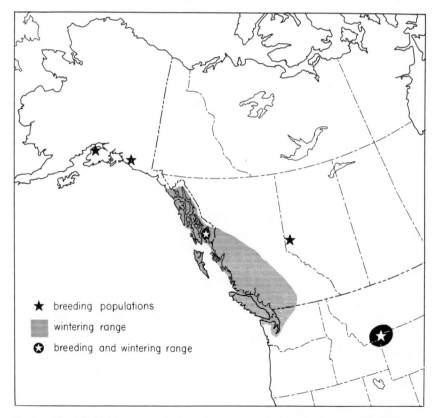

breeding populations

wintering range

breeding and wintering range

FIGURE 5.—Presently known breeding and wintering range, trumpeter swan.
469660 O—60——4

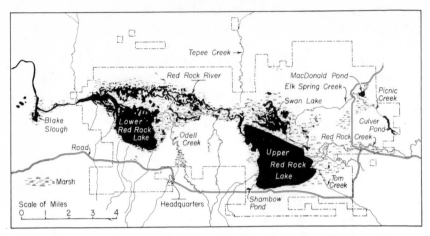

FIGURE 6.—Red Rock Lakes Migratory Waterfowl Refuge.

The following statement outlines some of the specific physical features of the trumpeter's breeding-habitat requirements:

1. Stable waters possessing a relatively static level, not exhibiting marked seasonal fluctuations.
2. Quiet waters of lake, marsh, or slough, not waters subject to obvious current or constant wave action.
3. Shallow waters of lake or open marsh, not so deep as to preclude considerable digging and foraging for lower aquatic plant parts, roots, tubers, etc.

RED ROCK LAKES REFUGE

Perhaps the best way to outline the characteristics of the trumpeter's present breeding habitat in the United States is to describe the principal nesting grounds of this species in the Red Rock Lakes Migratory Waterfowl Refuge. This area was acquired by the United States Government in 1935 and is now administered by the Bureau of Sport Fisheries and Wildlife principally for the perpetuation of this species. This splendid mountain-marsh system is located in the Centennial Valley (Beaverhead County) in southwestern Montana. Comprising about 13,000 acres of shallow lakes, productive open marsh, and extensive sedge meadows, it is a biotic complex not duplicated elsewhere in this country on such a grand scale. Its elevation of 6,600 feet, the relatively stable water supply which flows from numerous springs and creeks sustained by a dependable snow run-off, plus the exceptionally gradual gradient of the entire drainage are physical features which combine to perpetuate a stable virgin marsh of high quality, a rare feature of such generous proportions in these modern times.

FIGURE 7.—The Red Rock Lakes owe their stable waters to the Centennial Mountains which tower above them to the south, trapping abundant snows that feed the numerous creeks and springs entering the marsh system.

Geologically speaking, the Red Rock Lakes in the Centennial Valley of southwestern Montana lie in a broad trough bounded on both the north and south sides by two major faults. South of the lakes a continuous series of en echelon faults form the north face of the Centennial mountain range. The north side of the trough in which the lakes lie is marked by a series of faults along the front of the Gravelly range; thus the lakes lie in a down-dropped basin which comprises most of Centennial Valley. The gradient of the valley floor of Centennial Valley is extremely slight, and erosion is not down-cutting the exit of the Red Rock Lakes at any great speed. Therefore there seems little likelihood that within the next few hundred years there will be any marked change in the lakes themselves; they will neither be filled in nor drained by erosion, though many higher stands of the lake shore can be seen around the margins of the valley. These higher stands of the lakes probably correspond to wetter climatologic periods rather than any marked difference in drainage, and may perhaps be correlated with the various advances of the Wisconsin ice sheet and the extensions and retreats of the valley glaciers into the bottom of the valley floor.

Records of much dryer periods in the recent geologic past are also preserved. Immediately west of the Red Rock Lakes area are many square miles of anchored sand dunes, barchans; these dunes are now covered by vegetation and are nearly stationary. Their form and outline indicates that they were active moving dunes in the recent geologic past, and in a sense are now fossil dunes, testifying to a period of much lower rainfall than now occurs.

FIGURE 8.—Aerial view of Red Rock Lakes. Lower Lake in foreground is dotted with beds of bulrush. The marsh system is at the upper left, and the Upper Lake is in the center background.

The Red Rock Lakes and marsh were the subject of a formal flora survey, with transect control, in 1955 and 1956 by Biologist Watson E. Beed of this Bureau. His work, together with that of other individuals, forms the chief basis of present knowledge regarding the identification, distribution, and quantity of both submerged and emergent vegetation in this marsh. The following description is based on Mr. Beed's report.

All of the Red Rock Lakes bottoms are composed of a mucky matter, being a mixture of decaying vegetation, plankton, and mineral soil. Because of the relative low water temperatures, seldom exceeding 50° F., decomposition is slow and the deposit of decaying material relatively greater than the annual rate of deposition would indicate. It is this residual fertility of the bottoms, which combines with favorable water temperatures and levels during the short summer months, that produces the tremendous abundance of aquatic plants found in the Red Rock Lakes marsh.

The water itself, except for a stained condition in some of the bog bays, is normally clear except when disturbed by wind, feeding water-fowl, or by water movement during the spring run-off. The abundance of aquatic plants indicates a medium hard water with perhaps 20 to 30 ppm. of bound CO_2. The actual pH of four samples taken was 8.

With the exception of the north shore of the Upper Lake, which is subjected to considerable wave action, the shorelines of all waters are vegetated to the water's edge, chiefly with beaked sedge (*Carex rostrata*)[2], and exposed mud flats are absent. Shorelines are open rather than timbered except the south shore of Upper Red Rock Lake, which

[2] Botanical nomenclature, which follows Beed's report, was based on Norman C. Fassett's *Manual of Aquatic Plants*, Albert S. Hitchcock's *Manual of the Grasses of the United States*, and W. E. Booth's *Flora of Montana*, Part 1, as well as identifications supplied by Loran C. Anderson, Acting Curator of the Intermountain Herbarium, Logan, Utah.

FIGURE 9.—Trumpeter swan nest located on an old muskrat house on a cattail-sedge island in Lower Red Rock Lake. In the background the Centennial Mountains wear a snow mantle normal for June.

FIGURE 10.—Numerous channels, sloughs, and potholes set in a bog-mat environment of ·beaked sedge typify the Red Rock Lakes marsh. Darker shoreline vegetation is bulrush, cattail and rushes.

is bordered by a fairly continuous belt of aspens (*Populus tremuloides*). Along the higher better-grained soils, Engelmann spruce (*Picea engelmanni*) in a bog environment with willows (*Salix* spp.) along the immediate lake shore exist in certain locations about Upper Red Rock Lake.

Arrowhead (wapato, *Sagittaria latifolia*) and spikerush (*Eleocharis macrostachya*) are the principal emergent plants found in the Lakes and marsh between the normal sedge shoreline and deeper water. The stable low water levels explain the abundance of these plants in certain locations.

As might be expected, animal life flourishes in the water and around the shoreline. Frogs, toads, and polliwogs are extremely abundant locally in season, while snails and the fry of several fish species are also present in numbers. Water beetles, caddis flies, and rat-tailed maggots are also common in their appropriate ecological strata, while the production of small crustacea and plankton in maximum abundance is truly astounding, the water being literally alive during the summer season.

Swan Lake is a small but important shallow marsh of roughly 400 acres lying to the north of Upper Red Rock Lake and connected with it only by means of its drainage. Elk Springs Creek, which emerges from Swan Lake near the east end only a short distance from where it enters the Lake, is its principal source of water. The water table in this lake is very stable, though having no flow. Numerous emergent islands of spikerush and beaked sedge occur in Swan Lake, and several rather prominent beds of cattails (*Typha latifolia*) are also present. Water depths are extremely shallow, varying, from a few inches to only about a foot in the deepest area of any size, and averaging about 6 to 10 inches over the entire floor of the lake bed.

FIGURE 11.—A trumpeter nest located in the predominant sedge environment of the Red Rock Lakes marsh. Stem and leaf parts of both sedge and cattail form the bulk of the nest material both for the muskrat lodge nest foundation and the nest proper.

FIGURE 12.—Swan Lake is a shallow marsh sealed off from Upper Red Rock Lake by a natural sedge-willow anchored dike. Islands and peninsulas are chiefly sedge bog-mat while many extensive beds of spikerush also occur in these stable shallow waters.

Because the shallow, static nature of the water causes higher water temperatures than in the other areas of the Lakes, algae are conspicuous, especially during the late summer months. In spite of algal shading, the lake bottom is very fertile and supports a great profusion of aquatic plants. The following plants predominated in Swan Lake in 1955 and 1956. Percentages of area occurrence are: water milfoil (*Myriophyllum exalbescens*), 35; bare, 23; sago pondweed (*Potamogeton pectinatus*), 13; clasping-leaf pondweed (*P. richardsonii*), 12; leafy pondweed (*P. foliosus*), 7; slender pondweed (*P. pusillus*), 4; and miscellaneous, 6.

A glance at figure 6 will show that Upper Red Rock Lake is the largest lake on the Refuge; it is about 2,880 acres in expanse. It contains no "islands" of emergent vegetation, and even peripheral plants, such as bulrush or cattail, are not so prevalent as elsewhere.

Water depths in the Upper Lake vary from a few inches to over 5 feet, but almost all of the lake is less than 4 feet deep. The main water supply is furnished by Red Rock Creek, though the Elk Springs Creek–Swan Lake drainage, Tom Creek, and numerous fresh springs along the south side of the lake are also important and add a considerable flow, especially during the runoff season. Drainage of this lake is westward into the main marsh system.

The very fertile bottom of the Upper Red Rock Lake supports an almost unbelievably abundant and luxuriant growth of aquatic plants. In 1955 and 1956 the following tabulations of species percentages were recorded: waterweed (*Elodea canadensis*), 41; muskgrass (*Chara* spp.), 22; bare, 12; leafy pondweed, 5; sago pondweed, 4; and miscellaneous (chiefly *Potamogeton* spp.), 16.

The marsh surrounding Swan Lake and extending between Upper and Lower Lakes comprises the largest single habitat unit within the Refuge, over 8,000 acres. Of this area only about 10 percent is open water, most of the balance being nearly pure stands of sedge in a bog meadow community. Water depths vary greatly but outside the main channels are uniformly shallow. Current in the main stream is very slow and even less perceptible when divided into more than one channel. Many isolated potholes are found within this river marsh area. Most of these are small but a few are of considerable size.

The best of this river-marsh habitat, from a food-producing standpoint, is found along the stream beds of the slow-moving river and extensive shallow sloughs which border these outlet channels. Aquatic plants in the channels and sloughs of the main stream bed were found to occur in the following approximate order of abundance, with a high percentage of the area surveyed being covered: clasping-leaf pondweed, water milfoil, muskgrasses, sago pondweed, and arrowhead.

Common emergents in this area include at least two species of burreed (water burreed, *Sparganium fluctuans*, and *S. multipedunculatum*), hardstem bulrush (*Scirpus acutus*), and cattail. Ecologically, this unit is the most diversified of any on the Refuge, with the greatest variety of plant life.

The Lower Red Rock Lake is 1,540 acres in size and is supported chiefly by the dependable waters of Odell Creek, which arise in the mountains to the south. Several permanent sedge islands are found near the north side of this lake, while many prominent beds of bulrush are scattered over the lake at large. Water depths vary generally from 1 to 2 feet, placing this lake in an intermediate position between shallow Swan Lake and the moderately deep Upper Lake. The lake bed was covered by plants in the following percentages: waterweed,

39; bare, 19; algae, 12; clasping-leaf pondweed, 9; arrowhead, 5; sago pondweed, 2; and miscellaneous species, 14.

Several species of rushes (*Juncus balticus, J. parryii, J. longistylus*, etc.) and sedges (*Carex festivella, C. kelloggii*, and *C. laeviculmis*) are found most frequently on firmer ground between the marsh proper and upland meadows.

The northern slopes of the Centennial Mountains, which form the ramparts to the south of the Lakes, are covered with timber, principally Douglas-fir (*Pseudotsuga taxifolia*) and lodgepole pine (*Pinus contorta*) with a lower slope apron of aspen and willow (*Salix*, spp.). The slopes of the Gravelly Range which stretch away to the north of the Lakes are characterized by a more arid climate and sandier soil where numerous grasses and sages, principally big sagebrush (*Artemisia tridentata*), threetip sagebrush (*A.* tripartita), and silver sagebrush (*A. cana*) thrive.

By far the most common waterfowl associated with the swans in the Red Rock Lakes marsh are the lesser scaup (*Athya affinis*), many hundreds of which are produced annually. Other common marsh nesting birds include the long-billed marsh wren (*Telmatodytes palustris*), a sandhill crane (*Grus canadensis*), and coot (*Fulica americana*).

YELLOWSTONE NATIONAL PARK

In contrast with the Red Rock Lakes area, where the nesting territories are contained in a single marsh system, breeding swans in Yellowstone Park usually exist as isolated pairs on widely separated waters. Without exception, each of Yellowstone's swan lakes is occupied by only one breeding pair of birds.

The swan lakes of Yellowstone also differ physically in many ways from the rather uniform Red Rock marsh nesting habitat. In the Park, shorelines are often timbered, feeding areas are much more apt to be peripheral due to deeper water areas toward the center of the lakes, and lake elevations are generally greater. So the breeding grounds of the trumpeter in Yellowstone are a more marginal habitat than the vast uniform marshes of the Red Rock Lakes. This is apparent in the following description, based on a letter from Condon, of four Park swan waters found outside the plateau region.

The lakes of Yellowstone occupied by swan as nesting areas are pronouncedly different, each from the other, in their geological origin as well as in the general ecology of the area surrounding them. Trumpeter Lake, at an elevation of about 6,050 feet and with a surface area of about 20 acres, owes the origin of its basin to glaciation; it is surrounded only by a grassland-cinquefoil-sagebrush plant association. The waters are shallow, and one end of the lake provides cover

FIGURE 13.—A trumpeter pen on her nest in a shoreline stand of pure sedge, Upper Red Rock Lake. The Centennial Mountains escarpment forms a chilly backdrop.

for nesting birds in the cattails, bulrushes, and sedges. A detailed study of the vegetation within the lake has not been made, but its composition is very different from the vegetation in the lakes at high elevations, secluded in the evergreen forests of the plateau section of the park. There are no large beds of wokas, (yellow pondlilies, *Nuphar polysepalum*). Associated with the swans on Trumpeter Lake are found: ruddy ducks, coots, redwinged blackbirds, yellow-headed blackbirds, spotted sandpipers, mallards, soras, Canada geese, long-billed marsh wrens, muskrats, and a variety of smaller animals.

The Beach Spring Lagoon, with a surface area of about 29 acres, is off Mary Bay on Yellowstone Lake at an elevation of about 7,740 feet. It owes its basin to water impoundment behind a bar formed along the lake shore. Like Trumpeter Lake, this body of water is surrounded by a grassland-sagebrush vegetative complex. It does not have so much cover in the form of cattails, rushes, and sedges for concealment as does Trumpeter Lake. There are no large beds of wokas. The waters are shallow, and during the summer months are commonly visited by California gulls and white pelicans. Canada geese, buffleheads, mallards, scaup, and coots are commonly seen with young on its waters. Marshy areas are much more extensive around this lake than at Trumpeter Lake. The vegetative growth in the marsh areas is not sufficiently tall to provide cover for swans but does provide concealment for smaller birds and mammals.

Swan Lake, at an elevation of about 7,250 meet, owes its basin to glacial action. It is surrounded by a grassland-cinquefoil-sagebrush and sedge-marsh vegetative complex. Canada geese, coots, mallards, green-winged teal, scaup, goldeneyes, and buffleheads are seen with young on this lake. Yellow-headed blackbirds, spotted sandpipers, long-billed marsh wrens, and Wilson's phalaropes nest there. Muskrats are common, and otters are seen at times. The waters are relatively deep with extensive marsh areas on the northern end. Sedges and rushes predominate on the north end. Some small clumps of willow are present. Wokas beds are absent.

Geode Lake is a small lake at an elevation of about 6,150 feet with open rocky shores and virtually no plant cover. The waters are relatively shallow, impounded by an old beaver dam. This has silted over and thus established itself as a barrier which will probably retain water in the basin for many years to come. Very few other birds or animals use this lake. The absence of cover apparently discourages ducks and other waterfowl. There is undoubtedly overland movement of swans from this lake to ponds about ¾-mile distance under Crescent Hill.

The lakes secluded in the evergreen forests of the plateaus of the park are, in most instances, larger in size than the open-country glacial

FIGURE 14.—A female trumpeter, on her nest after returning from a feeding
period in the Lower Lake, shakes the water from her plumage. The nest is
located on a muskrat house behind a protective screen of bulrush. Note
elevation of nest in tall, dense cover, and discoloration of swan's head and
neck from contact with ferrous organic matter.

lakes. Their exact geological origin is somewhat obscure in some
instances, but the majority of them were caused by the damming of
old drainage basins or courses with glacial debris. Some are residual
lakes remaining in a depressed area of a once much larger Yellowstone
Lake. Virtually all of these lakes have beds of wokas in their shallower
waters. In most instances there is an absence of rushes and cattails.
This is not true of Tern Lake, Riddle Lake, or the small lake below
Madison Junction. In some lakes beavers are present and occasionally
their old lodges have provided a base for a nest site. Many of these
lakes have a fringe of meadow around them consisting of grasses and
sedges. Canada geese, mallards, goldeneyes, buffleheads, green-winged
teal, and scaup are seen with young on most of these lakes although
they are not present in any appreciable number. Grebes and coots
are also found on some lakes. The sora nests at White and Tern Lakes

Figure 15.—Geographical features of the trumpeter swan breeding and wintering areas in the United States.

and also at Riddle Lake, while the common loon has been observed nesting at Riddle Lake in association with the trumpeter swan.

COPPER RIVER BASIN, ALASKA

Notes on the Copper River area were furnished by Melvin A. Monson, U. S. Fish and Wildlife Service, who discovered the trumpeters there in 1951. I condensed his remarks as follows:

The Chugach Mountains, through which the lower Copper River passes, effectively divide the climate of the Copper River Basin into two categories. The south side of the range bordering the Gulf of Alaska has a climate maritime in nature with heavy precipitation and relatively mild temperature. . . . North of the Chugach Mountains the climate is colder and considerably drier. Somewhere in between these two general categories are the climatic conditions existing in the Bremner and Tasnuna River valleys.

FIGURE 16.—Trumpeter swan nesting site at Grebe Lake in Yellowstone National Park. Note exposed situation of sedge sod nest. Beds of wokas appear in the background, moulted feathers in the foreground.

Because of rugged topography of the region the deep Copper River canyon acts as a wind funnel so that high wind velocities are common in the lower Bremner and Tasnuna valleys. . . . During the summer the wind blows upstream . . . these strong winds pick up sand and silt from the valley floor of the Copper River below the confluence of the Bremner and Tasnuna Rivers and deposit this material as the wind divides and fans into the Bremner and Tasnuna Rivers. Such deposits are so great that the shallow lakes show evidence of filling up.

The Bremner River has a drainage area of 1,000 square miles and enters the Copper River 40 miles upstream from its mouth. . . . Only in the lower portion, the last 23 miles, does the river bed broaden into a relatively wide flat valley floor. Here there is evidence of great deposits of gravel and silt which have been carried down from the upper reaches. . . . In this stretch, the river does not possess a well-defined channel. Within this lower section small shallow lakes are scattered through the valley floor. It is in these small individual lakes that considerable nesting of swans occurs.

The Tasnuna Basin possesses characteristics similar to those described for the Bremner River. It has a drainage area in excess of 300 square miles and enters the Copper River from the west 40 miles above the mouth of this stream. . . . Here, as in the Bremner River, there is evidence of considerable deposits of gravel and silt laid down in the valley by retreating glaciers. . . . The river has no well-defined channel, and during high water much of the valley floor is flooded. Throughout the lower 10 miles are numerous shallow lakes where nesting swans have been observed.

Spruce is the only valuable timber in the two valleys. It is found up to elevations of about 2,500 feet above sea level. Above the timberline the mountain slopes are covered with a dense growth of alder. . . .

In the flat valley floors there are abundant growths of both willow and alder, which appear to be the dominant species. Also scattered throughout the area are

FIGURE 17.—Aerial view of trumpeter nesting habitat in lower Tasnuna River
Basin, Alaska. Trumpeter nest was found in small restricted slough in the
lower right-hand corner of photo.

limited stands of cottonwood and birch. Grasses are abundant throughout
much of the area, and in shallow lakes and along the lake shores in the valley
floors there are luxuriant growths of horsetail (*Equisetum* spp.).

WINTERING HABITAT

Within the greater Yellowstone region of southwestern Montana,
northwestern Wyoming, and northeastern Idaho, there are five prin-

cipal swan wintering districts. These are listed below in the order of importance, the first two being more vital to the United States segment of the continental trumpeter population than all the rest put together:

1. Island Park area, which includes Henrys Fork of the Snake River and its upper tributary waters (Idaho).
2. Red Rock Lakes Migratory Waterfowl Refuge (Montana).
3. Yellowstone National Park (Wyoming).
4. National Elk Refuge, Jackson Hole (Wyoming).
5. Madison River, and its tributary waters above the Meadow Lake Dam (Montana).

All of the areas listed contain shallow-water lake, stream, and pond habitat with varying amounts of aquatic vegetation. Because of warm springs these waters do not freeze over entirely during the long periods of cold winter weather which normally prevail. Forays by trumpeters outside the greater Yellowstone region described are occasionally observed, though probably these are chiefly exploratory flights. Most, if not all, of the trumpeters inhabiting the United States are believed to winter on suitable waters within the limits of the districts outlined.

These wintering grounds may be roughly divided into two main groups, being either spring-fed streams, or lakes and ponds which also receive warm water from some source. So far as streams are concerned, water movement alone is a factor of considerable importance in keeping such waters open during moderately cold weather, but some source of warm water is a necessity because prolonged periods of cold are common during the winter, with daily minimum temperatures well below zero. In such weather, water movement alone will not keep solid ice from forming completely across fairly active cold rivers.

This role assumed by warm-water springs in providing winter swan habitat in the greater Yellowstone region is all-important. For instance, on the main stem of Henrys Fork of the Snake River the abundant warm waters of Osborne, Harriman, Elk, and Big Springs are essential. On the Madison River within Yellowstone Park the warm waters from numerous geysers and springs collect in the famous Firehole River to keep both it and the Madison River free of solid ice for many miles downstream, and numerous other examples could be cited in the Park. Warm spring impoundments on the Red Rock Lakes Refuge provide the only swan wintering habitat in that area.

Without exception the numerous large warm springs within the greater Yellowstone region are primarily responsible for whatever winter waterfowl habitat is available; without the effect of their combined warm flow, the trumpeter as well as thousands of lesser waterfowl would be forced to migrate elsewhere, and this whole section of the Rockies would be nearly barren of wintering water birds. These warm springs provide wintering habitat for trumpeters conveniently near to suitable breeding grounds, a fact principally responsible for saving this species from extinction in the United States, sparing them the long dangerous migrations down heavily gunned flyways.

Besides open water, good swan wintering habitat contains a certain amount of level and open terrain allowing these large birds to loaf or fly without restriction of visibility or movement. On the smaller streams this becomes especially important since the air space over such water is limited, and trumpeters, perhaps more than any other waterfowl, require ample and unrestricted air space for take-off. Too, the presence of timber growing thickly along watercourses or around spring ponds provides convenient perches for avian enemies (eagles), cover for mammalian predators, and formidable obstacles to flight. Unobstructed snowfields on meadows adjacent to open streams or ponds are regularly used as loafing sites, especially later in the winter when the snow hardens with settling. During this season trumpeters are prone to convene in large flocks and become more active socially.

Because of these factors, the heaviest use of even a comparatively large open stream occurs in those areas which are not timbered or confined to a narrow canyon, and those portions of waters so restricted, even though containing an abundance of food at easily available levels, do not support their proportionate share of use.

ISLAND PARK

The waters of Henrys Fork of the Snake River, together with those of its upper tributaries, arise in the Island Park country (Fremont County) of northeastern Idaho along the west boundary of Yellowstone National Park. Here the terrain, physical characteristics of the stream, and warm waters from many contributing springs combine to produce hundreds of acres of shallow and productive riverbed and pond habitat, some of which does not freeze over even in the coldest weather.

The heart of this wintering area is located on or adjacent to the Railroad Ranch. This ranch with its adjoining lands contains the best and most intensively used trumpeter wintering area for its size on the continent. Old timers say that originally the preferred swan wintering area in this district was located on Shotgun Creek several miles to the north. When the desirable features of that area were eliminated by the completion of the Island Park Reservoir Dam in the 1930's, which flooded this Creek, the swans were forced to rely more heavily on the waters of Henrys Fork proper. (Likewise according to old residents the impoundment of Jackson Lake Reservoir in Jackson

FIGURE 18.—Aerial view of Henrys Fork (North Fork) of the Snake River below the Railroad Ranch, Island Park, Idaho. This stretch of river offers habitat to wintering trumpeters. The warm Harriman Springs keep these waters open even below −30° F.

Hole destroyed open-water areas caused by warm springs. This formerly constituted a wintering area of considerable importance to trumpeters.)

In the vicinity of the Railroad Ranch, the Henrys Fork is a moderately large, clear, shallow stream of relatively stable flow which meanders through open meadows. Several large springs and spring-fed tributaries provide the necessary warm water in strategic locations to keep at least some stretches of the stream open even in the severe winter weather. Beds of marestail (*Hippuris vulgaris*), leafy pondweed, and sago pondweed cover the stream bed in profusion, and with clasping-leaf pondweed no doubt form the bulk of the trumpeters' winter diet in this area.

FIGURE 19.—Aerial view of trumpeters wintering on Henrys Fork of the Snake River below the Railroad Ranch. Gray birds are cygnets-of-the-year. Trumpeters from the Grande Prairie, Alberta, region have wintered in this area.

RED ROCK LAKES REFUGE

Wintering habitat on the Red Rock Lakes Refuge is confined to two warm spring impoundments, MacDonald Pond, where the multiple Elk Springs furnish a plentiful supply of warm (58° F.) water, and Culver (Widow's) Pond where the equal but colder (41° F.) flow of the dual Picnic Springs is confined. At these two areas, located about 2 miles apart at the east end of the Refuge, a combined area of from 5 to 10 acres is normally open during the winter. Although these waters never freeze over entirely, the average open-water area may be reduced by half or less during the prolonged occurrence of −30° F. or colder nightly temperatures.

YELLOWSTONE NATIONAL PARK

Although regular counts are not taken owing to winter isolation factors, five main areas in Yellowstone Park are known to be regularly frequented or occupied by wintering trumpeter swans. A brief description of these winter habitats follows:

1. The Yellowstone River from the outlet of Yellowstone Lake north to its junction with Alum Creek normally furnishes winter quarters for a number of Park trumpeters as well as groups of Canada geese, mallards and goldeneyes. Various areas along about 2 miles

FIGURE 20.—Aerial view of 80 trumpeters in east Culver Spring, Red Rock Lakes Refuge, January 1956. Air temperatures —20° F. Note moose tracks in willow growth.

    of this stream furnish natural aquatic food at available depths as they remain open owing to thermal activity.

2. The Firehole and Madison Rivers offer dependable food supplies in open waters for the greater distance of their existence in the Park. A number of swans are regularly observed on the courses of these streams, even in midwinter, along with a number of mergansers, goldeneyes, mallards, and Canada geese.

3. Shoshone Lake geyser basin contributes enough warm water to the west bay of that lake to create a 10-acre expanse of open water there. Here a pair or so of trumpeters have been known to pass at least part of the winter, sometimes in company with a few Canada geese.

4. A 5-acre expanse of water normally remains open at the north end of Heart Lake near the entrance of Witch Creek. These waters usually support a pair of swans during most of the winter along with a few goldeneyes.

5. At the south end of the Park the Snake and Lewis Rivers, plus the open waters of Polecat Creek together with an adjacent slough, provide open water and aquatic food at an available depth to the small flock of trumpeters normally found wintering in this area. Mallards, geese, and mergansers are also found here with the trumpeters during this season.

NATIONAL ELK REFUGE

Several generous warm springs on the National Elk Refuge assist in keeping Flat Creek open during the winter months. This habitat is located for the most part within the Refuge and but a short distance from the town of Jackson, Wyoming. It has witnessed a rather remarkable increase in the numbers of trumpeters which have wintered here during the past decade. Together with other local warm spring-fed water areas in Jackson Hole, the National Elk Refuge promises to become a wintering area of major importance to the trumpeter in the future, particularly if some development of warm water areas could be accomplished without defeating other wildlife objectives.

MADISON RIVER

This drainage, below Park boundaries but above Ennis Lake Dam and including Cliff and Wade Lakes, normally winters several small flocks of trumpeters. These groups trade back and forth within the area or visit adjoining areas as the occasion demands. Specific areas containing winter habitat in this district are O'Dell Creek near Ennis, Montana, the upper Madison River near the head of Hebgen Reservoir, and spring-fed portions of Wade and Cliff Lakes located to the west of the Madison Valley proper.

WINTER COUNTS

Because of the poor winter flying conditions and the isolated character of the country, no true aerial census over the entire greater Yellowstone region has been made during the midwinter months. Fairly complete aerial or ground counts have been made as the opportunity arose in some of the districts listed. These observations have been made by rangers of the National Park Service on winter patrol, biologists of the Idaho Fish and Game Department, U. S. Fish and Wildlife Service personnel, and other local observers.

These count data are presented in table 4 in order to provide an index of relative use.

Small numbers of whistling swans have been observed (voice identification) during the midwinter months in the Island Park area. I have heard whistling swans on winter patrol trips in the vicinity of the Railroad Ranch, and Ed Kroker, foreman of the Ranch, has confirmed the regular occurrence of a few wintering birds in this area. The maximum number of the lesser species which has been noted is 8. These were reported by Frank Kennedy, winter keeper of the Elk Springs Ranch in the Island Park area. So although whistlers have been observed to winter in this area regularly, they are apparently never present in great numbers and the data in table 4 are therefore believed to represent trumpeters almost entirely.

Table 4.—Winter swan counts, Greater Yellowstone region, 1950 to 1957

Time of observation	Swans observed	Count method	Observer
ISLAND PARK AREA (IDAHO)			
Feb. 3–7, 1950	262 (208)[1]	Aerial	Shaw and Monaghan, Idaho Fish and Game Department.
Feb. 7, 1951	257	do	Do.
Jan. 10, 1952	330 (222)[1]	do	Salter, Idaho Fish and Game Department.
Feb. 2, 1953	356	do	Misseldine, Shaw, and Nielson, Idaho Fish and Game Department.
Jan. 6, 1954	419 (333)[1]	Aerial and ground	Salter, Idaho Fish and Game Department. Cromwell, U. S. Fish and Wildlife Service.
Jan. 6, 1955	271 (141)[1]	Aerial	Bizeau and Bross, Idaho Fish and Game Department.
Feb. 16, 1956	318 (288)[1]	do	Bizeau, Idaho Fish and Game Department.
Jan. 10, 1957	323 (250)[1]	do	Bizeau and Kaster, Idaho Fish and Game Department.
RED ROCK LAKES REFUGE (MONTANA) [2]			
Dec. 1949–Mar. 1950	105–80–200–150	Ground	U. S. Fish and Wildlife Service station personnel.
Dec. 1950–Mar. 1951	31–47–100–120	do	Do.
Dec. 1951–Mar. 1952	18–50–50–150	do	Do.
Dec. 1952–Mar. 1953	35–61–75–100	do	Do.
Dec. 1953–Mar. 1954 [3]	12–90–146–250	do	Do.
Dec. 1954–Mar. 1955	147–140–135–250	do	Do.
Dec. 1955–Mar. 1956	55–154–325–280	do	Do.
Dec. 1956–Mar. 1957	?–95–209–230	do	Do.
NATIONAL ELK REFUGE (WYOMING) [4]			
Season 1949–50	10	do	Do.
Season 1950–51	13	do	Do.
Season 1951–52	13	do	Do.
Season 1952–53	13	do	Do.
Season 1953–54	24	do	Do.
Season 1954–55	30	do	Do.
Season 1955–56	33	do	Do.
Season 1956–57	34 (56)[4]	do	Do.
MADISON RIVER DRAINAGE (MONTANA)			
Dec. 1955	30–50 (Cliff Lake)	do	Philip L. Wright, Montana State University.
Jan. 1956	20–30 (Cliff Lake)	do	Monte Neely, local resident.
Jan. 1956	6–8 (Wade Lake)	do	Do.
Jan. 1956	11 (O'Dell Creek)	do	H. W. Baker, U. S. Fish and Wildlife Service.
YELLOWSTONE NATIONAL PARK [5]			
Jan. 10–13, 1950	52	do	Unknown.
Jan. 8–12, 1951	No data	do	Do.
Jan. 1952	16	do	Do.
Jan. 13–15, 1953	33	do	Do.
Jan. 3–18, 1954	56	do	Do.
Jan. 7–18, 1955	18	do	Do.
Jan. 9–13, 1956	14	do	Do.
Jan. 4–9, 1957 (Madison River Only)	20	do	Do.

[1] Number in parenthesis represents numbers of swan on or adjacent to Henrys Fork through the Railroad Ranch or the immediate vicinity and upstream to I. P. dam.
[2] Highest count or estimate of numbers of birds seen during December, January, February, and March, in that order.
[3] MacDonald Pond winter-habitat development completed fall of 1953.
[4] Figure corresponds to maximum number of swans seen about Flat Creek feeding ground during winter. Average number accommodated each year is probably only slightly lower except for winter of 1956–57, when maximum number was present only a short time, hence is shown in parenthesis. Some of the maximum number shown in parenthesis may have been whistlers, though none were identified as such at the time. Identification of all individuals in entire flock of 56 was not possible.
[5] No concerted effort has been made to gather wintering trumpeter data in the Park. These figures represent swans seen while conducting the annual winter waterfowl inventory.

LIFE CYCLE

DESCRIPTION

The large size and general waterfowl conformation, white color, and prominent long necks of our native swans identify them whether seen on the water or in flight. Except for the occurrence of feral mute swans (*Cygnus olor*) along the eastern seaboard in the general vicinity of the lower Hudson River Valley or in Michigan (Grande Traverse County and vicinity), only the two native North American species are likely to be encountered in the wild. A detailed description of the external appearances of both species follows. For comparison, a number of weights and measurements of mute, whooping, and Bewick's swans can be found in Hilprecht (1956: 51–54). He also describes the appearance, flight, and voice of these foreign swans (1956: 19–31). From these we may conclude that the trumpeter is the largest swan in the world.

SPECIES DESCRIPTION

Trumpeter swan, *Olor buccinator* (Richardson), adult (sexes alike) : entire plumage white, head and neck commonly with a rusty stain from ferrous waters; iris brown; bill black, rarely with small grayish or yellowish spot immediately posterior to nostril; bill usually longer and broader terminally than in *Olor columbianus;* front edge of nostril usually 50 mm. or more from tip of culmen; four outer primaries emarginated terminally; and feet usually black or gray but sometimes tinged with brownish, yellow, or olive.

JUVENILE (sexes alike) : Gray Phase (common). Brownish-gray especially on the head, neck, and upper back, lighter gray ventrally; forehead, crown, occiput, nape, and upper cheeks light rufescent brown; plumage sometimes rust-stained as in the adult; feet yellowish or olive gray-black; bill becoming black but with basal portion of culmenary ridge behind nostril still salmon or light pink color; tomia of mandible dull flesh color. White Phase (rare). White down of young replaced directly by white feathers, identical to adult. Color of feet and bill as in gray phase.

Downy Young (sexes alike) : Gray Phase (common). Head and neck uniformly mouse-gray; body mouse-gray dorsally, lighter gray to white ventrally; feet yellowish; bill pinkish basally, dark gray terminally. White Phase (rare). Entire plumage white, feet yellowish, bill flesh colored.

Adult Male: [1] Wing 545–680 (618.6) ; tail 173–191 (182) ; culmen from tip of frontal feathering 104–119.5 (112.5) ; tarsus 121.5–126 (122.9) ; middle toe without claw 135–145 (141.1 mm.).[2] [Adult male (Kenai) : total length 59 in., wingspread 87.5 in., weight 27 lb. 6 oz.; (Yellowstone Park) : total length 60 in., wingspread 96.5 in., weight 27 lb. 9 oz.]

Adult Female: Wing 604–636 (623.3) ; tail 185–207 (196) ; culmen from tip of frontal feathering 101.5–112.5 (107) ; tarsus 113–128.5 (121.7) ; middle toe (w/o claw) 138.5–148 (143.3 mm.).[3] [Adult female (Yellowstone Park) : total length 58 in., wingspread 74 in.]

For comparative purposes the external appearance of the whistling swan is also presented here :

Whistling Swan, *Olor columbianus* (Ord), adult (sexes alike) : Entire plumage white, head and neck sometimes with a rusty stain from ferrous waters; iris brown; bill black when not with usual yellow or orange-yellow spot in front of the eye, front edge of nostril usually less than 50 mm. from tip of culmen; four outer primaries emarginated terminally; feet black or gray.

Juvenile (sexes alike) : Entire plumage ashy gray, usually darkest on the head and palest on the ventral portions of the body, sometimes plumbeous to sooty, brownish instead of pale gray due to staining from ferrous waters, bill basally flesh-colored with the nail and gape border black; iris hazel; tarsi and toes flesh color, livid to dusky.

Downy Young (sexes alike) : Plumage white, tinged with cartridge buff to ivory yellow especially on the head, neck, and breast; bill, tarsi and toes yellowish.

Adult Male: Wing 501–569 (538) ; tail 162–181 (170.8) ; culmen from tip of frontal feathering 97–107 (102.6) ; tarsus 105–117.5 (111.9) ; middle toe without claw 120–133 (126.4).[4]

Adult Female: Wing 505–561 (531.6) ; tail 146–186 (165.3) ; culmen from tip of frontal feathering 92.5–106 (99.9) ; tarsus 99.5–115 (107.2) ; middle toe without claw 110–126.5 (118).[5]

---

[1] Measurements in millimeters, giving the smallest and largest of the birds examined, with the average in parentheses (25.4 mm.=1 inch).

[2] Five specimens, from Idaho, Wyoming, Wisconsin, and Michigan.

[3] Three specimens, one from Montana.

[4] Eight specimens from Alaska, Maryland, Virginia, and North Carolina.

[5] Fifteen specimens from Alaska, California, Maryland, Virginia, North Carolina, and captivity.

Table 5.—Overlapping weights and dimensions of small trumpeter and large whistling swans

Age and sex	Olor buccinator—Minimum weights and measurements				Olor columbianus—Maximum weights and measurements			
	Number of specimens	Body wt. (lbs.)	From tip of bill to anterior edge of nostril (mm.)	From tip of bill to axis of eyes (mm.)	Number of specimens	Body wt. (lbs.)	From tip of bill to anterior edge of nostril (mm.)	From tip of bill to axis of eyes (mm.)
2+ years:								
Male	8	20	50	140	7	19.5	48	125
Female	14	16	50	133	21	19	49	138
1+ years:								
Male	8	18	47	131	2	17	41	123
Female	4	15	50	135	7	17	44	118

EXTERNAL APPEARANCE

If certain external characteristics are lacking or unobservable, it is easy to see why it is virtually impossible to distinguish these species positively without a postmortem examination. Richardson pointed out that the trumpeter tracheal route along the sternum detoured dorsally into the body cavity whereas the tracheal routes of other closely related swans did not. This detail is also naturally expressed in the pertinent adjacent portions of the trumpeter's anatomy, such as the sternum and furculum where structural modifications are necessary to accommodate the really unique dorsal tracheal detour which extends so prominently into the body cavity. More lately, Condon (MS) has focused attention on the syrinx and has been able to show significant differences between the trumpeter and whistling swans in the specimens he studied. The empirical anatomical differences between these two species are shown graphically in figures 21 and 22. Since a diagnostic autopsy may be impractical from many standpoints, even with the specimen in hand, the means of separating trumpeters from whistlers solely by external means will be explored briefly here.

The search for a valid external characteristic other than voice has perplexed both the field observer and the systematic scientist for well over a century.

Some of the points used in the past for species differentiation are taken up in some detail here to provide an understanding of the facts involved. On this basis a positive solution of the problem may some day be worked out.

With the exception of the voice criterion, 3 methods of identification based solely on external characteristics have been used in the past. These are the tail-feather count, bill coloration, and the measurements of various bill features, the last method being dependent upon size. A brief discussion of these 3 methods follows.

Tail-feather count. Many writers picked up John Richardson's remark that the trumpeter possessed a tail of 24 feathers, and have perpetuated a method of identification of such obviously limited value that it should, in my opinion at least, never have received more than passing attention in the first place. This was probably all that Richardson intended anyway, judging by his casual note. Leonhard Stejneger's early statement on this method should have pointed out once and for all the negative value of tail-feather counts when positive species determination is desired. He stated (1882: 216–217) :

> It has often been stated as a good criterion that *buccinator* has twenty-four tail feathers in contradistinction to *columbianus*, which only has twenty. Independent of the inconvenience of this character, when the birds moult their rectrices, I may confess that I only in a few cases have been able to count twenty-four tail feathers; and the inconstancy of the number of these feathers I have found pervading the whole group, this character changing individually, so that it is not at all to be depended upon.

Bill coloration. Most of the references of previous writers regarding this method of speciation refer to the area of the upper mandible (bill) immediately in front of the eyes, known as the "lores." Though the whistler is usually characterized by a yellow or orange-yellow spot on the lores, apparently this color is sometimes lacking and the entire bill is black.

On the other hand, the bill of the trumpeter is almost invariably black, though again this rule is not absolute. Dr. Ray Erickson, U. S. Fish and Wildlife Service biologist formerly at the Malheur Refuge, said that trumpeters kept in captivity at that Refuge sometimes exhibited an olive-yellow spot in the loral region. Apparently the abrasive or scuffing action given the bill when rooting out food from comparatively hard pond banks caused the underlying color to appear.

In 1957, I noted that the wild trumpeters at Red Rock Lakes sometimes exhibit a small indistinct gray spot of irregular shape behind the nostril. In two cases this was tinged with yellow, and in one instance the yellow could be discerned with the naked eye from a distance of over 50 feet. This specimen was collected and confirmed as a trumpeter by a postmortem examination of the sternum.

In conclusion it may be stated that while a completely black bill can represent either species, a prominent bright yellow or orange-yellow spot on the *lores* indicates a whistler.

F. H. Kortright (1943: 77) raises another point in bill coloration, writing of the trumpeter, "bill, black, with narrow salmon-red streak on edges of mandibles, lacking in Whistling Swan." My experience not only demonstrated that the salmon-red streak on the trumpeter was confined almost wholly to the basal section of the lower mandible edge, but that there was great variation in the degree to which it is

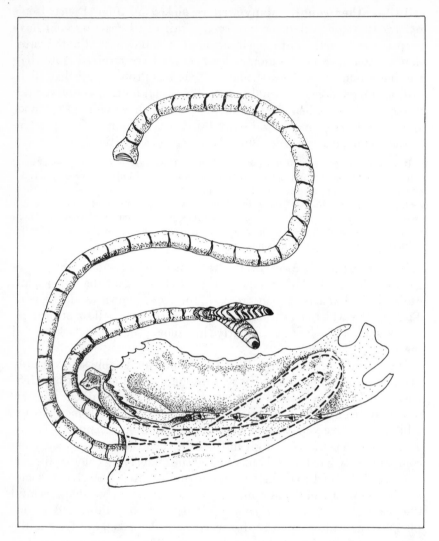

FIGURE 21.—Trachea and sternum of whistling swan.

present. This variance ranges from the quite prominent "grinning" streak" normally seen to a few very faint specks of vestigial salmon coloration which could be observed only upon minute and critical examination, the preponderant color for all practical purposes being completely black.

Furthermore, I have noted that some whistling swans complete with prominent yellow lores also exhibit the characteristic salmon-red "grinning" streak along the basal segment of the lower man-

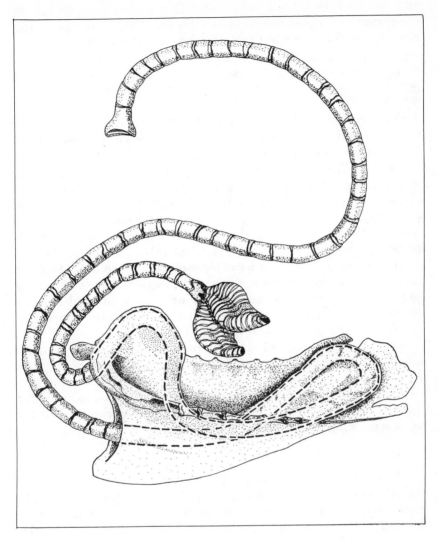

FIGURE 22.—Trachea and sternum of trumpeter swan.

dible edge, though not enough specimens have been examined in this regard to furnish a general rule. So, for all practical purposes, the salmon color usually present on the dorsal portion of the basal edge of the lower mandible cannot furnish a positive indicator of either species, since overlapping characteristics are commonly observed.

Bill measurement. From a comparison of considerable anatomical-measurement data on the subject, Stejneger correctly concluded that size alone is not sufficient to separate the two species since enough overlap exists to confuse the issue. This is true even though the trumpeter, the largest species of swan in the world, is on the average much larger than the whistler. He does state (1882: 217) :

> The position of the nostrils, those being situated more backwards in the Trumpeter than in the Whistling Swan, is thus the only mark by which it is possible to express in a short diagnosis, and which I have found constant and easily perceptible.

Measurements of the bills of a number of trumpeter specimens were made on the Red Rock Lakes Refuge during the summer molt period. With the cooperation of various Fish and Wildlife Refuge personnel at the Tule Lake and Sacramento Refuges, comparable data on whistling swans were also gathered. This information is summarized in table 5. These statistics demonstrate that, owing to the possibility of overlap, bill measurements alone cannot provide an absolute method of separating the species in question, though with the proper qualifications in mind an excellent rule of thumb can be demonstrated. Of course, in order to show overlap to the best advantage, maximum extremes of the weights and measurements of whistling-swan features and minimum extremes of the weights and measurements of the pertinent trumpeter characteristics in the appropriate age and sex groups were those listed.

When the voice and bill color characteristics of a given swan are missing or in doubt, any swan over 1 year of age, of either sex, which measures 50 mm. (2 in.) or more from the tip of the bill to the front edge of the nostril is probably a trumpeter. If the subject measurement is less than 50 mm., identification of the species as whistling swan is most likely to be correct.

VOICE

The voices of our two species of swans differ distinctly in the adult, doubtless owing to the extra loop of the trachea in the sternum of the trumpeter. Once heard, the trumpeter's call notes should not easily be confused with that of any other bird, least of all that of the whistling swan, whose voice resembles at a distance a high-pitched barking of "wow, wow-wow." Close at hand, as described by Lewis and Clark (Coues, 1893: 885), who gave to this species the common name of whistling swan, the "kind of whistling sound" can be heard. This noise "terminates in a round full note, louder at the end," the distantly audible *wow*.

Trumpeters are an expressive fowl, and their voices are often employed to show their feelings and attitudes. During the nesting and brooding seasons the mated pairs are fairly mute, though individuals in the nonbreeding flocks remain relatively communicative all summer. Through the fall and winter seasons the vocal natures of all age classes begin to ·be more fully expressed. During these months most of the swans are loosely bound into large informal flocks, and vocal expression is common, individually and in an occasional synchronized flock effort. Though they are perfectly capable of loud hissing, this has only been heard from cornered flightless trumpeters.

During the months of March and April, just before the occupation of the breeding grounds by the restless mated pairs, vocal efforts reach a climax. At this season the swans on the Refuge are still attracted to the open-water spring-heads at feeding time, though the pull of the breeding grounds must be growing stronger daily. The approach of twilight finds the large flock usually resident about the open water announcing with loud trumpet calls each flight of swans as they return from their daily visits to the still ice-locked lakes and marshes which will soon become their summer home.

It is difficult, if not impossible, to describe phonetically the notes of the trumpeter. E. H. Forbush (1929: 305) credits E. S. Cameron with the Kootenai Indian name for a swan, Ko-hoh, which when pronounced with a gutteral intonation is a very good reproduction of the notes of a trumpeter swan. The call has a definite hornlike quality over a wide vocal range and may be uttered from one to a number of times, at widely spaced intervals or in staccato fashion. The trumpeter gives voice perhaps most often in flight but also commonly while on land or floating on the water.

In general, the warning notes of the adult are sharp and terse, uttered infrequently; the decoy calls are longer and more apt to be repeated. Voices associated with simultaneous behavioral displays are much more conversational and when indulged in by more than two swans are apt to build up rapidly in participation and volume, finally reaching a crescendo and then ending in longer wailing notes. Since the range of an adult trumpeter's calls is well over a mile, the combined voices of noisy flocks can be heard at a distance of several miles if atmospheric conditions are favorable.

Flocked trumpeters especially may be heard after dark, and in all seasons, particularly on moonlight nights. At such times and when softened by distance their wild trumpeting calls heard afar over lake and marsh furnish musical reminders of their wilderness world.

If the call notes of the adults can be described as resembling a horn instrument, then the immature birds have the tone of a toy trumpet. Higher pitched and uncertain in overall quality, they bear the unmistakable characteristics of adolescence. By January, however, in place of the high-pitched fluting of the downy and post-downy periods, the birds utter a hoarse off-key imitation of the adult trumpeter.

PLUMAGES AND MOLTING

Cygnets and immatures. Young trumpeters emerge as downy cygnets in either of two color phases, gray and white (not albino). In the case of the gray individuals, by far the most common, the head, neck, and back are mouse-gray with the underparts quite white. Much the same situation prevails in the mute swan (Delacour, 1954: 63) except that the white phase has only been reported in captive birds (Hilprecht, 1956: 107–8) apparently as a result of inbreeding.

Although white cygnets have never been seen at Red Rock Lakes, they are regularly observed in Yellowstone Park, where broods with both colors occur. Condon (MS) reports:

Of the cygnets recorded during the period 1937–40, the following count of gray and white ones was secured: 1937, 23 gray and 6 white; 1938, 3 gray and 1 white; 1939, 16 gray and 1 white; 1940, 16 gray and 1 white.

Thus, over a 4-year period in the Park, 13 percent of the cygnets were those of the white phase. Moreover, Condon has said that the white down in these birds is replaced by white feathers, instead of those of the usual brownish-gray, so that when they have reached flight age they can only be told from their parents by their slightly smaller size, pinkish bill, and yellowish legs, which are becoming darkened with gray.

Only one record of white cygnets occurring in the wild outside of Yellowstone Park exists, that of three cygnets censused on the Icehouse Reservoir (Fremont County), Idaho, in 1956.

F. E. Blaauw (1904: 73), a Dutch aviculturist who bred the trumpeter in captivity at Gooilust (Holland) for more than 25 years, provides a good general description of the normal gray-colored young from his day-to-day familiarity with these birds, stating:

The chicks are white with a grey tinge on the back. The cere is covered with pure white down. The bill is flesh-coloured. The down of these chicks is very short and dense, quite different from the longer and more fluffy down of the chicks of *Cygnus nigricollis* and *C. atratus* [black-necked and black swans]. The result is that the chicks look much smaller in comparison. . . . At the age of about six weeks, the first feathers appear, and the birds then begin to grow very quickly. The first feathers are brownish-grey, without any markings as a rule, but one of this year's birds is remarkable for having transverse markings on the shoulders and greater wing coverts. After the birds are feathered the bills gradually acquire the black colour, the black beginning at the point and at the forehead, and gradually increasing. Later, the middle part, which is still pink, gets spotted with black, and in the course of the February following the first summer the whole of the bill usually becomes quite black. The legs by that time have also gradually darkened into dusky grey, which becomes black after the birds are a year old. About March white feathers begin to replace the grey plumage, except for some fine grey spots, which are still visible on the back of the neck and on the head.

FIGURE 23.—A pair of trumpeters on Grebe Lake, Yellowstone National Park, with 3 cygnets of the normal gray color phase and 2 cygnets of the uncommon white phase.

Usually the pinkish color of the cygnet's bill has become predominantly black by the time the individual is about a year old, though a close examination of the upper mandible will usually still show traces of the typical flesh-colored pigment at least until the individual's first flightless molt. By the time the bird has entered its second flightless molt, the bill is black.

During 1955 and 1956 Peter Ward, of the Delta Waterfowl Research Station, Delta, Manitoba, noted the general molting pattern of the young trumpeters furnished that station by the U. S. Fish and Wildlife Service in 1955, writing (correspondence):

> Although their exact age on arrival was not known, they were assumed to be four weeks old, this being based on our familiarity with growth rates of other waterfowl. This would have given them the first feathering of scapulars and flanks at six weeks. Body feathering was externally complete by the tenth [week]. The young birds seemed very conscious of the large wings and unable to hold them indefinitely at their sides.
>
> The first juvenal plumage was a dark grey-brown and remained thus until early in January when a gradual moult set in. Within the month this has changed the neck and breast to an off-white and is still in progress. Some evidence of the same change was visible in both scapular and wing coverts at this time where new feathers are appearing.

Adults. All of the closely related circumpolar species of swans are strictly white-plumaged birds in their adult plumage, except when a reddish coloration has been imparted to the head and neck feathers by ferrous organic compounds in the marsh or lake bottom they habitually frequent. At the Red Rock Lakes Refuge, swans feeding principally in shallow water during the summer months possess this distinctive reddish coloration to a much greater degree than those which customarily seek their food in deeper water.

During the winter, this coloration is much less evident on their heads and necks. Then the swans are feeding primarily in flowing spring and river waters where relatively clean (organically) rock, silt, or sandy bottoms prevail. Even during that season some rustiness is invariably observed upon a close examination of the feathers about the head, and I have never seen a wild trumpeter entirely devoid of the stain. With swans living principally in very shallow-water marsh areas, the whole neck and head and even some of the ventral plumage may be startlingly reddish.

While the leg color of most adult trumpeters can accurately be described as black, an off-black to distinctly gray color is also common. Various degrees of olive-yellow pigmentation are occasionally noted on the skin of the legs and feet of the adult trumpeter, but only rarely to the extent that the whole extremity could be said to have a yellowish appearance. The incidence of yellow pigment was noted on the skin of the legs, feet, and webs of the 102 nonbreeding swans captured during the summer of 1956 for fluoroscopic examination. Thirty-four of this group had at least some subdued olive-yellow tones in various skin areas. Frequently the yellow coloration was discernible on the skin of all three parts—legs, feet, and webs—with the most noticeable cases commonly found in the yearling age-class, and to some extent in individual birds of the 2-years-or-older age group.

Francis D. LaNoue (MS) implied that such coloration may be seasonal or local in nature in Yellowstone Park swans, as he records an unusual instance in this regard:

Early last spring 11 swans were seen possessed with yellow legs and feet. In addition all three of the dead mature birds [referred to] show the same color. Later in the season this color was not observed.

Immature and adult swans regularly undergo an annual molt during the summer period during which time they are unable to fly because of a more or less simultaneous loss of primary flight feathers. This molt most commonly occurs among the swans at Red Rock Lakes during the month of July, but may be completed during June in some cases or be delayed until August, September, or even October. This flightless molting period is important from a management standpoint since these birds can then be conveniently captured for examination and banding.

Several phases of this annual molt are as yet poorly understood. While the flocked nonbreeders molt more or less simultaneously, nest-

FIGURE 24.—Six trumpeters circle the open water at Culver Pond on the Red Rock Lakes Refuge in southwestern Montana. Seldom more than 6 or 8 of these birds fly together in local flights unless a large flock flushes together.

ing pairs do not usually follow such a regular molting pattern, on the Red Rock Lakes breeding grounds at least. Molting of the breeders appears to extend over a much longer period than that of the nonbreeders. Molted primary wing feathers are sometimes observed about the nest site in early June, and individuals of mated pairs have been captured for banding while in a flightless condition as late as October. During the summer of 1954, when it was desired to obtain pairs of known breeding capability intact with their young for transfer purposes, only the pen (female) and cob (male) of 6 pairs were simultaneously flightless and could be captured. Approximately 25 pairs were periodically checked for flight capabilities during the period of July 14–28 that year, and only 3 pairs were obtained on each of those dates. One member of each pair was able to fly in every other instance.

In the following 2 years, 1955 and 1956, even poorer luck was experienced. The mated-pair swan transfer program was suspended during those years chiefly because no more than a single known pair could be captured during any given attempt.

During the early part of the molting season, where only one of a pair was flightless it usually has been the pen, while most late-molting birds checked have been cobs. Peter Scott and James Fisher (1953:210) observed similar conditions among the wild whooper swans in Iceland.

Molting information on Yellowstone trumpeters which is contained in Park reports agrees generally with that from Red Rock Lakes, except for sex, which was not determined. The opportunity to check on the duration of the flightless molt of individual birds is somewhat greater in the Park, however, and Condon (MS) mentions in this respect, "The fact that some swan have been seen in flight as late as July 1 and as early as August 2 indicates that the interval of time when they are unable to fly is in some instances rather brief, probably not exceeding 30 to 40 days."

Oberhansley and Barrows (MS) record two exceptionally long molting periods in 1938 for the pair of trumpeters on Swan Lake:

The female remained flightless from May 14 to October 9, a period of 148 days, while the male was not seen in flight from June 11 to October 9, a period of 120 days. . . . Moulting in the pen occurred largely on or near the nest during the time of sitting. Most of the flight feathers were found in close proximity to the nest. A very small quantity of down was found on the nest eight days after hatching. The majority of the primary feathers were shed by the cob at a later date, many of them on or near the resting sites on the west bank of the lake.

FLIGHT

It is difficult to imagine a more beautiful and stirring sight in the whole waterfowl kingdom than a typically small flight of trumpeter swans as they cleave the air against a wilderness setting of dark conifers and the rugged Rocky Mountains. With the regular beat of their powerful wings and long necks undulating slightly from the exertion of each thrust, sometimes calling in flight but more often silent, they usually pass directly to their destination over the shortest route. If they chance to pass close to the observer, the clatter of their great flight quills can be heard distinctly above the usual rushing sound of moving air.

Local flights are usually low. This is especially true over familiar flat marsh or water where their wing tips sometimes appear to touch the sedge tops, or if they are over water, to pluck small jets of water into the air with each powerful lift of the wing. On longer flights over rugged mountain country, they are to be seen at much greater altitudes, gaining this height with considerable effort. Once they approach their destination, they may descend rapidly with a roar of cupped wings much in the usual manner of the more agile and airworthy smaller waterfowl, but their descent is usually slower and more gradual.

The trumpeters prefer to fly about their Rocky Mountain environment in small flocks, apparently family groups for the most part. Even when a large flock of trumpeters is roused suddenly, take-

FIGURE 25.—A pair of trumpeters show the 2 ways of carrying "landing gear" during flight. The normal method is by folding them back under the tail, but in sub-zero weather cold feet may be tucked up forward and be quite invisible in the warm feathers and down.

FIGURE 26.—The normal and "exerting" neck attitudes are shown by 2 trumpeters. Most commonly bent in this peculiar attitude during take-off, the neck straightens out in full flight.

offs are intermittent and by loosely formed groups. Upon becoming airborne they make their way in loosely knit small groups or flocks, though often to a common destination.

Their flying formation varies greatly, sometimes being on the order of an offset line, sometimes nearly abreast, or otherwise irregularly formed in an informal staggered formation. Even a pair in flight may follow no particular flight pattern. I have never observed a true V-formation of trumpeters. This flight formation is probably employed on certain occasions, especially on long flights when larger flocks would be the rule. A high V-flight of swans, apparently trumpeters, was seen by Ralph L. Hand, as previously noted.

H. F. Witherby et al. (1939:169) note of the whooper swan, "When travelling far flocks frequently fly in oblique lines or V's, but in [Outer] Hebrides parties rarely adopt any definite formation." This seems to apply to what is known of the trumpeters' flights as well. Audubon (1838:540) notes also, "If bound to a distant place, they form themselves in angular lines."

To my knowledge, the flight speed of the trumpeter has never been recorded. Though the swans generally have been credited with most astounding speeds by some writers, it is doubtful whether the trumpeter can, without a tailwind, fly much faster than the speed recorded for the whistling swan by C. S. Weiser (1933:92). Weiser estimated the full speed of the latter species at from 50 to 55 miles an hour, when tracked by a light airplane on several passes. With a strong tailwind, the trumpeter can probably approach or exceed a ground speed of 80 miles an hour with little difficulty.

Their legs and feet are normally carried in a streamlined manner tucked under the tail, nearly reaching its end. During the winter season, if the weather is very cold, they have been observed to fold their feet and legs forward in flight, carrying them quite buried in a warm "muff" of thick breast and down feathers (figure 25).

The feet with their great webbed area are usually employed both as an aid in gaining speed on the take-off and as an effective brake in alighting. After sufficient flight speed is gained following the take-off, the required distance for which varies greatly according to the wind, the feet are retracted into the customary position. In landing, the huge webbed feet are thrust prominently forward, acting like aircraft flaps to reduce flying speed and becoming effective hydrofoils as the swan contacts the water, skims briefly along the surface, then toboggans to a swimming position.

The long neck is often curved somewhat with the great effort required during the take-off and flight, apparently because of abnormal exertion. In normal flight position, however, it is carried fully extended, undulating slightly with the beat of the wings.

FIGURE 27.—Six trumpeters landing "flaps down" on Culver Pond, Red Rock Lakes Refuge. The feet are thrown forward before the moment of impact to ski the bird to a stop. Note various web positions guiding birds into landing.

F. E. Blaauw (1904: 74) mentions, "Young trumpeter swans when fully fledged are very active birds. They fly with great ease, rising directly from the water into the air, without running over it first with flapping wings as so many of the large waterfowl do." I have never seen this occur among trumpeters of any age class, though Richard Rodgers, the assistant manager at the Red Rock Lakes Refuge for several years, reported seeing an adult trumpeter rise directly into the air from the firm bank of MacDonald Pond. This was no doubt possible because of the great springing power of the powerful legs of these birds, but it is difficult to see how a similar take-off could be performed from the water unless it were very shallow over a hard bottom.

BEHAVIOR AND RELATED CHARACTERISTICS

Studies of swan behavior, per se, have never been reported, and as a result only a few fragmentary and scattered notes are available. Far from being a subject of only academic interest, certain actions of behavior of any species can be valuable indicators of inherent basic requirements. This subject should be studied by the wildlife manager in order to learn both the normal characteristic expressions of the species and those made under duress so that their management may be guided accordingly.

ESCAPE-DISTANCE

This topic, borrowed from H. Poulsen as it applies specifically to the swans, has been generally commented upon by some observers under other subject headings. The term, however, is aptly descriptive and so is adopted here. Poulsen (1949: 196) sums up some escape-distance characteristics of two Eurasian species of swans, stating:

> The escape-distance . . . of Whooper Swan and Mute Swan in winter in shore marshes was about 300 metres. In open lanes in the ice in winter in the harbor of Copenhagen the escape-distance is much less, that is they have then got used to human beings and have become tame. This does not influence the escape-distance in their breeding places. The Danish resident Mute Swans have a small escape-distance towards man and often breed close to habitations. But in the great Swedish lakes as for instance Tåkern the escape-distance of the Mute Swan is about 1,000 metres according to B. Berg (1926). The Whooper Swan is a more shy bird. According to Rosenberg (1946) the escape-distance in its breeding places in northern Sweden is about 1,500 metres. In enclosures the swans gradually become tame, the escape-distance gradually decreasing.

The escape-distance of trumpeters also varies, depending upon circumstances and the conditioning to human activity experienced by any given individual. Munro (1949: 712), speaking of wild trumpeters in British Columbia, relates:

> On many occasions in winter I have approached within 100 yards of a group of trumpeter swans standing on the snow-covered ice of a river margin. . . . When the trumpeter swans stand on some lake beach, it is usually possible to approach them within easy observation distance provided some caution is used. Thus at a small marshy slough near Vanderhoof a single immature bird remained standing on a muddy shore long after a flock of whistling swans, alarmed at my approach, had taken wing. Again, on a slough in the Cariboo region, two young of the previous year were observed at close range as they fed among a scant growth of dead rushes, 20 to 30 yards from shore. When two of us walked towards the slough the swans swam to the beach, walked up on it, and began dressing their plumage. At our closer approach they walked again into the water and swam slowly towards the centre of the slough. Many such instances could be related.

Supporting this testimony, the experiences of Frank Groves and a companion in "walking up to" a single trumpeter in Nevada and that of Donald McLean in approaching to "within 30 feet" of a trumpeter in California, previously related, should be recalled. Gwen Colwell (1948) also approached to within less than 50 feet of 5 wild cygnets of flight age on the Klinaklini River in British Columbia.

The escape-distance of trumpeters on the Red Rock Lakes, where these birds are captured periodically for banding and examination, is conspicuously great, even though they are fully protected at all times and fed regularly through the long winters. A long escape-distance is also prevalent in Idaho on the swan wintering area where some shooting occurs. In either locality alarm is shown at the first sight of man at whatever range, and the distance of their departure, whether by swimming or flight, probably averages well over 300 yards. Even in Yellowstone Park, infrequent molestation by tourists, fishermen, and photographers has apparently contributed to the great escape-distance noted there, in some instances.

While escape-distance has a measurable value for birds on the ground, it seems to lose some of its meaning when airborne individuals are considered. For instance, trumpeters which have flushed beyond 300 yards may fly back over the disturbing person well within 100 yards and even approach another person much closer if he happens to be in the path of flight. Other waterfowl frequently act in a similar manner. Unfortunately the usual low-flying habits of the trumpeter are not greatly affected by the fright factors which contribute to a long flushing range, and because of this they often provide tempting targets to waterfowl hunters who are strategically located, practically "flying down the gun barrel" if the hunter is partly hidden. This characteristic, coupled with their apparent inability to profit from learned wariness, which they practice on the ground, makes them especially susceptible to gunfire.

H. Poulsen (1949:196) notes that, "The swans do not show intention movements when they are going to fly up such as the geese and ducks. But the neck is held erect and the call notes are emitted preparatory to taking wings." Alarmed trumpeters hold their necks stiffly erect, with perhaps a slow nervous pumping action if flight is delayed, and emit single, terse, trumpetlike warning notes hinting of the intended escape. These short warning calls may be repeated while the escaping swan is taking off and for a short while in flight. Although the preflight behavior of swans does not include the striking head movements of geese and ducks, it is still a characteristic pattern that tells the observer that the bird is about to fly (Lorenz, 1937).

INTERSPECIFIC TOLERANCE

Some phases of this subject are of course closely related to the preceding topic, and its definition as applied to the trumpeter for the purpose of this discussion is simply learned escape-distance, or inherent escape behavior as it may be modified by remembered experience. Where interspecific behavior action is related to other birds, it will be discussed under the more appropriate topic of territorialism.

Condon (MS) furnishes a good general picture of the variability of learned escape-distance under various conditions among the Park's trumpeter population, under the topic "reaction to molestation or interference with normal solitude." He concludes, "Unless swan are in constant contact with man, they show a pronounced tendency to be alarmed by his presence and keep at what they deem a safe distance from him." The degree to which the normal (predator) awareness of these birds in wilderness surroundings contributes to this caution, or is learned by individuals from previous molestation at the hand of man, is of course not known.

Condon (MS) also points out that while trumpeters within Yellowstone Park are principally considered birds of wilderness character, this species has, in certain instances, accepted man and his activities to the extent necessary to incubate and raise its young successfully in spite of considerable human activity (photographers, fishermen, etc.). In some cases man's activity is not introduced into the breeding habitat to any extent until after incubation has been completed, and in others the adjustment to molestation apparently could not be made and the blame for the loss was laid on man-caused activity.

Duane Featherstonhaugh (1948: 375, 379) also notes that the trumpeter swan is to be found successfully living and raising its young on waters near active farmsteads in its northwestern Alberta environment. He even observed one pair nesting in a slough near the Grande Prairie airport, a principal stop on the Alaska-Edmonton run, where, he records, the roar of engines went unnoticed by the birds.

At the National Elk Refuge too, where breeding trumpeters were successfully established by the Fish and Wildlife Service, Almer Nelson, the former Refuge Manager, states (correspondence):

In 1944 the pair nested in the Flat Creek Marsh about 600 feet from the Jackson-Moran Highway. . . . one of the cygnets ventured through the woven wire game fence onto the highway and was killed by an automobile. In 1948 . . . one pair nested within 400 feet of the highway. This pair of swan left the nesting site two days following the hatch . . . [and] on July 1 the birds [parents] moved their young down Flat Creek to near the Flat Creek bridge at the edge of town within 50 feet of the Jackson-Moran Highway, and in showing off their family they caused a traffic jam on the highway which became crowded with tourists who stopped to see them. . . . This pair managed to raise three of the five young.

In summary, human activity may be tolerated within distances ordinarily considered within trumpeter nesting territory, certainly much closer than intruding swans would be permitted. (The latter trait will be treated later when the spatial requirements of breeding trumpeters are discussed.) The critical factors involved in the toleration of man's activity on or near the breeding territory seem to be not so much the actual presence of man, or even the relative distance at which this is experienced, as it is the degree and regularity of molestation.

At the Red Rock Lakes Refuge, these birds live in quite isolated wilderness surroundings at a considerable distance from humanity.

On occasion they are disturbed by census activities on the marsh as well as by capturing for banding, examination, etc. This apparently occurs infrequently enough so the "conditioning" does not occur. Hence, on the Refuge the swans are extremely wary and will avoid any approach by man.

Wild trumpeters, especially the young which have apparently never been molested or frightened by man, have been found to be very tolerant of man, sometimes almost unbelievably so. Featherstonhaugh (1948: 376) provides an interesting statement in this regard, telling of two stranded cygnets rescued and raised by Joe Tomshak in the Grande Prairie country, as he writes, "When we saw them [the yearling trumpeters] they were as tame as domestic fowl. They would waddle up to the kitchen door to beg for bread and drink from the rain barrel."

An even more remarkable example is provided by Gwen Colwell (1948) as she describes an unusual visit of five wild trumpeter cygnets one winter to the meteorological station at Kleena Kleene, British Columbia:

Peter, our goose, was fed his breakfast that morning on the ice ledge along the river bank. In no time the swans showed interest and were soon literally shovelling in mouthfuls of wheat. . . . They became so tame that they would scramble onto the ice when they saw us coming. . . . At the end of the first week they had found their way to the house door. . . . Upon several occasions we had all five huge birds in the telegraph office at once. They literally filled the room. Indeed, one felt that if they became alarmed and decided to take to the air, the roof would in all likelihood be carried off on their backs.

In captivity, trumpeters have lived for long periods and even bred regularly in favorable environments, so the presence of man or human activity, in itself, cannot be said to be inimical to their existence. When not molested, trumpeters can tolerate considerable human activity and actually thrive if other factors prove favorable. This tolerance may decrease as the birds acquire a certain amount of general predator wariness, which increases with age.

Trumpeters nesting in a wilderness environment are alert to any change in the appearance of the landscape within their nesting territory. Any such action as the erection of a blind is regarded warily. Nevertheless, Marshall Edson, photographer for the Idaho Department of Fish and Game, reports no difficulty in having breeding trumpeters accept a canvas blind located at no great distance from their nest, but these birds were familiar with man-made activity. My experience on the Red Rock Lakes Refuge wilderness breeding grounds is to the contrary, with one nest desertion resulting when I moved a blind from approximately 80 yards away, where it had been accepted during the incubation period, to only about 40 yards distant. Scott and Fisher (1953: 208) report similar extreme wariness in the whooper swan on its isolated breeding grounds in central Iceland, stating:

Most females left the nest as soon as the intruder came into sight. . . . Two pairs of swans showed extreme shyness when a photographic hide was erected more than *sixty yards* from their nests. One pair deserted and in the other case the hide was removed only just in time.

On one occasion a pen left a nest as a result of hearing the alarm note of a pinkfoot [goose], while the intruders were out of sight over a ridge. She apparently left in a hurry as the eggs had not been covered.

The high degree of tolerance displayed by trumpeters toward the presence and activity of other birds and animals persists even in the case of possible predators. Referring to their studies of the trumpeter in Yellowstone Park during the summer of 1938, Oberhansley and Barrows relate (MS):

Little concern was shown by swans at the approach of elk, moose, beaver, bear, or coyotes in observed cases and in no instance were they seen to be molested or greatly alarmed by any bird or animal other than man, at whose approach they were always alarmed. The first sight of a fisherman approaching Riddle Lake, for instance, would drive the swans from the small islands at the nesting site to the extreme north and east shore of the lake nearly a mile distant. At other lakes reactions were similar. Cover was resorted to if sufficiently distant from the intruder, while on larger lakes the swans swam rapidly away from the shore.

R. W. Patrick (1935 : 116), observed a pair of mute swans attacking a bullock twice, finally driving it away. Statements by other observers indicate that mute swans, especially in captivity, are generally more pugnacious than the swans of the genus *Olor*, though reportedly this trait is much less apparent in wild mutes (Witherby et al., 1939 : 175).

MEMORY

The memory characteristics of trumpeters seem to play an important role in such actions as escape-distance. From the standpoint of the wildlife manager, at least the fundamentals of the trumpeter's memory traits should be understood so that human activity can be planned accordingly, as this characteristic is unusually keen in this species.

Smith and Hosking (1955 : 116–117), in their experimental studies of the aggressive displays of some birds in the laboratory, found that:

Birds possess to a remarkable degree, a high retention of visual images, which become deeply "imprinted" on the bird's consciousness. . . . for birds are above all animals "eye-minded," and dominated by visual stimuli.

This is certainly true of the trumpeter. One characteristic which has impressed observers who have worked with this species has been its ability to remember visual experiences which have frightened it in the past and to govern its actions accordingly. For example, in the year 1950 I moved a small shed from Refuge Headquarters to the swan wintering grounds and placed it at the water's edge to serve as a swan observation post and photographic blind. During the following winter or two the swans became accustomed to this rough shelter, and having no reason for mistrust, accepted it as a part of the landscape and fed on occasion practically within its shadow. During the winter of 1951–52 I departed from this blind in full view of a large flock of trumpeters without first arranging for another party to preflush the flock as was customary, thinking that no harm would be done since it was the last observation of the season and any harmful effects would soon wear off. This abrupt action of stepping out of the blind directly into the full view of a hundred or more nearby swans naturally startled the flock, which, after a moment's hesitation and warning calls, took flight.

This event was apparently remembered in succeeding years, at least until the 1955–56 season, since they were never observed to "trust" the small building to the original extent again, always moving off in a wary attitude if they inadvertently fed or moved too close. Though the distance to which they would approach the blind decreased steadily as time went on, some mistrust was still evident during the spring of 1956, 30 feet being about as close as they would come in to feed, even when attempts to bait them closer were made. Apparently, the older birds which remembered the event communicated their feelings to others unconsciously by not approaching this shed too closely, for there must have been a considerable turnover in population during this 4-year period.

Erickson has mentioned that the trumpeters held in captivity at the Malheur Refuge remembered their capture and subsequent blood tests for avian tuberculosis, being much warier and more difficult to capture and handle the following season.

Leland Stowe (1957: 223) also noted, apparently from the testimony of the Ralph Edwards family of Lonesome Lake, British Columbia, that though wild wintering trumpeters at "The Birches" had taken grain from the hand of Trudy Edwards for years, after they observed the capture of several of their number which had been lured by grain into a trap, they would not accept hand-fed grain again during four subsequent winters.

Trumpeters are very alert to events, and recall detail well. John Holman (1950) quotes Ralph Edwards of British Columbia as writing, "The swans are very sensitive to any changes in routine, to any change in feeders, or even to any change in the garments worn by the feeder." Similar characteristics have been recognized in Canada geese (Hochbaum, 1955: 43).

SENSORY PERCEPTION

While no special work has been done on this subject, it has been my experience that their sense of sight and hearing are very keenly de-

FIGURE 28.—Trumpeters on Culver Pond display the 2 methods of plumage-shaking, 1 employing the wings. The elevated position necessary for either position is attained by rapidly treading the water.

veloped. Foreign sounds, such as the click of a camera shutter, are heard at considerable distances and may even cause an escape movement. Sight is also extremely acute, especially at great distances. Its long neck enables the swan to see above low forms of marsh vegetation far out over the water, and its keen eyesight can detect even a cautious approach by an observer.

SOME GENERAL BEHAVIOR ATTITUDES

Submerging and Diving. When hard pressed in close pursuit and unable to fly, all age classes will dive to avoid capture. The older cygnets as well as the immatures and adults are frequently surprisingly adept at this, and once submerged are often capable underwater swimmers.

Sometimes adults also display the curious ability to submerge almost their entire bodies in the water while the head and neck remain upright in a normal position. This is apparently accomplished by changing the web action, thus literally pulling themselves downward in the water while swimming. I have seen this phenomenon employed occasionally by flightless Refuge swans when they were attempting to avoid capture by boat in deep water. After diving a number of times, followed by extensive swimming under water, they become winded, and upon successive approaches by the boat they sometimes submerge their buoyant bodies gradually in this manner in order to avoid diving until the last possible instant.

Oberhansley and Barrows (MS) also note this behavior by swans in the Park, writing, "In some attempts at concealment they appeared to become less buoyant and drew their heads down to the level of the sedges in which they were hiding . . . becoming almost invisible."

Resting. All the various postures of relaxation appear to be assumed most commonly while out of the water. When in the water, individuals usually are moving about feeding, swimming, or engaging in some other definite activity. Even during the cold winter

FIGURE 29.—A small flock of trumpeters feeding with goldeneyes at Culver Pond, Red Rock Lakes Refuge. Typical drinking attitude is shown by swan with outstretched neck, right of center.

weather, when they are not actually feeding, most of their time is spent loafing or sleeping on the ice and snow.

In sleeping, whether prone or erect, the trumpeter curves its long neck to the rear, resting its head on the back between the wings and with the tip of the bill usually tucked under a wing up to the nostrils. I have never seen the trumpeter sleep floating in the water, although Condon has observed this in the Park.

Oberhansley and Barrows (MS) record of the Park swans:

Resting attitudes observed consisted of lying on the breast on land or in shallow water, floating on the water, and standing on either one or both legs with the neck usually recurved back across the body and the head tucked under the wing. Two swans at Geode Lake were each observed to stand continuously upon the left leg while alternately sleeping and preening for a period of 54 minutes. During most of this time the right leg of each was alternately trailed to the rear and downward at an angle of about 15 degrees, then drawn into the body or used to scratch the head and neck. In each case during sleep the neck was curved to the right across the body and back with the head tucked under the right wing. The more profound sleeper completely concealed the eyes, while the other one was more restless, never concealing the eye and frequently raising the head to a watchful position for a short time. It required much more care to approach swans when resting than when they were feeding.

Plumage-shaking. When swimming or feeding in the water, or shortly after coming ashore, the trumpeter commonly shakes the water from its feathers by one of two methods. When this action does not include the wings, the statement of H. Poulsen (1949: 196) applies, "When a swan is going to shake its plumage, the movement starts at the tail, which is swung rapidly side to side, and then the movement is spreading all over the body ending at the head." If this is accomplished by the trumpeter while still in the water, the whole body is first elevated by rapid treading. In any case the neck is held more or less in an outstretched position.

This method is not seen so commonly as a similar action which employs a full beat or two of the outstretched wings. The primary feathers are also frequently adjusted following this shaking, which is accomplished with the neck bent in a typical "exertion" attitude.

Attitude of Head. Erickson has noted with the captive trumpeters at the Malheur Refuge that the male commonly held its head in a nearly level position whereas the female often carried its head with the bill tilted slightly downward. If this holds true in wild flocks, it might aid the determination of sex in the field.

Drinking. The trumpeter drinks water in the general manner of other fowl, the water being first drawn into the mouth by submerging the bill and then transferred to the lower regions by elevating the head and neck. The latter movement is accompanied by a fairly rapid movement of the mandibles, a swallow of water visibly moving down the neck as a mobile swelling.

Foot Attitude. Some of the swans have the curious habit of occasionally holding one foot outstretched backwards, as if drying this appendage. This may be done either while on the water or when standing on the land, and is a much observed trait of the mute swan. A. C. Bent (1925: 282) records an observation of this habit in the whistling swan, but I have only rarely seen it practiced by the wild trumpeter (figure 43).

Carrying Young. Delacour and Mayr (1945: 9) state of the swans generally, "They seem to be the only Anatidae which have the habit of taking their downy young on the back when the young are tired or cold. This is the usual practice with Mute and Black-necked Swans. It is exceptional in the other species." To my knowledge this trait has never been observed in the trumpeter.

DISPLAY

Even in a group of birds noted for their display behavior, the trumpeter is an expressive species. Some of this reputation of swans comes from the frequent "threat" attitudes of the common mute swan of park and zoo. While the trumpeter does not exhibit this particular display, both its voice and prominent physical features are often employed in other ways to show its various feelings about aggression, recognition, territory, sex, etc. These emotions are expressed principally by the action and attitude of the wings, head and neck, general body demeanor, and voice, with many variations possible. But the true "courtship" or "nuptial" displays so prominent in the lesser waterfowl are notably lacking in the swans.

An attempt might be made to classify the fundamental behavior postures as expressions of "recognition," "triumph," "aggression," etc., but since these all have a common root in their display appearance, in which the voice is an integral part, such an appraisal should await that time when extensive recordings of their vocal efforts have

FIGURE 30.—A typical mutual display of 2 wild trumpeters on wintering waters, Red Rock Lakes Refuge. This basic display invariably is accompanied by vocal expression. It is used with variations in "recognition" and "aggression", and may have nuptial and other connotations.

been made in synchronization with motion pictures of their various actions. When these are available to the researcher for detailed comparison and analysis, we may begin to understand the behavior mechanism of these unique fowl. Without this, a fundamental knowledge of the species is lacking.

The most common display attitude is one in which the quivering wings are raised horizontally and partly extended. This posture, when accompanied by the pertinent vocal effort and extended position of the head, neck, and body, is used with some variation on greatly different occasions. In the water or on solid footing, the exact position and movement of the wings may vary considerably. The angle of the head at the end of a usually fully extended upright neck is nearly level in this basic display, contrasted with the definitely upward-inclined head and bill of the whooper swan as shown during its "mutual greeting ceremony" by E. A. Armstrong (1947: 192, 142).

Figure 31.—Trumpeters face each other in mutual display (right foreground)
and a swan indulges in a wing-flapping plumage shake (center background)
while an adult bald eagle watches from a background snowbank in March
on Red Rock Lakes Refuge.

This basic display attitude has only been seen exhibited as a mutual
action. It is shown on occasions when aggressiveness is involved
among flocked birds that are socially active, or during the breeding-
nesting-brooding season when a member of a breeding pair flies back
to its mate after successful defensive action towards another swan
trespasser. It may also be employed first by a single adult and result
in mutual action when aggressive tactics are employed within the
territory. During such times, both birds apparently recognize each
other as foes and rush together with loud staccato trumpeting, exhibiting with outstretched quivering wings and extended head and neck

as they plunge in to do battle, or turn to escape. O. Hilden and P. Linkola (1955: 524) report very similar behavior in the whooper swan, as do Witherby et al. (1939: 170).

Essentially the same display behavior, but with some notable variations, commonly occurs among the individual members of late-wintering flocks as they gather about the chosen feeding areas or on their extensive loafing grounds of snow, which at that season has become packed and hardened. This attitude appears to arise from less justified reasons than territorial protection. Commencing with bobbing heads and gradually increasing wing action, it develops into positive aggression, apparently as the result of self-assertive tendencies which seek expression before territorial establishment. It also occurs to some extent whenever large flocks of nonbreeding trumpeters gather together, and so may be a result of population pressure.

One variation of this display may involve as many as 4 or 5 birds, if the efforts of 1 or 2 are successful in getting action started. In this group action, which may occur either on land or on water, the body position is more erect than in the simple mutual display, and the wings are also usually slightly more extended and are apt to be held at a higher angle, thus showing off the underside of the wing primaries to a greater extent. Treading increases their stature in the water, while wing movements are much more active as each swan strives to maintain or improve his performance in the circle of displaying individuals. After the preliminary head-bobbing procedure, the bird holds its neck quite fully extended with the bill about level, facing its fellow demonstrators in voluble expression.

The trumpetings of the group exhibitors are truly remarkable, even from the start, but especially so when they rapidly increase in tempo and intensity as they are joined by other swans. When the climax has been reached, it usually ends in lowered-head aggressiveness as various individuals shoot rapidly in pursuit of others in a regular free-for-all amid a noteworthy outburst of trumpeting from the always interested onlookers. It is impossible to say whether these exhibitions are made up principally of any particular sex or age group since those observed have been of unknown sex and in the white dress of the adult.

This performance is, in general, the usual aggressive expression of these birds, which they may assume either in defense of their breeding territory or in pursuit of personal victory in a spontaneous dispute. In the case of breeding birds on the territory, a warning display and calls by one or both of the resident pair usually suffices to turn approaching strangers away. Occasionally an intruder alights in an active territory of a pair, or more rarely mates from pairs in adjacent territories come to blows.

Figure 32.—Two trumpeters landing on Culver Pond are greeted by displaying swans. Band on left leg of lower bird marks it as a pen (female). Both Barrow's and common goldeneye ducks are present in this scene.

Aggressive action on land or water begins when an individual with head lowered for action propels itself decisively by wing or web in the direction of the trespasser. In the air the pursuing swan closes the distance to the trespasser by rapid flight. The victim, perceiving its predicament after a losing race, usually turns steeply upward and is followed for a brief time by the pursuer, after which the action is abruptly terminated by the pursuer turning back. In the water, actual feather pulling and wing pummeling may occur before one is successful in routing its opponent. Such punishment seldom lasts more than a few moments, but it can nevertheless be formidable and effective and seems always to result in the defeat of the trespasser. Invariably the returning victor is met in the home territory by its mate which joins in a mutual display of quivering wing, bobbing head, and staccato trumpeting, ending with reclining neck and wings and wailing notes. This is comparable to the "triumph ceremony" described by Heinroth and Lorenz for the geese and shelducks.

The aggressive attitude may also be assumed by any flightless trumpeter when it is confronted suddenly or is pursued by man and is unable to escape. It is usually displayed in such cases when an individual is captured in a confined location or cornered on solid footing in an unfamiliar environment, when the aggressive posture or action is accompanied by considerable hissing. Swans on water have never been reported to take an aggressive action toward man. Possibly the bird feels that it is in its native element and escape is possible until the moment of capture.

From the foregoing remarks it might be concluded that the trumpeter is a pugnacious and quarrelsome bird. This is not generally true, however, at least in the wild population with which I have been acquainted. Minor emotions are usually expressed initially by voice, and many times these feelings are not further developed. Hours have been spent observing these birds on their breeding grounds when not a single aggressive action was noted. During the fall months when the breeding birds and their families rejoin the nonbreeding flocks, the pair formation which apparently occurs then among maturing individuals (Delacour and Mayr, 1945:8) adds to the general unrest resulting from the change of season and impending migration, and more frequent emotional displays take place. This is also true when early spring unlocks their traditional nesting marshes, since the birds are still confined to limited feeding areas about the few warm springs. The approach of the breeding season, with its sexual stimulation and welcome seasonal change after the winter's hardships, ushers the population into its greatest social season. At this time display attitudes are commonly observed among flocked birds. As soon as the marshes open up and the birds disperse, the display activity shifts to the nesting territory and is less frequent.

Delacour and Mayr (1945:9) describe the precopulatory display of swans:

Swans, geese, and whistling ducks (tree ducks) have essentially the same precopulatory display, both birds of a pair repeatedly dip the whole head and neck until finally the female flattens herself out on the water and sinks deeper with the neck half extended.

On several occasions a similar display, but without the dipping ceremony, was observed on an open-water area while the birds were still on their wintering grounds during March. In these cases, the posturing was not followed by copulation, and perhaps expressed some other mood or was not even a formal display attitude. A description of copulation by trumpeter swans provided by Frank McKinney (correspondence) reveals that this act does not differ from that noted with other large species of waterfowl.

Intraspecific strife and display among the confined trumpeters at the Malheur Refuge is described by Erickson, who relates (correspondence) :

FIGURE 33.—"Solo" display, trumpeter swan on Culver Pond, Red Rock Lakes Refuge.

A pecking order is established with each group of swans in the pond. With the very young cygnets, size seems to be the main factor determining the position of each bird in the order, but as the smaller individuals approach the previously larger ones in size, vigorous tussles ensue as members of the order attempt to maintain or improve their positions. The scuffling usually is most noticeable during feeding when the swans are grouped more closely.

In an evenly matched fight, the swans will approach and attempt to intimidate the adversary by carrying the head and neck low. If the opponent stands his ground, the aggressor will drive in and each will grasp the neck or feathers of the head, neck, or anterior part of the body of the other swan, both birds thrashing against each other, breast to breast, and each attempting to tread the other one under the water. This may last as long as two minutes, though usually the outcome is forthcoming within a few seconds, and the weaker or less experienced member of the match turns and flees, the victor grasping the rump or tail feathers of the loser and being towed for some distance around the pond, accompanied by much splashing and flailing of wings.

The wings are less commonly used in striking the opponent, but the loser always uses them in running from the fight. When the loser reaches the cover of the willows or races up on shore, the winner will turn and face an apparently admiring group of other swans who have been watching the performance, will draw its head far back on its back, half spread its wings on each side, and promenade back towards the flock in an extremely pompous and swaggering fashion.

The cygnets appear more interested in these engagements than the older swans, and will gather along the fence in their part of the enclosure and pay tribute to the winner in the form of rapt attention and juvenile "trumpeting" as the winner slowly swims by in full display. Sooner or later after the match, both participants will rise on the water and flap their wings.

If the winner is a member of a mated pair, he then will rush forward, and be met in like fashion by his mate, both facing each other closely with quivering wings partly outstretched and trumpeting their congratulations in staccato fashion, usually ending these expressions in a longer wailing sound.

FIGURE 34.—Rear view of "solo" display (left).

Judging from my observations of wild trumpeter populations, Erickson's report indicates that behavior becomes much more formal and stylized in captive birds, where certain features may be more fully practiced and developed. Though strikingly similar, they do not appear to be truly representative of similar actions among a wild population. A fertile field for further study in this direction awaits the research worker.

BREEDING

Although a basic knowledge of breeding characteristics and habits is essential to a grasp of population dynamics, very little on this

FIGURE 35.—While a pair of trumpeters engages in mutual display (left center), 4 gather in a group exhibit (right). Mallards and pintails in the irregular foreground.

subject is now known about the trumpeter in its breeding habitat in the United States. Only from detailed observations by various individuals over a period of years, coupled with notes on similar characteristics of better-known species of swans, can we throw light on the important aspects of reproduction.

The breeding biology of mute, whooping, and Bewick's swans, including notes on pair formation, courtship, territorial traits, nesting, and hatching success, is treated in Hilprecht (1956: 55–89).

PAIR FORMATION

Literally nothing is known of the ages of wild swans in their pre-pairing associations.

The behavior of captive trumpeters should provide clues regarding the formation of pairs as it occurs in the wild, and Erickson furnishes an interesting observation in this regard, writing (correspondence):

Although the cygnets form friendships during their first year of life, they seem to serve no sexual function, and it is as common to see three associating amicably with one another as it is with pairs. The first mated pairs develop during the third year, when they seem to resent intrusion by other single or paired birds.

Writing in a more general sense of the swans as a group, Delacour and Mayr (1945: 8) state:

Pair formation, which occurs in the fall in all temperate zone swans, takes place without elaborate displays. According to Heinroth (1911), birds that are in the process of pairing swim in close proximity, press the plumage close to the body, and hold the neck in a peculiar position, the head appearing thickened.

BREEDING AGE

Assuming that the ages of both birds are equal, pairs do not appear to become firmly mated until well along in the third year of life. Possibly the earliest breeding of trumpeters may be accomplished as the pair enters the breeding season completing their fourth year of life. It is conceivable that if one of the paired birds is older, or has had previous breeding experience, successful pairing and nesting may be initiated somewhat earlier than would otherwise be the case. (W. H. Watterson [1935: 238] reports mute swans nesting at 2 years of age.)

Referring to captive trumpeters again, Erickson furnishes another pertinent statement on the earliest ages at which copulation was observed among trumpeters in the Melheur flock, writing:

No pairs were observed copulating until in the five-year-old class, although it may well have occurred unobserved. One three-year-old pair, which was separated from the others, made a rather listless attempt at nest construction, but the effort was abandoned before the "nest" had passed the "platform" stage. This same pair again attempted nest construction and were seen copulating two

FIGURE 36.—Aggressive action of trumpeter following group display, Culver Pond wintering waters.

years later. However, the female developed a lameness and did not continue nest-building, dying about three months later.

Whatever the average minimum breeding age of trumpeters may be, the initial age at which a wild pair comes into breeding mood and nests may be influenced somewhat by the quantity of unoccupied territory located in suitable nesting habitat. Delacour's statement (1954: 72), on the four closely-related circumpolar species of swans may apply to the trumpeters of the Red Rock Lakes:

Although the adult state is assumed in the third year, it seems that most of these swans do not breed until the fifth or sixth year, perhaps because it is often difficult for young birds to appropriate a nesting territory.

We do not know if a high breeding population of swans occupying a limited area has any effect in postponing the initial breeding age of nesters. It will be shown later that while the number of breeding swans at Red Rock Lakes has increased in proportion to the whole population, it is breeding *success* which has declined markedly during these years.

Examples of the nesting of 3 pairs of trumpeters of known ages may throw some light on the subject. In the first case, a pair of trumpeters, forming from 3 cygnets-of-the-year, which were taken from Red Rock Lakes to the National Elk Refuge in 1938, nested successfully in 1944 when they were entering their sixth year of life. Though these individuals were established within easy flight range of

the Yellowstone swan population and had the ability to fly unrestricted during this period, they were seen so consistently on the Refuge following their transplanting, where none had been observed for
many years previously, that the identity of the pair is assured. It is
also interesting to note here, in reference to Jean Delacour's remarks,
that while these were the only swans in the habitat, they did not
nest until practically 6 years old.

Two pairs of trumpeters have since bred several times in the limited
marsh area available on the Elk Refuge. The second pair nested first
in 1948. Since only 1 cygnet was produced in the original nesting attempt in 1944, the second pair (if natives of the Elk Refuge) must
have been mated either from a combination of brood members of the
1944–45 hatches, or that of 1945 when 3 cygnets were produced. In
either case at least one of the mated pair would have bred at its hypothetical minimum breeding age, when just completing its third or
fourth year of life. Of course, there is no proof that either of the
mates comprising the second nesting pair were native Elk Refuge
birds, but in view of the general tendency of the Anatidae to return
to their natal breeding marshes following the wintering period, at
least one and probably both mates of the second pair were Elk
Refuge-bred birds.

In the third instance, a pair of trumpeters which formed from
several cygnets-of-the-year transferred to the Ruby Lake Refuge
from Red Rock Lakes in 1949 were seen on nearby Franklin Lake
in their third year of life, during an October 1952 aerial waterfowl census. On October 7, 1953, another aerial census revealed
a pair of swans with a lone cygnet, again on Franklin Lake.
Because identification of this pair was not confirmed by a ground
check, and because whistling swans have arrived from the north at
Ruby Lake as early as mid-October and no nesting swans were noticed
on an earlier spring flight over Franklin Lake on April 16, this record,
like the others, can be classed only as hypothetical. If it is a valid
trumpeter nesting record, as the refuge manager assumed, these birds
would also have begun nesting at a minimum breeding age, just completing their fourth year. Thus the only evidence at hand, which is
admittedly sketchy, indicates that nesting may begin as early as
the fourth year of life (3 years, 10 months) or as late as the sixth year
(5 years, 10 months).

MATING FIDELITY

The oft-repeated truism that "swans mate for life" has been established more by a lack of evidence to the contrary in semidomesticated
captive birds than by a thorough study of the facts with wild swan
populations. While a general rule of life-mating appears to be valid

FIGURE 37.—Aggressive pursuit terminating a group display of 5 trumpeters, Red Rock Lakes Refuge.

for swans, it is reasonable to suppose that a wild swan which loses its mate early in life may remate.

H. Poulsen (1949: 197) furnishes an interesting general statement on the mating fidelity of swans among those pinioned in the zoological gardens of Copenhagen, Denmark, writing:

The Mute Swan is strictly monogamous. Among the 60–100 tame (hand amputated) Mute Swans kept in the parks of Copenhagen, each pair always sticks together for life. In the cases in which it has been attempted to pair a swan with a new mate instead of the dead one, no success has been achieved in contrast to the statement of HEINROTH (1911) that the re-pairing is not difficult.

There is a real attraction between particular individuals of the opposite sex. Unfaithfulness between the mates is rare. During the last ten years only three cases have occurred among the tame swans in Copenhagen. Thus a wild male had paired with two tame females. Just as mentioned by PORTIELJE (1936) the pairing with the second female occurred when the first one was sitting on the eggs.

In captivity, bonds of naturally monogamous species sometimes break down, and the trumpeter apparently is no exception. Dr. G. C. Low (1935: 147) records that in England:

Polygamy in the Mute Swan is very rare indeed, and I have only heard of one instance, in addition to one case of a female Swan that paired with two males, all three living together on harmonious terms. There was for many years at Woburn Abbey a breeding trio of Trumpeter Swans, but I was never able to discover whether the odd bird was male or female. . . . Many years ago a ludicrous instance occurred at Abbotsbury, where two male swans [mutes] not only associated together, but even built a nest every year, upon which they took turns in sitting!

Dr. J. M. Dewar (1936: 178) published a short but interesting paper in which he outlined some aspects of the mating infidelity of captive mute swans as it has been observed in certain rare instances over the years in England and Europe. In his article Dr. Dewar proposes the apt phrase "ménage à trois" to describe "the association of three individuals of a bird species for the purpose of nesting." Dr. Dewar continues his explanation of the term and its pertinency to the mute swan as follows:

As a label, ménage à trois is preferred to its synonym, bigamy, because ménage à trois implies the setting-up of an establishment, which bigamy does not necessarily do. . . .

Ménage à trois has to be distinguished carefully from homosexuality and other sexual relations. Homosexuality, which has been recorded several times in the Mute Swan, is an association of two individuals of the same sex, leading to pairing and nest-building, and in the case of females the laying of eggs which are necessarily infertile.

Altogether I have been able to collect from the literature six examples of ménage à trois in the Mute Swan and to add a seventh case coming under personal observation.

John Ellis (1936: 232), commenting upon Dr. Dewar's paper, establishes at least one and possibly two apparently valid cases of ménage à trois among mute swans on an English park lake.

A similar aberrant relation existed among three trumpeters living south of the Red Rock Lakes Refuge on a small reservoir in Fremont County, Idaho. I noticed them while flying the summer census on August 29, 1956, in the Island Park area. Three adult swans were together with three cygnets on the Icehouse Creek Reservoir. All six birds formed a typical family group which did not break up in spite of repeated low flights directly over them in the pond. Conversation with a rancher familiar with the swans on this Reservoir later confirmed that observation, and further established the fact that these three adult birds spent most of the spring and summer together, from breeding season until fall, although one departed for about a month during this period only to return later and remain until autumn. In 1957 the three adult swans returned to the Reservoir and one female again nested successfully. This trio was broken up later in the summer by the death of one of the adults. The sex of the extra bird was never determined. As far as is known, only one nest was built each season and only one brood was ever seen. Of the hundreds of pairs of wild trumpeters I have observed with cygnets in their breeding territories during the period 1948–57, this was the only record in which more than two adults were seen with young.

PRENESTING HABITS AND BEHAVIOR

Long before the winter season has ended, sometimes 3 months before any open water appears, pairs or small groups of trumpeters may be found loafing about their still-frozen breeding habitat on the Red Rock Lakes Refuge. This bleak, wintry landscape is 6 or 8 miles from the nearest open water at the spring-fed ponds. Water is not generally open in the Red Rock Lakes and marsh until after mid-April. But both paired birds and small flocks have been seen far out on the vast snowfields which overlie the breeding habitat as early as February 2 (in 1949) and February 21 (in 1950). This practice becomes commoner as the season advances. By the time the ice on the Lakes is ringed with run-off water from the surrounding meadows in April, it is immediately occupied by the swans, which then no longer need return to their winter feeding waters.

Early occupation of the breeding grounds is apparently instinctive, as several Yellowstone Park observers have testified to the same behavior pattern. In Yellowstone these early visits to breeding habitat may occur considerably later than at Red Rock Lakes, since early April is the earliest that swans have been seen visiting their still-frozen Park breeding habitat. Perhaps before April other loafing areas in Yellowstone are more convenient to winter feeding waters, and at Red Rock Lakes the breeding habitat may first be occupied coincidentally as loafing grounds during the late winter months, with no special territorial significance. With only one exception, the early literature states that the trumpeter was invariably the earliest waterfowl to arrive on its Arctic breeding grounds in the spring, preceding even the geese or whistling swans.

Whether a given pair occupies in the late winter the area to be claimed as a territory later has not been determined. While pairs often occupy the same snowfields, more consistently as the season advances, their positive identity as the same pair was not established then, or related later to the breeding pair which nested in that area. It would appear logical to assume that in the last few weeks preceding the advent of open water some territorial claims are being staked. Specific observations of the beginning of territorial defense actions are lacking. At first, just the pair's presence in an area is enough to show that the territory is occupied.

During the period just before the spring breakup, especially on the warmer days and nights, vocal efforts and flight activity reach a climax. The long winter with its hardships and severe cold is drawing to a close and the excitement of the breeding season is at hand. Singles, pairs, and small groups move frequently about from one open patch of water to another, spending long periods feeding or loafing on the ice in the warm spring sunshine. The successively later twilight increases this activity, and vibrant sonorous trumpetings from the marsh are then audible far into the night.

TERRITORY AND TERRITORIAL BEHAVIOR

Territorial behavior in the trumpeter is characterized by the defense of the "mating, nesting, and feeding ground for young," the "type A" territory classification of Margaret Morse Nice (1941: 471). Territorial defense of areas other than that concerned essentially with reproduction is apparently unknown in wild swan populations; hence, the discussion of territory here will be confined to this definition of the term.

Many observers writing from firsthand experience have agreed that swans as a group are among the most territorially minded of any birds commonly kept in captivity, setting up wherever possible relatively large areas of habitat where various other forms of competing bird life, especially other swans, may not be tolerated during the breeding season. It also appears that paired swans, wild or "kept," differ a great deal in degree of territorial behavior, both interspecifically and intraspecifically.

H. Poulsen (1949: 195, 198), writing of swans both in the wild and in the Zoological Gardens of Copenhagen, says:

In the Mute Swan the well known threat display (imposing posture, Imponiergehaben, HEINROTH) serving to intimidate intruders in its territory was observed chiefly in the adult male, but also in the female when I approached the nest at a time when it had left it in search of food. . . . but never in the Whooper Swan. . . . Outside the breeding season the swans are sociable birds, and outside their territories they even in the breeding season agree well. A strange female, which settled in a territory, was seen to be chased off by the owning male in threat display, whereas outside the territory he dropped this attitude, the feathers now being close to the body. Thus a strange female may have two different valences (TINBERGEN, 1942). Inside the territory: enemy, outside the territory: female to copulate with.

Intolerance in the mute swan is apparently modified by captivity. H. F. Witherby et al. (1939: 175) remark on this:

Mute swan, much more than Bewick's and Whooper, is naturally predisposed to association with man and easily tamed. O. Heinroth found that behavior of wild-caught birds from the Black Sea differed in no respect from that of semi-domestic swans. Usually aggressive and vicious towards other birds in the semi-artificial conditions in which it often lives, but both Naumann and E. Christoleit stress that this trait is less noticeable in fully wild birds.

*　　　*　　　*　　　*　　　*　　　*　　　*

In wild state usually nests on islets in swamps or in shallow water in reed grown lagoons, but in semi-domesticated state almost anywhere near water, sometimes in colonies of great size.   In protected areas of this kind, the nests may be only a few yards apart.

*   *   *   *   *   *   *

The swannery at Abbotsbury (Dorset) is not only the largest individual congregation of Swans in this country, but is unique.   Though foot-marked and living under conditions to some extent artificial, the birds are all fully winged and virtually wild.   Dependent to some extent on annual fluctuations of food-supply, numbers vary between under 200 and over 500 pairs.

The interspecific relationships of mute and whooping swans are also noted in Hilprecht (1956: 89) to vary from "extremely tolerant" in captivity to "far more tolerant" in the wild.

Erickson makes an interesting comment on the trait of interspecific intolerance among the confined trumpeters at the Malheur Refuge, stating (correspondence) :

The trumpeters are intolerant of intrusion by whistling swans and several whistlers have been seriously injured when they attempted to mingle with the larger birds and had to be rescued or they would have been killed.   Trumpeters seem to disregard ducks and geese.

E. A. Armstrong (1947: 284) notes yet another aspect of territorial behavior in swans, writing, "Where a pair of territorial birds, such as whooper swans, are constrained to remain on a lake dominated by another pair they do not breed."

Wild trumpeters usually show territorial aggressiveness toward their own kind by a combination of loud calls, tremulous movements of half-raised wings, and general hostile body attitude.   In most cases, the defending resident pair is located on the water when the possible trespasser is spotted in flight some distance away.   If the distant flyer approaches, one or both of the swans occupying the territory assume the aggressive posture with their wings while trumpeting with extended head and neck their unmistakable staccato warning notes. If this display is ignored by the approaching swan and a close passage or landing appears likely, no time is lost by the defender in getting into the air in immediate pursuit.

In flight, the pursuer always seems able to overtake the departing intruder, though if both territorial defenders take to air, only one, presumably the male, approaches the trespasser closely.   When with great effort the defending bird has succeeded in overtaking the fleeing invader, the latter invariably climbs sharply upward, only to be followed closely by its pursuer.   This seems to be the signal for the conclusion of the chase, for the successful defender, now far from its territory, turns and heads homeward, announcing its return with triumphant trumpeting.   Gliding downward, it splashes into the water near its waiting mate where both birds approach each other trumpeting their mutual staccato congratulations with outstretched

FIGURE 38.—Observations on the territorial traits of trumpeters can be made by a single observer over several thousand acres, since the high mountains provide ideal vantage points. Here the birds on Lower Red Rock Lake are studied from an observation post on the northern flank of Centennial Mountains.

tremulous wings, ending with a dipping motion of their head and neck and longer prolonged wailing notes. A display of the whooper swan on similar occasions has been reported by E. A. Armstrong (1947:142).

Sometimes the defending resident bird is on solid footing when a flying intruder draws near. In this case the wings of the hostile defender are held in an even more outstretched drooping attitude than is possible when it is on the water. Here, since the extending of the neck appears more pronounced and the body is visibly erected, an even more threatening attitude results than when the displaying bird is on the water. In either case a direct attack by air follows shortly if the warning is ignored.

Though both sexes usually partake in aggressive warning displays toward a trespassing swan, usually only one departs from the territory if pursuit or eviction is necessary, but both swans may take wing when prompt action is made necessary by an overt violation.

Some territorial demonstrations occur from before the time that the nest is constructed in the spring until late in the summer when the cygnets are half-grown, though they are not shown uniformly during this period. They begin sometime after territories are taken, are most common during nesting and early brooding, and then taper off.

Even during the height of the breeding-nesting season, however, aggression and discord are not common. When breeding populations have been highest on the Refuge, paired swans appear to spend the vast majority of their time feeding, loafing, incubating eggs, caring for young, etc., actually geting along quite harmoniously with neighboring pairs if territorial boundaries are respected, as they usually are. Too, the large flock of nonbreeders scatter out on the vast shallow expanses of Upper Red Rock Lake, feeding far out from shore on the extensive underwater aquatic pastures or loafing along the shoreline wherever breeding territories are not established, and seldom venture into the established breeding territories.

At the other extreme, I observed a lone trumpeter, apparently a "lonesome" nonbreeder, warned or actually evicted from five different territories within the space of an hour. In some cases this individual, which appeared to be seeking the company of its kind, would be allowed to settle in a distant corner of an occupied territory for a few moments; however, the hostility of the residents would increase visibly with each passing minute until cob or pen, or both, would fly at the trespasser in a show of aggressive eviction.

This is not the general rule, as mated pairs seem to learn neighbor relations quickly, just as the nonbreeders are apparently impressed with the importance of staying clear of the breeding areas. By the time of the flightless molt in July, few acts of aggression are observed. Movement is naturally more restricted at this season, but even after the molt, when flight activity picks up, aggression never appears to regain its former level, though it is displayed on occasion by breeders throughout the rest of the summer.

During the incubating period, mated swans rarely leave their territory unless one makes a short aerial inspection or defensive flight. Sometimes the departing bird may land some distance away in a "neutral" area where either alone, or congenially with others, it feeds or loafs, returning to the territory some time later. Breeding pairs nesting along the line of flight usually make aggressive warning displays upon seeing the commuter in flight, and this usually causes the vagrant mate to move on. Except for such short absences, the mated pair usually remains resident within its nesting territory until late summer or early fall. Towards the end of summer, territorial bonds definitely become weaker; this is especially true of broodless pairs which may desert their home area altogether.

On one occasion a mated pair, together with their brood, deserted their territory, travelling about 2 miles across Upper Red Rock Lake to settle along the opposite shore. Before this change of territory, the brood had been reduced from 6 to 2 from unknown causes, so it is possible that the parents wished to move from the cause of mortality and/or molestation. The area selected for the new home was the shore-line of a rather exposed bay about midway between two other active but distantly spaced territories. The season being well advanced and the site well separated from adjacent territories, the shift of residence was a successful move and permanent for the season.

Some variation of territorial behavior is evident among individual pairs, depending upon their familiarity with each other. Also, the size of the territory defended, and the subsequent spacing of nests, indicates the appeal of a given habitat. Once the territory is estab-lished, adjacent resident pairs recognize their neighbors and modify their aggressiveness accordingly. The pursuit distance at which the defenders will take aggressive action is much greater when a stranger has been sighted than when a mate from an adjoining territory is observed.

In one unique case of tolerance, 2 pairs nested for several successive years a measured 885 feet from each other on the same shoreline of a large widening of the Red Rock River. However, the nests were hidden in a dense growth of bulrush and the areas used in common were at a minimum, each pair keeping to its end of the opening and the adjacent stretch of narrower river channel. The distance be-tween nests is usually much greater.

Interspecific aggressive behavior by trumpeters on their nesting territory appears to be directed chiefly against the larger birds. Usually, territorial aggressiveness is not shown towards the larger mammals, including man. When such an intruder approaches nest or young, even at a distance, trumpeter pairs discreetly desert. Trum-peters generally disregard the ducks. Both ducks and coots swim unmolested among trumpeters in close association and perfect har-mony. Ducks and coots feed intimately within the trumpeter "family circle" in the territory, where they compete with cygnets for surface food stirred up by the parent swans. When ducks and swans are present in large numbers and compete excitedly for grain in the restricted areas of open water of the Refuge wintering areas, a trum-peter may take an annoyed jab at some passing duck that gets in the way, but this is infrequent.

In Denmark, K. Paludan and J. Fog studied the effects of in-tolerance displayed by wild mute swans against ducks. This study was made in response to the claim by many sportsmen that the swans in that country interfered with the reproductive success of wild ducks. While testimonies of swan intolerance with ducks were noted on small and restricted sites, the swan, mallard, and gray-lag goose bred close together without inimical effects in other instances. Paludan and Fog (1956: 44) concluded, "Under no circumstances can the Mute Swan be of any importance to the Danish duck population in general."

The trumpeter is not so tolerant of the larger water and marsh birds. While Erickson (correspondence) mentions that nonnesting, captive swans held in an enclosure at the Malheur Refuge ignore these lesser companions, this may not always be the case with wild pairs on their breeding territory. Featherstonhaugh (1948 : 379) writes of trumpeters:

The swans also drive off any geese (in addition to other swans) that may land in the vicinity of a nest, but they pay no attention to ducks or other marsh birds. We found nests of the mallard, the ruddy duck, the lesser scaup, and the American coot within a few feet of swans' nests.

In observations made between May 11 and August 30, 1949, I noted 11 instances of territorial defense, 8 against other swans and 1 each against a white pelican, a great blue heron, and a Canada goose. Charles Hotchkiss, ranger-naturalist of the National Park Service at Teton Park, reported to me seeing a swan chase away a sandhill crane which came close to the swan nest.

Interspecific intolerance involving muskrats has been observed in at least two cases. W. Verde Watson, a Park Service naturalist in Yellowstone Park, furnishes an account of a trumpeter swan killing a muskrat, supposedly in defense of its cygnet brood, writing (1949: 49):

The pair of adults were lazily swimming about off shore sounding rather plaintive, deep toned "words" of instruction to some of the cygnets. These youngsters had just given some heed to the old folks and were making way toward them when one of the adults, with a great flurry of feathers and beating of the water, half-flying and half-running upon the water, bore down upon the muskrat intruder which was apparently swimming past some 25 to 50 feet farther out in the lake. Arriving at the spot where the 'rat must have been she beat the water furiously with both wings, seeming literally to walk about on the water as she darted very quickly from side to side and round and round following the quarry. All the while she hissed loud and angrily and periodically pecked vigorously at the object of her wrath. \ . . . A quick look through the telephoto finder of the Leica revealed that the animal was a muskrat, and observations during the succeeding couple of minutes or so indicated that it was probably done for. . . . Thus we were really amazed when it emerged again and swam almost directly at the same swan that had abused it so badly shortly before. . . . The old bird saw it coming and with determined bearing swam to meet the muskrat. This time the initial shock was delivered as a vigorous and meticulously aimed peck followed by the same unmerciful wing beats and much loud hissing. . . . This encounter probably did not last over

30 seconds, and then when the bird sailed away from the scene and the water settled down the unfortunate 'rat came up and lay motionless on the surface. . . . Subsequent autopsy . . . revealed a considerable bruised and bloody area in the neck, and it was thus considered likely that the fatal blow may have been the first well aimed hammerlike peck delivered at the opening of the second round.

R. O. Hart, a District Ranger in Yellowstone Park, furnishes (1952: 56) a similar eye-witness account of an encounter between a swan and a muskrat. This time, however, the skirmish did not end in a fatality.

The presence of pelicans, cranes, herons, geese, or muskrats, does not necessarily arouse aggressiveness in swans, even mated birds within their breeding territory. Most of these species have often been seen in close proximity to swans with no territorial action or other aggressive behavior resulting. Swans with young are most apt to take offensive action against such species.

Despite the variations and flexibility in the defense of territories such action is the main factor regulating the distribution of pairs in an area of breeding habitat. There is no direct evidence yet that territorialism limits breeding numbers in all cases, although it is a factor in determining nesting success.

In the complex pattern of the Red Rock Lakes marshes, territories are generally established where they existed the previous year, often with exactly the same nesting site occupied. Various observers agree that breeding pairs remain attached to their territories year after year. Oberhansley and Barrows (MS) state of their 1938 Yellowstone Park observations, "At each nesting site studied, old nests were used and the actual time devoted to their repair was brief." Condon (MS), Yellowstone Park, stated, "In nesting, pairs have in most instances returned to their previous year's nests and repaired the old nests for re-use."

In the contiguous marshes of the Refuge, the desirable features of these territories with a long breeding history are apparently recognized by other pairs who quickly appropriate areas unclaimed by former owners. As Albert Hochbaum (1944: 78) found in his studies of the canvasback on prairie marshes, "I believe that . . . a delicate arrangement of terrain, if it remains relatively unchanged from year to year, is recognized by any individual duck as desirable and thus is occupied." This is apparently true of the trumpeter as well, since a normal population turnover would dictate at least some change if the selection of territories were not governed by inherent instincts. What appears as desirable nesting habitat to a human observer may remain barren of breeding swans year after year, even in the face of a rising population of breeding swans, while territories which appear similar may be occupied.

During years of increasing numbers of breeding pairs at Red Rock Lakes, expansion has occurred chiefly into less desirable (previously unoccupied) habitat, not in the compression of the additional breeders within previously occupied territories. This may contribute to the low reproductive success which characterizes the years of high breeding population, but just how it does is unknown.

If the former nesting site is missing or unusable for any reason, the swans select another location within essentially the same territory. For several years a pair nested on a bit of shallow marshland which protruded from an otherwise open lake shore unoccupied by other swans. One season this small area was destroyed by the winter's ice action, and with the loss of the only suitable nesting site, the otherwise acceptable territory has not been occupied since.

Whatever determines the trumpeter's selection of territory, the most obvious result is the distant spacing of nests. For four successive years, during the nesting seasons of 1954–57, swan nest locations were plotted on aerial maps showing about 6,000 acres of water and marsh, about 50 percent of the nesting habitat in the Red Rock Lakes marsh. The Upper Red Rock and Swan Lake areas are shown in figure 39, and the Lower Red Rock area in figure 40.

This nesting distribution data is highly accurate, since the incubating swans are very conspicuous when viewed with a $20\times$ spotting telescope from lookout posts on nearby hills. Most of the nests shown were subsequently checked by boat, and no errors were found in the plotting data. Any errors would probably be those of omission. A total of 109 nests were thus plotted during the month of June in the 1954–57 period considered.

Of 74 nests observed on the Upper Red Rock and Swan Lakes in the 4 seasons, 57 (77 percent) were located on or within a few feet of previously or subsequently used sites. Three (4 percent) were occupied during all 4 seasons. Much the same situation prevailed on the Lower Red Rock Lake where a total of 35 sites was checked, with 25 (71 percent) located on substantially the same bit of marsh used the previous year. Here only 1 site was used all 4 years.

Shorelines are not selected in the same proportion for nesting territories as is island habitat, and relatively straight shoreline is almost totally ignored. Whenever territories are established on comparatively open shorelines, the pursuit-distance at which one of the mated pair will take aggressive action against an intruder is noticeably greater than if a bay or island is occupied. The highest concentration of nests per acre is found on shallow Swan Lake where the irregular shoreline combines with numerous stable sedge islands to provide the greatest variety and interspersion of water and marsh habitat. In 1957, for instance, approximately 500 acres of water, island, and

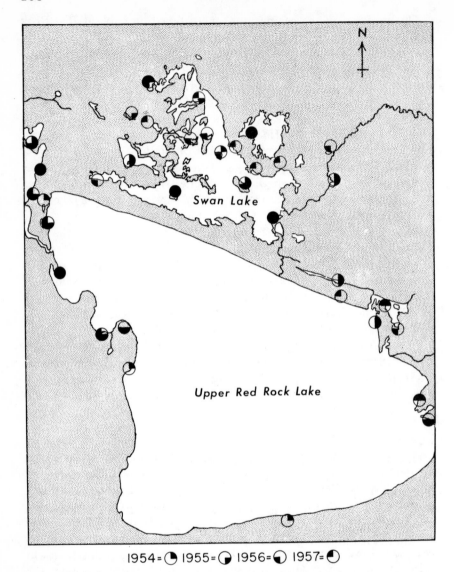

1954 = ◐ 1955 = ◑ 1956 = ◕ 1957 = ◔

FIGURE 39.—Nest locations, 1954–57, Upper Red Rock Lake and Swan Lake marsh. (Approximately 8,000 acres in map.)

peripheral habitat of Swan Lake supported 7 pairs of nesting swans, or about 70 acres of territory per nesting pair; on deeper Lower Lake, where nesting sites are most frequently located atop bulrush muskrat-house sites, only 10 pairs nested on the 1,500 acres, or about 150 acres per nesting pair. The relation of shoreline to interspersed nesting habitat will be shown later under Population Mechanics.

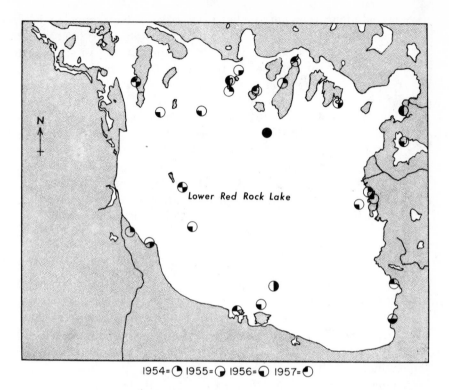

1954=◐ 1955=◑ 1956=◒ 1957=◓

FIGURE 40.—Nest locations, 1954–57, Lower Red Rock Lake. (Approximately 3,000 acres in map.)

The amount of territory claimed by a mated pair of trumpeters may seem to be related to the quantity of food available at a given distance from the nest. On an open shoreline, the territory defended is normally greater than that of an island-nesting pair in shallow-water territory where a great deal of food may be available within a short radius of the nest. A shoreline nesting pair will, however, frequently select a small bay for the nest location where territorial defenses are limited principally to the confines of the bay itself, and in spite of the comparatively smaller amount of food available, the pursuit-distance is found to approximate that of island-nesting swans. So, quantity of feeding area alone does not necessarily determine either the size or the appeal of any given area as nesting territory. The arrangement of the various terrain features within the area, as well as the number of potential nesting pairs, are also important factors.

The area of marsh or lake required to support a pair of trumpeters and their brood adequately must be but a fraction of the size of the territory claimed, and depends upon the quality of food produced as well as the quantity and availability. For instance, trumpeters have nested along very narrow but productive water channels where food was abundant and where travel to larger waters for food would not appear to be necessary. They do not prefer to nest on closed channels or ponds of a size equal to or even larger than the channel if egress by swimming to larger waters is restricted, though the food supply within such an area may appear adequate to support a good-sized family. M. M. Nice (1941 : 469–470), speaking generally of song birds, states: "Many birds, like the Song Sparrow and House Wren . . . , at first claim far more land than they really need; under pressure of competition they decrease their holdings *but not beyond a certain point*. In other cases, territorial behavior adapts itself to circumstances, and the type changes, so that many more pairs are accommodated on a certain area than would otherwise be possible." This may also apparently be true of the trumpeter to a limited extent.

A certain amount of water space, presumably to meet flight take-off requirements, appears necessary within each territory, and the large number of potholes over the Refuge which often produce considerable food are not an important segment of the breeding habitat because of such restrictions. The marsh next to these potholes is heavily vegetated; thus, landing or take-off near the nest is difficult or impossible.

Condon (MS) found in Yellowstone Park that:

Of the 29 lakes used by trumpeter swan during the past 10 years, only 4 are smaller in size than 16 acres, and of these 4, all are 9 or more acres. This tendency to choose lakes of 9 or more acres indicates the need for a reasonably large territory for the rearing of young. . . . none of the 29 lakes used have harbored more than one nesting pair of trumpeter swan. Many of the lakes have adequately cared for several nonnesting adults, but only one nesting pair has been found to utilize a lake.

Mated pairs sometimes guard territories but have never been observed to nest. This situation may be noted in the same territory from year to year, when the same pair apparently returns. It is not known whether these pairs have been shunted by competition to areas in which breeding may be inhibited for some reason, or merely are incapable of breeding. There does seem to be some correlation between the areas occupied in this manner and their specific location. Too, the percentage of nonnesting pairs appears to increase when the breeding population is high, but no figures are available to support this generalization. In 1957, there were 3 pairs of nonnesters in addition to the 10 nesting pairs on Lower Red Rock Lake, while the Upper Lake contained 2 pairs of nonnesters in addition to the 6 pairs of nesting swans.

NESTING

NEST SITES

Muskrat houses furnish the great majority of swan nesting sites at Red Rock Lakes. On the Lower Lake where bulrush beds are plentiful, the trumpeters prefer to nest on muskrat lodges located in this growth, and few nests are placed on the shoreline proper. On the Upper Lake where bulrush is found only occasionally, all of the nests are located by necessity along the shore proper.

Even while the breeding marsh remains frozen, the tops of muskrat houses which protrude from the snow are visited by swans and used as loafing sites. Whether their attraction at this season is due to their potential as nesting sites or to their convenient location as observation posts is not known, but their prebreeding season appeal is certainly more than just casual.

Nests are usually located so that all or part of the site is bounded by a moat of water. During a year with an abnormally high spring water table, one swan nest was located on a solid sedge meadow, a measured 298 feet from the nearest waters. The dried remains of algae at the base of the nest, however, showed that the nest was actually built in a few inches of water during the runoff. The great majority of nests on the Refuge are placed on muskrat houses located on semi-floating sedge bog-mats.

Any suitable feature located somewhat above the general level of the marsh terrain may be used as a nesting site. Oberhansley and Barrows (MS) mention in their Yellowstone report:

Old muskrat houses furnish excellent nesting sites, and in one instance at Little Robinson Creek, an old beaver house was used. At Riddle Lake, beavers were observed in the act of converting an old swan nest into a home for themselves by piling limbs and dead tree sections over it. On the other hand, old beaver houses form islands which were used by swans.

Condon (MS) adds to the subject of nest locations in Yellowstone Park by stating:

In some instances, small islands removed from the mainland are used as nesting sites, and islands visited at Riddle and White Lakes afforded sites for nests made of reeds and grasses which were piled into small mounds hollowed to accommodate the clutch of eggs. . . . Many nests are built on the lake shores in open unconcealed areas, with very little vegetative cover for concealment and with the nest itself consisting of only a small mound of grasses, reeds, twigs, and rushes. Such nests and nest sites were used at Geode, Grebe, and Madison Junction Lakes.

NEST BUILDING

Nest-building activities are shared by both sexes, though the female probably contributes the bulk of the effort. Nest materials on the Refuge consist chiefly of sedge sod and plant parts, though any material nearby may be used. These materials are not moved farther than a neck-length away. In one instance, a pair of swans in Upper Red Rock Lake was observed in what seemed to be nest-construction activities. Both birds remained prone on a small sedge island near the mouth of Shambow Creek and busily picked up vegetative debris, rootstocks, and plant parts with their bills, stacking these in a mound to the rear. This continued for perhaps 5 minutes with vigorous enthusiasm. Then one of the swans departed and began feeding some distance away, completely ignoring the activities of the other bird. The mate remained and continued to tug and wrestle with desirable bits of tough sedge and fibrous matter, adding these materials to the small heap already accumulated to the rear. It was still at the task when the observer left the observation post some 15 minutes later.

This particular nest foundation was begun late in the season and was never completed. The pair of swans which were so intent on its construction were not observed engaging in this activity again, nor did they nest at all that season, although they remained in the territory and defended it against other swans.

An observation in Yellowstone Park of a pair of trumpeter swans engaged in nest-building activities is given by Oberhansley and Barrows (MS):

In repairing the nest at Swan Lake the cob and pen cooperated. The old nest material was rearranged by adding material from the sides of the nest to the top. Some of the submerged portions of the nest were brought above the water and other materials (chiefly sedges) near at hand were gathered and added. As the swans gathered sedges they would throw them to the rear in the general direction of the nest to be added later. This particular nest is located upon an old muskrat house and has been used for several years. It has a fibrous, mucky base and gradually becomes coarser toward the top where the fibrous material blends with sedges and a few scattered leaves of willow and birch in the nest proper. The nest is partially surrounded and supported by several clumps of mountain bog birch (*Betula glandulosa*) and a few willows (*Salix*, sp.) which [formed] a rather poor screen until the surrounding sedges had grown tall enough to serve better. All approaches are well guarded by water to a depth of about four feet, gradually sloping to a width of approximately 10 feet at the bottom of the pond. The total height of the nest was 61 inches, with top protruding 22 inches above the water line.

Swan nests constructed on the Red Rock Lakes Refuge average somewhat smaller than the nest just described but the general account is typical. Condon (MS) records, writing again of his observations in Yellowstone Park:

The type of nest constructed by trumpeter swan in Yellowstone Park varies greatly and the material from which it is made is governed entirely by the type of cover and vegetation near the nest site. . . . where an abundance of grasses, sedges, reeds, and rushes is available, nests of large proportions are at times built. Such nests have been built at Swan and Trumpeter Lakes. Their large size is, in all probability, due to the necessity of keeping a dry nest and the desire to have the nest removed from dry land by a strip of water. Nests of this type have been constructed only where vegetative cover and water depths have been favored with suitable sites.

MacFarlane (1891: 425) gives a general description of the nests of Arctic trumpeters which were observed near Fort Anderson (east of the Mackenzie River delta), stating:

> Several nests of this species were met with in the Barren Grounds, on islands in Franklin Bay, and one containing six eggs was situated near the beach on a sloping knoll. It was composed of a quantity of hay, down, and feathers intermixed, and this was the general mode of structure of the nests of both swans.

Only a trace of down and a few molted feathers have been observed about the nest areas of trumpeters on the Red Rock Lakes area. The material of which the nest bowl proper is constructed differs little from that of which the upper part of the nest is fashioned, the finer leaf and stem parts of the sedges being the usual material used there.

For a month, more or less, after the eggs are hatched, the nest becomes a favorite site for the brooding of the cygnets at night and loafing by day. By midsummer, as a result of these activities, the nest is an odoriferous mound of decaying vegetation and defecation. The hatched egg shells and unhatched eggs, if any, are buried to a depth of several inches with fecal deposits in addition to the vegetative material which has become mashed down from the nest bowl or piled on the site by muskrats. Of course the nest by this time is unrecognizable, with usually only a few molted white feathers nearby to indicate that the unattractive heap was once a tidy swan's nest.

EGG DESCRIPTION

Trumpeter eggs are somewhat granular in texture, elongated ovoid in shape, and off-white in color when freshly laid, becoming nest-stained a brownish color a short while after incubation.

In 1955, 109 eggs representing the complete clutches of 21 nests were measured for length and greatest diameter (see appendix 3). Longitudinal measurements ranged from 123 mm., which was the longest and which had a diameter of 74 mm., to the shortest, which measured 104 mm., there being 4 of the latter (2 in a clutch of 6, 1 in a clutch of 5, and 1 in a clutch of 4) which were 69 mm., 71 mm., 70.5 mm., and 70.5 mm., respectively, at their greatest diameter.

The egg of greatest diameter measured 77.5 mm. and was 109 mm. long, being one of a clutch of 6, while the egg of shortest diameter was 68 mm. and measured 113 mm. long, being one of a clutch of 8.

The average length of the 109 eggs checked was 110.9 mm., while the average diameter was 72.4 mm. It is interesting to note that the average trumpeter egg from the Red Rock flock is noticeably smaller, 110.9 x 72.4 vs. 121.3 x 77, than the average measurements of 3 eggs (from 2 nests) obtained from the Copper River, Alaska, flock by Melvin Monson (1956: 445). The smaller egg-size ratio of the Red Rock Lakes trumpeters also holds true when compared with that reported from the Kenai trumpeter flock (Dave Spencer, correspondence). The average size of the eggs obtained at Red Rock Lakes compares very closely with that reported by A. C. Bent (1925:297) in the measurement of 25 trumpeter eggs.

CLUTCH SIZE

Sizes of completed clutches of eggs in various trumpeter nests on the Red Rock Lakes Refuge show this annual variation: 1949, 12 nests containing 3 to 9 eggs each held a total of 61 eggs for a mean of 5.1 eggs to the nest; 1951, 13 nests containing from 4 to 7 eggs held 73 eggs for a mean of 5.6; 1952, 17 nests containing from 2 to 7 eggs held 88 eggs for a mean of 5.2; 1955, 32 nests containing from 4 to 8 eggs held 157 eggs for a mean of 4.9. The 74 completed clutches observed over an intermittent span of 7 years contained a total of 379 eggs, the mean being 5.1 eggs to the nest.

These figures agree well with the clutch size noted by MacFarlane (1891:425) among Arctic-breeding trumpeters, as he states, "It usually lays from 4 to 6 eggs judging from the noted contents of a received total of 24 nests."

EGG LAYING

The rate at which eggs are laid and the length of the incubation period were not studied on the Refuge since gathering such data on a single nest would unnecessarily disturb several nesting pairs. Other observers have made some pertinent notes.

H. F. Witherby et al. (1939: 177) state of the mute swan, "According to O. Heinroth, eggs laid on alternate days; confirmation desirable;" which H. Poulson (1949) obligingly furnished, writing, "The female Mute Swan in the Zoo laid 5 eggs in 1947 and 4 eggs in 1948 on alternate days."

Witherby et al. also report that whooper swans in confinement laid eggs on alternate days (1939: 170). For lack of specific information on the subject, the production of about 1 egg every 48 hours is assumed to be normal for the trumpeter also.

INCUBATION

Although Witherby et al. (1939: 177) report that in the case of the mute swan the male assists the female in incubating the eggs, this has never been observed or reported in the trumpeter. Poulsen

(1949) corroborates Witherby's mute-swan statement but adds that in the case of the whooper swan the male did not participate in incubation duties.

Several records have been compiled on the length of the incubation period. Dr. Ward Sharp, writing of 5 trumpeter swan eggs which were set under bantam hens, records in a Bureau report:

> The little hens could not keep the eggs warm, faithfully as they tried. One end of the egg was always cool. A few days before the [other] eggs hatched (about 3 or 4) two eggs became warm and hatched soon afterward. The incubation period was about 33 days.

Oberhansley and Barrows (MS) in their Yellowstone Park observations also report an incubation period of 33 days, but Almer Nelson, formerly Refuge Manager at the National Elk Refuge, writes of a period of 36–37 days. Inasmuch as the incubating period lasts more than 4 weeks, the variation of a few days' time would be expected under the varying conditions found in the wild. A normal incubation period of from 33 to 37 days seems reasonable.

Again referring to the much-studied mute swan, Witherby et al. (1939: 177) state, "incubation begins before completion of clutch in some cases." This tendency may also be present in the trumpeter to some extent, as unhatched eggs containing well-developed embryos are sometimes found in nests from which the female has departed with her first-hatched cygnets.

HATCHING DATA

The Red Rock Lakes–Yellowstone region has short, cool summers. Thus the average hatching date is important, since the nesting lakes and marshes freeze over rather early, dooming any late cygnets which are still flightless.

Of 12 nests closely watched in 1949, 9 had produced broods between June 15 and 21. The first brood was seen on June 15, and the last nest under observation apparently hatched about June 26.

In 1952 hatching was much later. On 7 nests checked that year, only 1 had produced young by June 17, 3 more had hatched by June 28, and the remainder had hatched by July 3. The average hatching date in 1952 was later than at any time during the period 1948–52, presumably because mating was delayed by abnormally high water levels during the initial spring breakup period. Fortunately a long, unusually warm autumn followed, and no cygnet mortality seemed to result from this late hatch. Normally, hatching on the Red Rock Lakes marsh occurs between June 15 and June 25.

In 1946 Sharp reported seeing the first cygnets on June 10, and earlier A. V. Hull mentioned, "The first egg date that we have is April 26." Both of these records indicate unusually early nesting.

Condon (MS) records a late-nesting case in Yellowstone Park in 1940. The trumpeters were not seen on the lake until May 30, and no cygnets appeared until July 18, probably too late to survive the fall freeze.

Judging from the egg-laying rate, average clutch size, period of incubation, and the known hatching dates of many nests, egg-laying normally commences on Refuge marshes shortly after May 1 and most clutches are completed by May 15. Thus, nesting is underway in many cases before the ice has disappeared. This is many weeks before the ducks commence to nest in earnest.

David Spencer (correspondence) states that on the Kenai National Moose Range in Alaska in 1957 most of the hatching was completed by June 25. This indicates that the nesting seasons on the Kenai and in the Red Rock Lakes marshes are coincidental to a surprising degree, the great difference in latitude (16°) apparently being well compensated for by the contrast in elevation (sea level vs. 6,600 ft.)

RENESTING

All the white northern swans raise a single brood each year, if successful in nesting. No instance was found in the ornithological literature to the contrary, either in the wild or in captivity. In captivity, both the black swan and the black-necked swan will produce 2 or even 3 clutches of eggs in a single year if the eggs are removed successively after each clutch is completed. If a brood is raised by the parents from the first clutch of eggs laid, this precludes a second nesting for that year.

An unsuccessful attempt, sponsored by outside interests but permitted by the Service, was made in 1944 to increase trumpeter swan production artificially at the Red Rock Lakes Refuge. In this case a clutch of 5 eggs was removed from a wild trumpeter nest on the Refuge and incubated artificially. Jean Delacour (1944: 135–136) states of this attempt, "We had hopes that the robbed pair of swans would nest again, but they refused to do so, and the only supposed advantage of taking eggs rather than cygnets was thus denied."

One valid case of renesting may have been found. While on a routine inspection of swan nests in Refuge marshes, I encountered 2 fresh nests within 25 feet of each other. In one nest, which was deserted, there were the broken pieces of 5 eggs, which had apparently been destroyed not too long previously, while the active nest located nearby held 2 eggs. The smaller clutch was being incubated, and in addition 3 eggs were floating near the new active nest.

Presumably when the eggs in the first nest were destroyed, possibly by predation, the clutch was in the process of completion, and the pair promptly renested close at hand. The 3 floating eggs may have been lost in the interval between the destruction of the first clutch and the completion of the second nest to the point of being able to hold eggs. Thus, a total of 10 eggs was apparently laid by the one female, as an association of 3 breeding swans has never been observed on the Refuge, and territorialism would prevent the nesting of 2 pairs so closely.

In the case of the failure of a trumpeter pen to renest, as reported by Jean Delacour, the eggs may have been removed from the nest after egg laying had stopped and incubation was actually under way. If the eggs had been quietly removed as they were laid, leaving one or two in the nest to restrain the inclination to desert or nest elsewhere, a much greater production by the female may have resulted.

CYGNET DEVELOPMENT

In common with other birds, the young of the trumpeter are equipped with an egg tooth believed to help in breaking out of the shell. Oberhansley and Barrows (MS) noted, "This sharp point is a special adaptation designed only for pipping the shell and disappears sometime after hatching. . . . The shells average 1 millimeter in thickness and are very strong."

Only one record of the weights of newly hatched cygnets seems to have been made. Regarding this, Sharp, referring to the cygnets artificially incubated, states, "The two cygnets weighed 7 and 7½ ozs. respectively when hatched on June 19, 1944." No other figures are available, but these data are believed representative.

How much time is spent by the wild pen brooding the newly hatched cygnets on the nest before leading them to water is not known. The presence of unhatched eggs or cold inclement weather might prolong brooding, while a complete hatch and warm weather might shorten it.

F. E. Blaauw (1904: 74) made a note regarding the persistence of brooding in his captive trumpeters, stating, "During the first days of the life of her chicks, the old female trumpeter often retires to her nest for hours together, warming them under her, and she continues to do this during the night for a long time."

Much attentiveness is shown the young cygnets by the parents, with both adults usually present. How aggressively the parents might defend their young from predators is not known. The treatment of muskrats by aroused trumpeters suggests that very vigorous action is possible. But the parents' close supervision of the young gives very few opportunities to predators.

When the presence of humans threatens the swan family, the adults will usually desert their young without protective action, with little if any reduction of the normal escape-distance. If time and opportunity allow, the adults try to lead their young into dense growths of emergent aquatic plants, leaving the scene unobtrusively shortly after hiding their cygnets. The cygnets will then usually remain quiet and well hidden, though sometimes flushing from their hiding place when deliberate search is commenced in the immediate vicinity. Scott and Fisher (1953: 209) report that among wild Icelandic whooping swans:

> Older cygnets would feign death when handled, having their necks in a lifeless attitude. This was particularly noticed in a brood estimated to be about two weeks old, and again in one of about four and a half weeks. . . .
>
> The behavior of parent whoopers with cygnets was also variable. Some deserted their brood and flew away at a range of several hundred yards. Others

FIGURE 41.—Newly hatched trumpeter cygnet, Lower Red Rock Lake; egg in mid-foreground being pipped.

FIGURE 42.—Close-up of trumpeter cygnet showing fine, grayish-white down.

remained to protect their young and were photographed at less than thirty yards.

When not disturbed, parent trumpeters spend most of the time swimming, feeding, or loafing, with the more active cygnets busily moving between or immediately around them. Close family ties result in a tightly knit family formation which reduces vulnerability to predators.

This characteristic, coupled with a pair's territorial proclivities, virtually eliminates the possibility of two or more broods combining, especially in the younger age classes when both factors are more strongly expressed. On one occasion, however, during the August 29, 1955, aerial census of the Refuge, a single pair was seen accompanied by 10 cygnets. Specific nest checks in that vicinity earlier in the year to determine clutch size establishes that in this instance the abnormal size was due to an association of at least 3 broods. The actual circumstances surrounding this unusual case are unknown. (Earlier observations of the 4 broods nearest this occurrence had revealed that hatching originally produced broods of 5-3-3-1.) Sharp, in a trumpeter census report in Refuge files dated June 28, 1943, also reports a brood of 7 cygnets which he believed was a compounding of 2 broods of 4 cygnets seen in the same general area 12 days earlier, so such cases apparently do occur.

Although swan brood amalgamation appears to be rare, older broods of preflight age sometimes contain individuals of marked size differences. These cases probably represent variations in individual growth rates rather than examples of brood combinations, though the latter may occur to a limited degree. Hochbaum (correspondence) notes that the two Montana cygnets raised at Delta showed marked differences in size from the start. The larger bird proved to be male, the smaller, female.

The rapid growth rate of this species is assisted by the long daylight hours of summer which the young spend feeding in their fertile marsh environment. It was previously noted that the two cygnets hatched in captivity on the Refuge on June 19 weighed 7 and 7½ ounces. On September 2 these same birds weighed 15¼ and 15⅜ pounds respectively, a thirtyfold increase in 75 days. In the wild, growth must be at a comparable rate, as I have weighed 19-pound cygnets of preflight age captured for banding in early October.

Because of the early freeze-ups on their breeding grounds, the average age at which cygnets are capable of flight is important. Oberhansley and Barrows (MS) report that in one case a cygnet hatched June 23 was observed on its initial flight on October 9, a period of 109 days. James R. Simon (1952:462) checked the flight capabilities of 3 trumpeter cygnets, hatched on June 16, 1951 in Grand Teton National Park, from October 4 to 16. Two cygnets could fly by the 14th, and 2 days later, 122 days from hatching, the whole family departed the pond on the wing. The cygnets transferred from the Red Rock Lakes Refuge to the Delta station in 1955 made initial flights when about 13 weeks old, a period of 91 days. A development period of from 100 to 120 days would apply to the average Red Rock Lakes cygnet, as young hatched about June 20 are frequently seen in flight before October 10, though seldom before September 20. There is considerable variation in the individual development so that some cygnets, though hatching on time, might be flightless and vulnerable at the final freezeup. This has occurred as early as

FIGURE 43.—Swan family at loafing cite, Grebe Lake, Yellowstone National Park. The special foot position of the adult is commonly seen with mute swans. This brood is approximately a month old.

October 28 for the Red Rock Lakes and marsh, though the 16-year average final freezeup date compiled during the 1938–53 period, is November 8.

Though family ties remain strong, the "apron strings" of the parents tend to loosen as the young grow older. On one occasion, a brood of cygnets was left alone for about 30 minutes while the parents moved briefly to another part of the lake. This occurred on August 30, when the young were half grown.

Only two notes exist regarding the duration of family ties after the offspring's first winter. I once noted two immature trumpeters, in their initial flightless molt during July, closely together when a large loosely scattered nonbreeding flock was approached. These two individuals were so attracted to each other that the long pursuit by boat did not separate them, as usually occurs among unrelated swans. Both were subsequently captured for banding, and were found to have been banded the previous autumn when they were pre-flight cygnets of the same brood.

This observation suggests that associations of brood mates may persist for some time after the offspring are left by their parents upon the approach of the breeding season, at least until their first flightless molt. This period would appear to be confirmed and even extended by R. H. Mackay (1957: 339), who reported that three brood mates banded in 1955 were shot virtually together in Nebraska in late October 1956. Family ties in the trumpeter are apparently strong.

FOOD

Swans spend long hours in their endless quest for food and consume enormous amounts of succulent green vegetation when given an opportunity, all parts of the various aquatic plants being taken. Witherby et al. (1939) mention that pondweeds, buttercups, mannagrass, eelgrass, waterweed, muskgrass, and clover, besides others, constitute the food of the Eurasian species of swans. Hilprecht (1956: 96–100) also mentions their foods and feeding habits. Many of these plant forms are an important part of the diet of our native swans as well.

The findings from several unpublished food studies of the trumpeter in its Yellowstone and Red Rock Lakes environment, plus the laboratory analysis of stomach contents of trumpeter casualties and pertinent notes by other observers are combined here to furnish a summary of the food of this species. Much more remains to be learned, particularly of their winter food habits and requirements.

FEEDING HABITS AND FOOD OF YOUNG

From the beginning, downy cygnets are much interested in food, and are very active in their quest for it. For a long period following hatching, the swan family feeds in a tightly knit group, the adults usually remaining near each other in the shallow water while the cygnets swim busily about between them, frequently with coots or ducks intermixed, seeking the morsels which are stirred up by their parents.

Writing from close-hand observations of swan families feeding on lakes in Yellowstone Park, Oberhansley and Barrows (MS) describe these early feeding activities:

The first food of the cygnets was presented [brought up] to them on the surface of the water by the adults and consisted principally of aquatic beetles, with some insects and crustaceans, together with small quantities of the white, tender basal part of sedge. The young birds were very adroit in snapping up morsels that floated to the surface near the parent birds as they fed from the bottom or scratched food loose. Droppings in each case studied averaged over 95% animal matter for the first three weeks. Plant life became increasingly important with age and varied from sedges to water milfoil, pond weed and other aquatic plants as the season progressed. Beginning in August snail shells (*Lymnaea stagnalis jugularis*, Say) began to appear in the cygnet droppings. These snails are abundant near the east shore of the lake.

Condon (MS) reports:

The cygnets that have been observed during their first two weeks after hatching were seen to feed in very shallow waters of six inches to one foot in depth, and when feeding where the water was deeper, they were gathering the food stuffs brought to the surface from the bottom by their parents while feeding. In shallow water, where they can reach the bottom or the vegetation growing up from the bottom, their feeding is carried on by the simple process of stretching their long necks down and securing the food by working over the plant and animal matter at hand and selecting those desired.

That swan cygnets tended to cut down on the animal matter in their diet after about five weeks was noted by their tendency to feed in deeper waters and to be feeding primarily on vegetative foods. Droppings collected at Grebe, Riddle, Geode and Swan Lakes all gave evidence of a preponderance of vegetable foods and very little animal. Those animal forms eaten were undoubtedly of the softer forms, for evidence of them did not appear in the droppings collected at resting areas.

These observations agree generally with the feeding habits of the cygnets at the Red Rock Lakes Refuge, though close observations of feeding families of swans are impractical in the vast marsh system. On one occasion five Refuge cygnets from a single brood and one cygnet from another brood were recovered soon after they had died, presumably of exposure, and a determination of their stomach contents was made by the Fish and Wildlife Research Laboratory in Denver, Colorado. These data, as well as information concerning the stomach contents of a predator-killed cygnet in Yellowstone, are presented in the Appendix, part 4. In the case of the Refuge cygnets, practically no animal matter was present, with leaf and stem fragments making up from 80 to 100 percent of the stomach contents, and the seeds of sedge and spikerush also present. In the single Yellowstone cygnet of comparable age, fresh water fairy shrimp (*Eubranchipus* sp.) were represented as well as sedge fragments.

The young of the trumpeter have been successfully raised in captivity in at least two instances, without natural parental care, and under varying conditions. This indicates that their early food habits or requirements are not critical or fixed. The first case was demonstrated on the Red Rock Lakes Refuge when two were raised by Sharp, as mentioned previously, while a pair of month-old cygnets were reared at the Delta Waterfowl Research Station after having been transferred from their Red Rock Lakes Refuge natal environment.

In the case of the Refuge cygnets artificially raised by Sharp, bantam hens served as both the method of incubation and source of parental care. This attention inspired no apparent attachment to the foster parent, nor to the humans helping care for the cygnets. Initial foods fed in this case were broiler chow, milk curd, and dandelion leaves. Wheat and lawn clippings were added to the diet later. Development of these birds appeared comparable to those in the wild except for a weakness of the legs, which became apparent after each weighed about 10 pounds, and from which they subsequently recovered.

At the Delta Station the month-old trumpeters were successfully started on a ration consisting of duck grower pellets, with a constantly available supply of lesser duckweed (*Lemna minor*) serving as the green vegetation supplement. Later the leaves and stalks of arrowhead were introduced and were much relished, as much as a bucketful being consumed by a single cygnet in a day. Upon the exhaustion of the local supply of arrowhead, the leaves of cattail were substituted with equal success.

The young developed normally at Delta except again for an apparent weakness of the leg bones, which supported the body with difficulty out of water as the birds rapidly gained weight before the bone structure hardened. This weakness was eliminated by permitting the cygnets access to a supply of swimming water, where their body weight was supported much of the time by water instead of the individual's legs on the hatchery's cement floor.

FEEDING HABITS AND FOOD OF OLDER CYGNETS, IMMATURES, AND ADULTS

Even before the development of contour feathers changes the appearance of the wild downy cygnets, they seem to rely progressively less on food material provided by the adults and become more interested in obtaining it by their own efforts. At this stage any emphasis on the high protein diet of aquatic insect and crustacean life shifts to vegetable foods. Feeding is still accomplished very much as a family unit, and after the cygnets are 2 or 3 months old their food-gathering actions indicate that their diet is approaching that of their parents.

While the feeding of the cygnets appears to be confined solely to water, that of the immature and adult, though predominantly aquatic in nature, may include a limited amount of feeding or grazing upon land. Audubon (1838: 540) noted, "This swan feeds principally by partially immersing the body and extending the neck under water. . . . Often, however, it resorts to the land, and then picks at the herbage, not sidewise, as Geese do, but more in the manner of Ducks and poultry." Swans have rarely been observed feeding on land on the Refuge.

Trumpeters most frequently feed in shallow-water areas where they are able to use their long necks to the best advantage, or if deeper water is encountered they may "tip up" in the manner of puddle ducks. Although they are quite capable of diving and swimming under water, they apparently resort to diving solely to escape when flightless.

Oberhansley and Barrows (MS) contribute an interesting note on the feeding of a pair of trumpeters within Yellowstone Park, writing, "A typical observation on September 18 of a pair of swans feeding on a small lake near Madison Junction showed 2 birds suspending 15 and 13 times respectively in 30 minutes. . . . There was no system of timing, sometimes both birds submerged alternately and again simultaneously; neither appeared to be on guard." This description also typifies the feeding of trumpeters in the shallow water areas of the Refuge.

Tubers and rhizomes of the various aquatic plants are a staple food item, along with the stems and leaves of such plants, and the swans spare no effort in excavating for these starchy plant parts. Their powerful legs, large webs, and prominent toes are especially efficient in stirring up the soft mud of their shallow marsh environment. Great holes, sometimes over a foot deep and several feet in diameter, on the shallow bottoms of the Red Rock Lakes marsh bear witness to this method of exposing food materials.

Erickson describes the feeding of the Malheur captive flock (correspondence):

Swans are also disposed to feeding along the shorelines and river banks, where they gouge out and undermine the banks in search for roots and shoots. Their stout, muscular necks and heavy bodies aid them in performing major excavations when undercutting the banks. In the swan pond they have been successful not only in eliminating much of the hardstem bulrush growth, but also in the destruction of the tough rootstocks of the tule.

Many references to the food habits of the native swans are to be found in the early literature. It will be recalled that Lewis and Clark noted that both species of swans fed much on the root of the "wappatoo" in the Columbia River.

Later observers confirmed Lewis and Clark's statement that the swans fed much on the root of the wapato or duck potato. George Barnston of the Hudson's Bay Company noted that (1862: 7831), "In the scarcity of their favorite food, the tubers of

the *Sagittaria sagittifolia* [probably *S. latifolia*], they have recourse
to the roots of other plants, and the tender underground runners of
grasses in the higher latitudes." J. C. Hughes (1883:283) also
recorded that along the Columbia River the favorite food of the
trumpeter was the wapato, listing the species as *Sagittaria variabilis*
[probably *S. latifolia*], stating that a Mr. Allard observed a trumpeter which had been strangled by a large tuber of this plant which
had become lodged in its throat.

A. C. Bent (1925:286) quotes Major Bendire as stating that about
"20 small shells, perhaps half an inch in length" were found in a
stomach of a whistling swan, while E. S. Cameron was noted to have
observed this species to feed, presumably in Montana, as follows:

> The swans were engaged in feeding upon the soft-shelled fresh-water snails
> which abound in this lake and explain its great attraction for them. During the
> several days that I watched the swans I never saw them eat anything else, but
> doubtless they pick up vegetation as well, being accustomed to walk about in the
> grass at the mouth of Alder Creek. Marsh Lake is so shallow (only 2 feet deep
> over most of it, and 4 feet in the deepest part) that the long-necked birds can
> generally reach the mollusca without much tilting of their bodies in characteristic
> swan fashion.

In a recent study of the food habits of whistling swans wintering
in the Chesapeake Bay region, Robert E. Stewart and Joseph H.
Manning (1958:209–210) examined the gullet and stomach contents
of 49 birds. They report:

> In the series studied, submerged aquatic plants furnished 100 percent of the
> food in fresh estuarine waters, 60 percent in brackish waters, and 47 percent in
> estuarine marsh ponds. Mollusks [chiefly long clams and Baltic macomas],
> although comprising 31 percent of the food in brackish estuarine waters, were
> not listed for other types, while rootstalks and stems of emergent marsh plants
> were important only in the estuarine marsh ponds.

Witherby et al. (1939:177) mention that the mute swan has been
noted to eat "small frogs and toads, tadpoles, worms, fresh-water
Mollusca, occasionally small fish (*Alburnus*) and insects with their
larvae" in addition to its more staple diet of plant foods. Fish were
also recovered from the gullets of several trumpeters which died at
the Kellogg Bird Sanctuary in Michigan (Dr. Miles Pirnie, correspondence), but it is doubtful that these represent a part of their
customary diet.

From this, and data to be presented later, it appears that the
trumpeter will eat a variety of vegetable foods. Mollusca and
vertebrates do not occur as a staple fare but are apparently eaten
when readily available.

Several observers have contributed to the knowledge of the specific
foods of the trumpeter in Yellowstone Park. Oberhansley and Barrows (MS) state:

Identification of two principal plant foods (from small lake near Madison Junction) was positive and later determined as pond weed (*Potamogeton filiformis*) and water milfoil. . . . The droppings of adult birds consist almost entirely of vegetable matter, with an occasional large quantity of grit. . . . Four species of sedges used as food have been identified from Swan Lake, the most important of which is *Carex rostrata*, which serves also as an excellent cover. . . . Seeds of various aquatic plants, principally sedges, were found in the stomach of the swan that died on Trumpeter Lake. One small snail shell and traces of crustaceans were also present.

Condon (MS) gives a more detailed list for the swans in Yellowstone Park:

The principal plant types on which the trumpeter swans have been observed to feed as identified by examination of plants taken at various places feeding occurred are: Pondweed (*Potamogeton*, sp. undet.), Water Milfoil (*Myriophyllum*, sp. undet.), Musk grass (*Chara*, sp. undet.), Waterweed (*Elodea canadensis*), Duckweed (*Lemna trisulca*), Tules (*Scirpus*, sp. undet.), Spatterdocks (*Nymphaea polysepala* [*Nuphar polysepalum*]), Bur-reeds (*Sparganium augustifolium*), Wapato (*Sagittaria cuneata*).

In watching the trumpeter swan feeding it was found that they eat the foliage of each of the above-named plants. The opportunity to examine the stomachs of the adult trumpeter swan for food content has been limited and only one has been secured in the past 2 years. This contained all vegetative matter, parts of which were identified as being: Muskgrass (*Chara*), Waterweed (*Elodea*), and Duckweed (*Lemna*). This stomach contained an ample quantity of quartz and obsidian sand grit.

Collections of droppings . . . from Geode, Grebe, Swan, and Madison Junction Lakes . . . were so nearly 100 percent vegetative in character that no animal matter was discerned. . . .

Another interesting item was the abundance of the seeds of the spatterdock . . . in the droppings collected from Grebe and Madison Junction Lakes where large beds of these plants abound. . . . From one dropping taken at Grebe Lake on September 21, 1939, a total of 272 seeds of the spatterdock were secured and 497 small seeds from an unidentified plant. All the droppings at resting areas at Grebe Lake gave evidence of heavy seed eating. The failure to digest many of these seeds was of interest. All seeds were highly polished. That the preponderant percentage of the foods eaten by swans are of plant origin was evidenced in droppings examined at resting areas on all lakes visited.

Dr. O. J. Murie, former U. S. Fish and Wildlife Service biologist, collected 17 samples of swan droppings from the shores of Grebe Lake on September 2, 1943, and analyzed them. Prominent plant parts in these remains included filamentous green alga, sedge spikes, pond weeds, and wokas, with traces of animal matter (Tricoptera).

In 1938, A. V. Hull, who was manager of the Red Rock Lakes Refuge at the time, found the fresh carcasses of two trumpeters on the Refuge in December and June and sent the stomachs to the Service's Denver Wildlife Research Laboratory for analysis. In both, the tubers of sago pondweed dominated. In the December-taken bird, with the fragments of rootstocks, they comprised 100 percent of the contents

(443 tubers) while in the case of the June-taken bird 597 tubers constituted 90 percent of the contents, with leaf and stem material of the same plant bringing the total up to 96 percent. (See appendix 4 for an analytical breakdown of data.)

Earlier, Hull submitted 3 trumpeter swan stomachs taken from lead-poisoning fatalities at Culver Springs April 3–7, 1937, on the Red Rock Lakes Refuge. White water buttercup (*Ranunculus*) and mosses (*Amblystegium* and *Fissidens*) were the most prominent plants represented in the 100-percent vegetable contents. (See appendix 4 for further details.)

Most of the foregoing information has concerned the food habits of the trumpeter other than during the months when they are restricted to the limited areas of open water in winter, about which little is known.

An aquatic plant survey along portions of Henrys Fork of the Snake River used by wintering trumpeters indicates that the following plants are available (in the probable order of their importance to the swans) : Sago pondweed, leafy pondweed, water milfoil, white water buttercup (*Ranunculus aquatilus*), marestail, water moss (*Fontinalis*), clasping-leaf pondweed, and mannagrass (*Glyceria elata*).

Munro (1949 : 712) notes that in British Columbia their winter diet includes the following items:

From observations of feeding trumpeter swans, it has been determined that the following foods are attractive to them, namely, the seeds of yellow pond lily, *Nuphar polysepala*, and water shield, *Brasenia Schreberi;* the tubers of sago pondweed, *Potamogeton pectinatus*, and the stems and foliage of similar species. Late in the season, when the supply of more desirable foods is low, the birds eat water moss, *Fontinalis* sp., the stems and roots of sedges, *Scirpus* sp., and whatever other aquatic vegetation can be secured. The gullet of an adult male that died from lead poisoning at Itatsoo Lake, Vancouver Island, in February 1938, was packed with stems of grasses and sedges; the stomach contained 12 seeds of *Ceratophyllum demersum*. In an examination of the stomach contents of seven adults and two juveniles, killed by lead poisoning on Vancouver Island in January 1946, Dr. I. McT. Cowan identified the following items, namely, stems, leaves and roots of grasses, sedges (*Carex* sp.), and rushes (*Juncus* sp.), seeds of *Polygonum* sp., *Carex* sp., and wild cherry (*Prunus emarginata*). Another from Steveston, at the mouth of the Fraser River, had eaten grass roots, and seeds of a spike rush (*Eleocharis* sp.).

Swans kept in captivity adjust their food habits to whatever is available. Their bulky-green-food requirements usually cannot be entirely met with the limited supply of aquatics available, and some sort of supplementary feeding becomes necessary. At the Malheur Refuge, where a number of trumpeters were kept for several years on a fairly large spring-fed pond, a daily ration of barley and wheat supplemented their natural green foods, which they obtained either in the pond or by gouging roots and rhizomes from the banks.

At the Delta Waterfowl Research Station, the green-food requirements of the trumpeters in summer are met largely from the endless supply of duckweed which floats through the pens, as well as the occasional addition of the leaves and stalks of arrowhead. Their main diet requirement is provided in the form of wheat, soaked and fed in automatic dispensers. In the winter they are fed wheat, duck pellets, and lettuce trimmings.

Bulk green foods fed in quantity may be important when reproduction is desired in captive birds. This point was stressed by Mr. C. L. Cunningham, a successful breeder of swans at Woodinville, Washington, who advised that his captive swans, including the whooper, mute, black-necked, and black, daily consumed enormous quantities of fresh lawn clippings before the egg-laying season and that this plentiful supply of bulk green food was all-important in bringing his birds to a breeding condition. In this regard, the Heinroths (1928: 149–150) also mention that whooper swans in zoos rarely produce fertile eggs. They cite Blaauw's success in propagating trumpeters, giving them abundant greens in the form of watersoldier (*Stratiotes*) before the nesting season. Similar results were obtained with whoopers in Berlin by feeding cabbage and other greens. The nutritional requirements of the swans are unknown. This may explain in part the generally poor breeding success experienced more recently with the trumpeter in captivity.

A number of swan studies have been conducted by various governments over the years at the insistence of fishermen and sportsmen who accused these birds of interfering with livelihood or sport. In Germany, a food habits investigation of mute swans was conducted by the Reich Health Administration before World War II (Hilprecht, 1956: 96). In 1954, Danish sportsmen instigated a study of mute swans in their country, claiming wild duck production was being adversely affected by the aggressive behavior of the swans on mutual nesting habitats (Paludan and Fog, 1956).

In the United States, several swan studies have been carried out from time to time as the result of complaints to the Federal Government. As early as 1919, W. F. Kubichek conducted a field survey in Currituck Sound, N.C., for the U. S. Biological Survey, investigating charges that the large number of whistling swans which winter in this area were consuming most of the natural aquatic foods, leaving little or none for the ducks. A study with a somewhat similar objective is currently in progress on the Bear River Migratory Bird Refuge, Utah, under the direction of the Cooperative Wildlife Research Unit at Logan. The study of the food habits and status of whistling swans in the Chesapeake Bay area by Stewart and Manning (1958: 203–212) was undertaken in part to obtain information to answer the charges by shellfishers that these birds were making inroads in the commercial clam beds.

In all cases, either in this country or abroad, the swans were substantially cleared of these charges, although in certain instances some inimical relationships were noted.

LIMITING FACTORS

EGG FAILURE

The hatching success of trumpeter swan eggs on the Red Rock Lakes nesting marshes has been low compared with that of lesser waterfowl. In 1949 for instance, 30 of 61 swan eggs laid in 12 nests failed to hatch—a loss of 49 percent. In 1951, the loss was 34 percent in the 13 nests checked, when 25 eggs remained in the nest from a total of 73 incubated. Examination of 178 eggs in 36 nests in 1955 revealed that 36 percent failed to hatch for one reason or another. Thus, in the limited number of cases studied, hatching varied from 51 to 66 percent. In Denmark the hatching rate of the eggs of wild mute swans was about 60 percent as reported by Paludan and Fog (1956: 44). In studies of the trumpeter on the Kenai Peninsula, Alaska, Spencer (correspondence) reports about a 65-percent hatching success in a limited number of clutches.

For various reasons, the roles played by infertility and mortality of the embryo in the trumpeter egg are not known. Often the embryo has died after it was well developed. In such cases, incubation may have begun before egg laying was completed, or the eggs failed to hatch together for other reasons. The trumpeter pen then apparently departed with the cygnets which hatched first. Other causes of egg failure are even more obscure. These undoubtedly include cases of infertility or physical handicap, fatal chilling of the embryo after incubation has commenced, or abandonment of the nest before incubation has been completed. Loss of productivity due to egg failure is a major factor in the present low production of cygnets on the Refuge.

Predation is not important to hatching success on the Refuge. In the data presented, for a total of 61 nests observed in 1949, 1951, and 1955, not a single case of predator-caused egg loss was observed. Only 4 nests containing predator-destroyed eggs have been found in the 7 seasons during which swan nests have been examined. Furthermore, eggs which failed to hatch remained exposed but unmolested in the nest long after incubation had been terminated.

In Yellowstone Park, however, a number of random studies and observations made through the years show that egg destruction by predators apparently occurs to a significant degree. Joseph Dixon (1931: 454) writes:

The pair of swans which Mr. Wright and Mr. Thompson watched at Tern Lake on June 11, 1930, were not successful in driving off the marauding ravens, for when the mother left to feed, a raven appeared and was observed to fly directly to the nest. . . . Mr. Wright recorded in his notebook what took place, as follows, "At first the raven just poked about in the nest with its beak. . . . It stuck its head down once more and pulled from an egg in the nest a long pink and whitish object, apparently an embryo from one of the swan eggs, and started to fly away with it just as the parent swans rushed back and drove it away from the nest."

Condon (MS) records an incident of nest destruction by a bear, and George M. Wright and Ben H. Thompson (1935: 34, 35) furnish another account:

A black object loomed by the swan nest. With field glasses glued to our eyes, we saw that it was an otter stretching its full length upward to peer down into the nest. From one side it reached out toward the center and pushed aside the material covering the eggs. Then the commotion started. With rapt interest, the otter rooted around in the dry nest material, heaving up here and digging in there, until it was more haystack than nest. Then the otter started to roll, around and around, over and over. This went on for a number of minutes. At frequent intervals its long neck was craned upward, and the serpentlike head rotated around to discover (we supposed) if the swans were returning. At last the otter seemed to weary of this play. It climbed from the nest to the outer edge, then slid off into the water. . . . It never turned back, and was finally lost to sight. . . . Seeing that the damage was already done, and another year's potential swan crop for the Mirror Plateau lost irrevocably, we saw no further reason for caution. So we stripped off our clothes and waded out across the shallows. We were amazed to find all five eggs intact. There they were, all together, rolled to one side, but perfectly whole. . . . We covered the eggs and hurried away in confusion as huge hailstones pelted our bodies. We hoped that the parents would return to protect the eggs from chill. The storm obscured the scene, obliterating the next chapter in the story. Later we learned from ranger reports that no cygnets were raised on Tern Lake that year. Which meddler should shoulder the blame, the otter or the scientist?

Even in Yellowstone Park, the low hatch is due principally to causes other than predation. Observers agreed that human intrusion was the most significant known cause of egg failure in the Park.

PREFLIGHT CYGNET MORTALITY

Although the relative paucity of predation records on swans of flying age indicates that predation is of little consequence in determining overall swan population levels, it may be an important cause of death to preflight cygnets. Swan broods suffer serious losses in both the Red Rock Lakes and Yellowstone Park breeding populations. While casualties of preflight youngsters may approach or possibly exceed 50 percent during some years, very little is known regarding causes of such mortality.

The information in table 6 is believed representative of the overall cygnet mortality on the Refuge during 1949. Since some of these observations were accomplished at distances over 2 miles with a 20× spotting scope, counts may not be absolutely accurate for any given count and brood. A high degree of accuracy was achieved by frequent observations over a period of 3 months, and as the cygnets became larger and moved in a less compact brood, tabulation was easier and more accurately made. The habit of swan families to remain in the nesting territory until the approach of flight age, plus the characteristic of each family to remain apart from other similar groups, makes the accurate tally of cygnet mortality by individual brood possible.

In the broods under consideration, mortality was widespread and significant, with losses heavier among the newly hatched cygnets than among those approaching flying age. The causes of these losses are undoubtedly varied but unknown. Perhaps because the remains of a small cygnet resulting from a kill are few and inconspicuous and may be entirely consumed by predator or scavenger, few records are available regarding specific predation on young cygnets in Red Rock's marshes.

In 1949, I saw a large gull kill one cygnet and wound another after the young were separated from the parents. The old swans were distracted by my presence in the boat, and failed to defend their young. Normally, the young cygnets remain very close to their parents, and without my presence, the attack would not have been made, or the parent swans would probably have repelled it.

In Yellowstone Park the opportunities for discovering the remains of dead cygnets are greater than in the large marshes of the Red Rock Lakes. Condon (MS) furnishes a specific account:

> Those cygnets on Swan Lake, however, are thought to have been killed by a large male otter, whose presence there was discovered on July 10, 1939, when a thorough survey of this lake area was made in an endeavor to locate the lost cygnets, and the cause for their disappearance. One cygnet was found dead and floating in the lake near the northwest bank within ten yards of the swan nesting site. This cygnet, upon examination, revealed a crushed sternum, ribs, and two tooth punctures. . . . The otter den was located on the east bank of the lake and at several sites around the lake otter droppings were collected that contained down, bones, leg and foot skin. These fragments were examined in the laboratory and compared with the down and leg skin from the cygnet found. The comparison revealed that these undoubtedly came from a swan cygnet, and it is felt that in this instance the otter was responsible for the loss of part, if not all of the family of five cygnets from Swan Lake.

Although otters have only rarely been reported from the Red Rock Lakes Refuge, minks have at times been suspected of cygnet predation. Sharp relates in a Refuge report:

> A family of mink worked at the Idlewild boat pier during late July. I counted 36 coots and 31 ducks and 1 young muskrat that were dragged upon the pier along the edges of tall overhanging sedges. A family of three cygnets that used this area disappeared during this time.

Table 6.—Cygnet mortality at Red Rock Lakes Refuge, 1949

Nest	Eggs hatched	Number of cygnets observed per brood									
		June		July				August			
		21	30	6	14	21	28	6	15	19	30
No. 1	3	3	3	2	2	2	2	0	2	2	2
No. 2	3	0	3	3	3	3	3	3	3	3	3
No. 3	5	3	5	0	3	3	3	3	3	3	2
No. 4	3	2	2	3	3	3	3	3	0	3	3
No. 5	4	4	4	4	4	4	2	1	1	1	1
No. 6	4	1	1	0	0	0	1	1	1	1	1
No. 7	4	0	4	4	4	4	4	3	2	2	2
No. 8	1	0	0	0	0	0	0	0	0	0	0
No. 9	3	0	2	2	0	2	2	2	3	0	3
No. 10	1	0	0	0	0	0	0	0	0	0	0
Total	31										17
Cygnet loss since previous check		5	0	1	2	2	1	1	1	0	1
Broods affected		3	0	1	1	1	1	1	1	0	1

With the exception of minks and skunks, no mammalian predators of any consequence are to be found in the dense, sedge-covered, soft bog-marshes of the Red Rock Lakes. Though dead cygnets are occasionally discovered on the water areas, they are invariably intact, with no evidence of predation. The densely vegetated shores preclude a systematic search.

Although gulls, falcons, eagles, and ravens are occasionally sighted over the marsh during the summer, they have never been seen molesting the swans, either young or old. Presumably, the usual close swimming and feeding formation of the swan family presents little opportunity to the predator, with the size and potential defense capabilities of the adults an obvious deterrent. Although great horned owls have been mentioned as possible predators, no record exists.

MORTALITY OF IMMATURES AND ADULTS

Except for man, trumpeters in the wild appear to have few important natural enemies after flying age is reached. Both golden eagles and coyotes may take swans of any age class under certain local conditions which present favorable opportunities. Even in such cases it is doubtful whether the trumpeter is a normal prey of either eagles or coyotes with any degree of regularity. Some of the captive trumpeters at Malheur and Ruby Lake Refuges have been lost to bobcats on several occasions. The following instances outline the circumstances under which losses have occurred among unconfined trumpeters.

The natural enemies and causes of mortality, especially parasites and diseases, of other swans are discussed in detail in Hilprecht (1956:101–107).

Avian predation: Probably the only winged predator capable and willing to tackle a full-grown swan in flight is the eagle. Apparently even these great raptors will attempt this only occasionally.

On several occasions, eagles have been observed to knock trumpeters out of the air and kill them. Sharp (1951 : 225) witnessed the following cases of eagle predation on cygnets of flight age concentrated on their Red Rock Lakes winter feeding waters, writing:

On one occasion in late November of 1944 the writer observed one of the eagles [golden] make three stoops over a flock of swans on a snow covered meadow. The swans stood motionless and apparently had no fear. This eagle was apparently sporting over the swans as no kills had been made up to this time. . . . A cygnet was killed at Culver Pond on December 26, 1944, and another was struck in the air and killed on January 1, 1945. . . . A total of three cygnets was killed during this winter.

A local rancher in that area, James F. Hanson, reports occasional harassment of the trumpeters by eagles, but only rarely a killing.

Henry W. Baker, Jr., Superintendent of the Federal fish hatchery near Ennis, Montana, provides an eyewitness account of eagles killing a swan in the Madison Valley (correspondence) :

When first observed, the encounter was approximately 1,000 feet elevation. The two eagles worked together, first one would hit the swan and then the other until they brought it to the ground, at which time they both attacked it . . . killing it in the matter of a couple minutes. I was approximately 600 to 700 yards distant at the time.

Ralph Edwards (Holman, 1933 : 169–211), the early settler of Lonesome Lake, British Columbia, relates, "I have noticed during the hard winters that the grey ones fall prey to the eagles and starvation before the white ones. This winter I have seen two cases of eagles killing swan. The eagles do not seem to be able to catch the swan when they are stronger or on a straightaway flight."

Though eagles can and apparently do kill adult swans on occasion, the effect on overall trumpeter numbers is believed insignificant. To my knowledge, no other winged predator has ever been observed to prey upon adult swans.

Mammalian predation: Swans may occasionally be molested by coyotes, but direct evidence that they have actually killed swans still is lacking. Even in Yellowstone Park, where coyote populations exist at natural levels, reports of actual kills are nonexistent. Condon (1950 : 1, 2) reports some ineffective coyote molestation:

During the fall of 1947 after Swan Lake had frozen over it was common to see a lone pair of trumpeter swans resting on the ice. . . . The tracks in the snow showed that their siesta was interrupted by a coyote which . . . apparently was either persistent, hungry, or just playing a game, for it had each time approached cautiously to some point where it was screened by a cinque-foil bush or clump of grass at the ice's edge and then had made a dash toward the resting swan. Each time failure was its lot.

Dr. Adolph Murie (1940: 135), after a thorough study of coyote prey relations in Yellowstone Park, wrote:

At some of the lakes where swans have been raised, coyotes are concentrated. At Trumpeter Lake, where seven cygnets were raised in 1936 and again in 1937, coyotes and coyote signs were frequently noted at the lake. . . . The only evidence of waterfowl predation consisted of some remnants of a green-winged teal found on the bank and in one dropping.

Dr. Murie concluded his field study and a review of available information on the subject within the Park by writing, "It 'was rather unexpected to find that the coyote in Yellowstone exerts no appreciable pressure on the trumpeter swan population. . . . The data available at the present time indicates that the coyote does not represent an important mortality factor for the trumpeter swan."

At the Red Rock Lakes Refuge, too, no definite coyote kills of swans have been recorded, though Hull (1939: 381) states, "During the winter coyotes have been known to capture adult swans in deep loose snow before the birds were able to get into the air or open water." Sharp also reported, "Ranchers hauling hay off the refuge near Upper Red Rock Lake reported seeing coyotes on two occasions flush swans off the ice or snow. In both cases, the swans were too alert and agile in the take-off to allow the coyote to come close to a catch."

From the foregoing evidence it is concluded that the coyote is not an important predator of trumpeters, either in Yellowstone Park or on the Red Rock Lakes Refuge.

Condon (MS) also relates a case where circumstantial evidence pointed to a bear as the suspected killer of an adult swan in Yellowstone Park, writing:

a dead male was found floating near the northwest shore of Fern Lake. . . . A thorough examination of this bird revealed a transverse cut straight across the breast region 6 inches long and 1¼ inches deep. . . . After inspecting the area around Fern Lake where this swan was found, I concluded that a bear was, in all probability, responsible for its death. There were abundant fresh signs of bear around the lake and the extensive damage done the swan seemed greater than that which any other animal might inflict.

From the foregoing testimony it would seem that 4-footed predators are even less effective than their avian counterparts in preying upon swans of flight age.

Hunting. From the earliest times on this continent swans have been taken by the native peoples by whatever method was available, snare, arrow, or gun. Though the primitive peoples presumably killed principally for food, the white man also killed the swan in great numbers over wide regions of its range not only for domestic needs but also because of the ready commercial market established for its down and quills. Man is, by far, the greatest enemy with which they have had to contend.

Although the enactment of the Migratory Bird Treaty Act by the United States Congress in 1918 made it illegal to kill either species of our native swans, shooting and lead-poisoning still account for more casualties, in the case of the trumpeter at least, than the aggregate of all other known causes of adult mortality.

During the last 20 years, illegal kills of trumpeter swans have occurred chiefly during the open waterfowl season in Idaho along Henrys Fork of the Snake River and its tributaries, and to a lesser extent in Montana and Wyoming. Since trumpeters commonly fly along the water courses at a low level, they furnish a conspicuous target well within range of waterfowl hunters, many of which cannot resist the temptation to shoot. The kill is believed to have increased in the past decade with the appearance of greater numbers of nimrods afield.

Fifteen years ago, Condon recognized this danger to the swan population in the Yellowstone region, stating (MS) :

That there is a definite mortality among the swan due to shooting by hunters during the open season on waterfowl is evidenced not only by the above incident [that of finding a swan containing shot in the Park] but by the arrest and conviction of hunters in Idaho and Montana for killing trumpeter swan. Many instances of this type have come to light and undoubtedly many are shot that no one knows about. . . . Adults known to have lost their lives at the hand of man far exceed the records that we have of death due to natural causes.

In an effort to determine the gunning pressure to which the trumpeters are subjected while on their comparatively unprotected winter ranges, the U. S. Fish and Wildlife Service arranged with the Illinois Natural History Survey to make a fluoroscopic examination of a number of swans during their flightless molt on the Red Rock Lakes Refuge. Frank Bellrose of that survey supervised this investigation in the summer of 1956, using a portable fluoroscope borrowed from the Delta Waterfowl Research Station, Delta, Manitoba.

During the period July 20–28, 100 trumpeters from the Refuge's nonbreeding population were examined fluoroscopically by Bellrose to determine the presence of lead shot. In addition to this sample, I subsequently examined 3 birds in August.

Of the 103 trumpeters thus inspected, a total of 15 (14.6 percent) were found to be carrying lead shot. Numbers of shot present in any individual bird varied from 1 to 9 and included shot sizes ranging from 7½'s to BB's with 2's and 4's most common. Of 4 swans banded in 1951 or earlier, 2 were carrying lead. Owing to the large size of these birds and the difficulty of locating the shot on the dimly illuminated fluoroscopic screen, some may have been missed. Thus, it is probable that the actual percentage of swans carrying lead shot was somewhat greater.

The actual number of trumpeters killed each year in their United States range is unknown, but it probably exceeds 25. The number of known swan casualties was 17 in 1933 (Beard et al., 1947: 140) and 19 in 1939 (Condon, MS). The average number of swans known to have been lost to hunting during later years continues to be serious. The known loss was reported to be 23 in 1951, 17 in 1952, and only 9 in 1953. In 1955, Eddie Linck, the Idaho State Fish and Game Officer covering the Island Park area, estimated a total of 25 trumpeters illegally killed in that area alone, with 12 casualties known for certain. According to Walton Hester, conservation officer for the Island Park district in 1956, a known loss of 15 hunter-killed swans occurred with at least another 5 estimated as being taken. Mr. Hester also expressed the thought that some of the cygnets may be selectively shot for food, since the adults are noted for their general unsavoriness. Evidence supporting this view is lacking.

The concern of those interested in the welfare of the trumpeter resulted in the appointment of a new U. S. Fish and Wildlife Service enforcement agent in eastern Idaho in 1956, principally to cope with this illegal killing of trumpeters while on their main wintering grounds in the Island Park area. Increased local publicity in the past few years via radio, TV, newspapers and posters has focused attention on the problem. It is hoped that the increased attention will serve to stop the indiscriminate killing of these birds.

Lead poisoning. This factor is irrevocably related to hunting and causes mortality among swans that feed, even for short or intermittent periods, in habitat shot over in previous years. Hull recovered 4 trumpeters which died on their Refuge feeding grounds at Culver Pond during late March and early April, 1937. Material from these birds was sent to the Denver Research Laboratory where E. R. Kalmbach diagnosed the fatalities of 3 as due to lead poisoning. The gizzard pads of all 3 exhibited the characteristic greenish coloration and hardening, with the contents containing 3, 11, and 17 pellets respectively (0.248, 0.498, and 0.857 grams of lead). In the fourth case, Hull made a similar diagnosis, with 19 pellets in the gizzard of the dead bird he examined. No other trumpeter cases have been reported in the United States. No hunting has been permitted on the wintering waters of the Refuge since it was established in 1935; hence, the possibility of further losses is lessened.

In British Columbia, the problem of lead poisoning among wintering flocks of trumpeters has presented a recurring threat. J. A. Munro (1949) documented the loss of at least 9 trumpeters of the

Vaseaux Lake wintering population in 1925. These birds were forced out of their regular winter quarters by ice and used other open waters which were heavily contaminated with lead shot. The stomach contents of 1 of these victims contained 451 shot. More of this group were believed to be subsequent victims of ingesting lead shot on this occasion, as only 6 of the original group of 17 returned to Vaseaux Lake the following winter and the flock later disappeared completely. Munro also records the loss of at least 13 trumpeters from a flock of 15 wintering on Vancouver Island in 1946. The stomach tracts of these victims held from 2 to 29 pellets each.

On Idaho's lower Coeur d'Alene River, a form of metallic poisoning diagnostically similar to lead poisoning has resulted in irregular but substantial mortality in the waterfowl over the years. Whistling swans, stopping in migration, have occasionally suffered heavy losses in this area, but as contamination is local these losses have never involved trumpeters.

Weather and mortality. Unseasonally cold weather undoubtedly affects hatching success and survival of trumpeter cygnets. These effects are not completely known, but some influences have been observed and are cited here.

Cygnet Development vs. Weather. Uneven development rates of cygnets are not uncommon and, when combined with late hatching, result in some loss when the ice forms earlier than usual. The average hatching date on the Red Rock Lakes Refuge is about June 20. Over 100 days is normally required for a cygnet's development to flight age, and the Refuge has become icebound as early as October 28 (twice) with November 8 the 16-year average (1938–1953).

Final freezeup is invariably preceded by a period when ice is prevalent over the marsh and lakes, so development may be retarded in the critical preflight stage of the growing cygnet through food shortage and injury to the wing from hitting the ice during flight attempts. Although it is possible occasionally to rescue such birds, as well as unharmed individuals which have simply not matured sufficiently to fly, it can hardly become a regular practice, since travel conditions on the new ice over the vast river and marsh area are often treacherous by foot and impossible by boat.

In 1949 at least 20 cygnets on the Refuge were still incapable of flight by October 15. Fortunately, the final freezeup did not occur until November 18 that year. This additional time may have allowed all of these particular cygnets to develop sufficiently to fly.

Condon raises a point about some other hazards, found in Yellowstone Park:

One factor that may contribute to cygnet mortality after they reach flying age is that many of the lakes on which the swans establish themselves are small and may not offer sufficient space for them to learn to fly well, and when the families leave these lakes they must fly for some distance over land before reaching water upon which to alight and on such occasions cygnets may become fatigued, fall to earth and may not again get into the air. It is felt that such was the fate of one of the cygnets from Geode Lake in early October 1939 and that such mishaps may occur more often than we think where lakes are small and separated by rough canyons and timbered areas such as exist on the north side of Yellowstone Park.

MORTALITY OF GROWN BIRDS. The formation of ice over normally open wintering waters, as a result of very low temperatures, may prevent adult swans from feeding in these traditional locations. When this ice remains for a prolonged period, starvation may result rather than movement out of the region to where food may be available. Such instances seem to be rare within the United States however, judging from the lack of evidence or reports. Dr. Olaus J. Murie documents such an occurrence (correspondence) :

A number of years ago (March 22, 1932) I found two dead swans north of Moran in Jackson Hole, where they had been wintering in a small piece of open water on a stream (Second Creek) near Jackson Lake. They had evidently starved to death since they had eaten all the available food in that little piece of water. . . . The male weighed 18 lbs. 4 oz. The female 16 lbs. 12 oz.

As a general rule in the major Island Park–Red Rock Lakes– Yellowstone wintering habitat, at least some open water and food are available to swans wintering in these warm spring-fed water areas. This is true even during prolonged periods of winter weather where nightly minimums drop below −20°F. Though food supplies are undoubtedly short until moderating weather arrives, they never fail entirely, and I know of no other cases of trumpeter starvation in this country.

In British Columbia, starvation has caused greater losses of wintering trumpeters. Munro (1949 : 713) records:

The number of trumpeter swans dying from starvation in winters of more than average severity probably is a significant factor in population reduction. Many swans winter in sub-marginal territory where food is not abundant at the best of times and may become completely inaccessible at times of sub-zero weather, or at periods of high floods. In such times the swans stay on, in what probably is their ancestral wintering ground, to starve or to become, in their weakened state, victims of predators, rather than seek feeding grounds elsewhere. The situation is being met to some extent by artificial feeding, as has been noted, but winter populations in remote and inaccessible territory cannot be helped in this way.

Swan mortality resulting from the icing up of swans' plumage by severe winter weather has also been reported from Canada, though never to my knowledge from the United States. The notes of O. J. Murie record this instance related to him by Dave Hoy, a river freighter familiar with wintering trumpeters:

Fort St. James, B. C., June 13, 1934, Mr. Hoy says that a number of years ago the trumpeter swans numbered 250 or more but they winter killed. He says the water does not freeze over for long but the short period of freezing may be fatal. About three years ago a number got frozen into the ice. They were found in that condition on a number of occasions, eaten by coyotes. Slush ice would gather on their wings so they could not fly.

The icing of swans' plumage has never been reported from the Island Park area where slush ice is seasonally common on the streams frequented by wintering trumpeters. The water-shedding capacity of a swan's plumage is definitely related to the overall health of the individual, so it is difficult to see how the plumage of a healthy adult swan could collect ice, or how such an individual would allow itself to become frozen into the ice no matter how severe the weather might become. Low food supplies may play the determining role in such cases.

Disease. Trumpeter swans within the United States exhibit the alertness and vigor associated with most wildlife populations. Dead, sick, or weak birds are rarely observed without reason for their condition being obvious, and disease does not appear to contribute significantly to mortality in the wild.

While disease has apparently never been reported in adult wild trumpeters, small cygnets occasionally possess deformities of their feet. Sharp stated in a Service report:

Three nests did not hatch and a fourth failed due to feet deformities of the cygnets. The latter nest, when checked on the Upper Lake, had three dead cygnets and another alive on the nest. Careful study revealed that the living cygnet could not stand. An examination of its feet showed that they were pitifully deformed. Then the dead cygnets were examined, and their feet were deformed in a similar manner.

A cygnet which I rescued from a gull's attacks possessed a deformed foot as described by Sharp. On the other hand, the broodmate of this cygnet, which was killed by the gull, had normal-appearing feet. This abnormal condition may be a cause of some mortality in preflight age classes, since it has not been noted with the older trumpeters.

The incidence of several diseases has been reported from trumpeters in captivity. Confinement often increases the opportunities for sickness and infection, and facilitates the observations of afflicted birds. One of the adult trumpeters at the Delta Station died during the winter of 1955–56 after displaying signs of weakness and sickness, one of which was trouble in keeping its plumage dry and free of ice. A thorough postmortem examination was not possible at that time, though symptoms of both aspergillosis and fowl cholera were apparently present.

Dr. E. M. Dickinson of the Veterinary Department of Oregon State College found and cultured bacilli typical of avian tuberculosis from a captive trumpeter at Malheur Refuge which exhibited the lesions of this disease, dying there apparently of this cause. Several other losses in the Malheur trumpeter flock had these symptoms, although no successful testing for this disease was developed. Three casualties listed for the Ruby Lakes trumpeter flock were attributed to avian tuberculosis. The greatest incidence of loss in these cases seemed to occur in the younger age groups, especially those less than a year old, with a reduced rate of loss as the birds grew older. A more recent trumpeter loss at Malheur in 1956 was diagnosed by Dr. Dickinson as having aspergillosis.

Of the captivity record of the trumpeters which have been kept at the New York Zoological Park, William G. Conway (correspondence) advised, "Four specimens are said to have died of aspergillosis; . . . two, probably, from botulism." Since the natural conditions necessary for botulism contamination do not normally occur in the Red Rock Lakes–Yellowstone region, this sickness has never been reported in the native trumpeter flock, but in late October 1957 two cygnets in Malheur's captive flock apparently died from botulism. In one case the diagnosis was fairly certain, while in the other the evidence was only circumstantial (David Marshall, correspondence).

Dr. T. T. Chaddock (1938: 25) examined 8 wild whistling swans postmortem, from April-June carcass recoveries in Wisconsin, reporting the presence of aspergillosis (in 4), pneumonia (in most), silicosis (in 2), "dropsy" (in 2), besides parasites (in 5) plus other pathological factors.

Parasites. Trumpeter swans, in common with other wild species, are frequent hosts to various parasites. Judging from the occurrence of parasites in other fauna, the level of any given parasite population is usually determined more by the general health of the host than by any other single circumstance. Healthy birds normally support low numbers of parasites, while sick or weak birds frequently exhibit heavy infestations. In the latter instances, while parasites may combine with other factors to hasten death, they are usually considered only a contributing cause of mortality. Thus, there seems sufficient justification to document several cases in which parasites were either believed to have caused mortality or were present in such numbers that they probably contributed substantially to the reported sickness or death.

Dr. Ian McT. Cowan (1946: 248, 249) stated that the death of a wintering British Columbia trumpeter found in a weakened condition near Vanderhoof, B. C., was due to gross multiple parasitism. He relates, "Both the cestode *Hymenolepis* and the filarial nematode *Eurycerca* were present in numbers apparently sufficient to induce pathological changes in the host, and it is not possible to determine in this case which of the two was most harmful."

LIFE CYCLE

In another instance Cowan found the white swan louse *Ornithobius cygni* abundant in the plumage, and 3 specimens of *Eurycerca* in the heart muscle of a trumpeter which apparently died of lead poisoning, as 30 pellets of lead shot were found in the gizzard of this swan.

Parasites were noted in 5 of the 8 whistling swan carcasses examined in Wisconsin by Chaddock (1938: 25–27). Five cases exhibited pediculosis (lice infestation) around the fluff of the vent, the presence of gizzard worm (*Spirotera hamulosa*) was demonstrated, and the eggs of common poultry roundworm (*Ascaridia liniata*) were found when a fecal examination of the 5 internally parasitized individuals was made.

Leeches are common to abundant during the summer months in most of the waters inhabited by the trumpeters in their United States range. As one might expect with waterfowl accustomed to seeking their food in the soft mud and vegetation of such areas, leeches frequently become attached to their bodies. While these blood suckers apparently possess little more than nuisance value on the larger swans, they may be a contributing cause of mortality with small cygnets. Sharp reports that on one occasion:

Cygnets taken from the north side of the Lower Lake revealed that their under parts had from a dozen to fifty small leeches crawling over their wet feathers. Swanlets on two occasions taken from this area when placed in the boat within a few minutes shook their heads violently and finally threw out a leech; the latter were gorged with blood. These leeches were from one-half to three-quarters of an inch in length, and when crushed were filled with blood, as much as could be held without apparently bursting. One cygnet on the Upper Lake also disgorged a large leech.

One of 3 cygnets transferred from the Red Rock Lakes Refuge to the Delta Research Station in 1955 died after only 3 days. The post-mortem examination was conducted by the Ontario Veterinary College at Guelph, Ontario, and revealed that the cygnet had died from an infestation of thornyheaded worms (*Polymorphus baschadis*). These worms require crustaceans as an intermediate host and are fairly pathogenic, causing anemia and cachenia (Peter Ward, correspondence). The cygnet probably was infested at Red Rock Lakes, and this may be a cause of some mortality there.

Trematodes are occasionally observed in the cloaca of Red Rock Lakes trumpeters when they are being examined to determine the sex. Two of these parasites were identified as *Echinostoma revolutum*. Feather lice (*Mallophaga*) are also commonly observed. Determinations of the specific identity of these parasites was made through the office of Dr. William Jellison, Parasitologist, National Microbiological Institute, at Hamilton, Montana.

In 1950 and 1951 blood smears from various Refuge trumpeters were prepared and forwarded to Dr. Carlton M. Herman, Wildlife

Pathologist, Patuxent Research Refuge, for a routine examination for leucocytozon, but no positive report was received.

Hilprecht (1956: 103–104) reports that swans in Europe become infested with parasites, the tape worm *Hymenolepis aequabilis* and the leech *Protoclepsis granata*. The latter becomes especially abundant during summers of low water levels when it is thought to contribute to mortality on a large scale.

Accidents. As one might expect from such large, specialized fowl, trumpeters appear to be "accident prone" under certain circumstances. In confinement at the Malheur Refuge, death of several swans resulted from drowning when their heads and necks became caught in an underwater section of fence while trying to obtain grain beyond easy reach. In the New York Zoological Park a trumpeter was reported to have died of injuries sustained when it was caught in a gate.

In the wild state, the known accidents seem to be confined largely to striking power, telephone, or fence wires in flight. At least 3 cases of known trumpeter fatalities have been reported for the Island Park area from such causes, as winter fog is common along open watercourses. Besides these, 2 other similar cases, 1 on the Refuge and 1 in southeastern Montana, have occurred. In 4 of the 5 known cases the accident was fatal.

LONGEVITY

From earliest times swans were known to be very long lived. The ancient naturalists of Greece bore testimony to this (Evans 1903: 121) as well as early English ornithologists who presumably were writing of the mute swan in captivity (Swann 1913: 164). Some age data of other species of captive and wild swans are furnished by Hilprecht (1956: 100–101).

The Refuge swan banding project is comparatively recent and may eventually contribute valuable data on the longevity of wild trumpeters. Despite the considerable success of F. E. Blaauw and others in breeding the trumpeter over a long period in Europe, specific records of longevity appear to be lacking. The Philadelphia Zoological Garden had eight trumpeters on display from 1895–1939, one of which lived for 29 years. F. H. Kortwright (1943: 80) noted that a trumpeter lived for 32½ years, presumably in Canada. This seems to be the present record for this species in captivity.

POPULATION

Little information was uncovered regarding the status of the swan population which existed in the Rocky Mountains of Montana, Wyoming, and Idaho, before the specific swan surveys were initiated by the National Park Service in 1929. The few breeding pairs and immatures which then inhabited this vast region were even more thinly dispersed over their widely scattered mountain lake environment than they are today. (See "Distribution and Status" for a few clues to precensus status of swans in Yellowstone Park and Red Rock Lakes Refuge.) The important general conclusion to be drawn from the scattered data available seems to be that this species was not abundant in this region since the turn of the century, and by the 1920's must have nearly disappeared from its last breeding grounds in this country.

ANNUAL SWAN CENSUS, 1929–57

The life history studies in the Park and Refuge have progressed only sporadically in the three decades since the National Park Service's trumpeter swan survey began in the fall of 1929. Fortunately, the annual census which was initiated in 1931 has been effectively conducted during most of this period. When properly qualified, this accumulation of data offers a remarkably complete 27-year record of population levels. The large size, prominent white color, sedentary habits, and use of only a comparatively few water and open-marsh habitats combine to make these birds an ideal species to locate and census accurately. Too, with few exceptions, census methods and coverage were generally expanded in time to keep abreast of the growing swan population. For these reasons I believe the census data which follow are exceptionally reliable and representative.

144

Although it is assumed that little or no interchange has occurred between the trumpeters living in this tristate region with other populations in Canada and Alaska, this possibility has never been thoroughly explored. But in view of the attraction the waterfowl show for their natal marshes generally, and the absence of banding data to suggest the possibility of populations mixing, it is concluded that the factor of interchange has been insignificant thus far.

The results of the 27 years of swan-census effort, first solely by the National Park Service and then with the cooperation of the Fish and Wildlife Service, are presented in detail in table 7 and in appendix 5. The distribution of the swans during their 1954 peak year census, and the pertinent references, are given in appendix 2.

Not all of the census data in table 7 will be found to agree exactly with figures released for news publication by the Fish and Wildlife Service over the years. A few discrepancies were subsequently discovered in the field and corrected but were not released as a news followup owing to the small difference in numbers involved. In each case, the data in table 7 are the most comprehensive and representative which could be found.

POPULATION DYNAMICS

The rise in trumpeter numbers in the United States which began a quarter century ago is closely correlated with the establishment of the Red Rock Lakes Refuge and the increased protection and attention which then became possible. The relatively few departures of the annual census numbers from uniform rates of change can be explained by incomplete censuses, departures of sizable segments of the population, and actual variations in productivity.[1] Information obtained from the annual trumpeter censuses is presented in tables 7 to 12 and shown graphically in figures 44 to 50.

As related earlier, ground counts conducted from 1931 through 1945 were made under great handicaps of personnel and equipment compared with the coordinated aerial censuses which were developed later. Since a complete coverage of areas occupied by trumpeters was not accomplished during the earliest years, 1931–35, it is likely that the actual populations were somewhat larger than were located, but the numbers recorded then are believed to be highly representative.

Since 1936, when more complete ground coverages of the trumpeter-occupied areas were begun, only two complete censuses, in 1950 and 1957, produced results which did not compare well with counts made during the preceding and following years. The low count of im-

---

[1] For purposes of this discussion, "productivity" is measured by the number of cygnets censused annually.

Table 7.—Swan census data, 1931 to 1957

Year	Red Rock Lakes Refuge			Yellowstone Park			All other areas			Total, all areas		
	Adults	Cygnets	Total	Adults	Cygnets	Total	Adults	Cygnets	Total	Adults	Cygnets	Total
1931	(1)	(1)	(1)	18	12	30	2	3	5	20	15	35
1932	19	7	26	29	2	31	9	3	12	57	12	69
1933	15	9	24	27	8	35	7	0	7	49	17	66
1934	16	26	42	16	17	33	16	6	22	48	49	97
1935	30	16	46	16	11	27	(1)	(1)	(1)	46	27	73
1936	31	26	57	38	13	51	7	2	9	76	41	117
1937	34	51	85	38	26	64	9	0	9	81	77	158
1938	28	42	70	40	4	44	25	9	34	93	55	148
1939	50	59	109	47	17	64	26	0	26	123	76	199
1940	58	48	106	39	14	2 53	26	6	32	123	68	191
1941	52	44	96	44	15	59	47	10	57	143	69	212
1942	45	43	88	(1)	(1)	(1)	53	10	63	98	53	151
1943	88	25	113	(1)	(1)	(1)	49	9	58	137	34	171
1944	106	58	164	41	8	49	60	6	66	207	72	279
1945	113	50	163	(1)	(1)	(1)	67	5	72	180	55	235
1946	124	46	170	43	8	51	122	18	140	289	72	361
1947	131	49	180	45	8	53	116	3	119	292	60	352
1948	121	73	194	49	13	62	142	20	162	312	106	418
1949	132	61	193	54	21	75	162	21	183	348	103	451
1950	106	40	146	57	16	73	140	17	157	303	73	376
1951	170	76	246	63	11	74	184	31	215	417	118	535
1952	184	55	239	58	10	68	236	28	264	478	93	571
1953	211	38	249	51	10	61	216	51	267	478	99	577
1954	352	28	380	64	23	87	144	31	175	560	82	642
1955	242	41	283	58	10	68	195	44	239	495	95	590
1956	293	39	332	48	9	57	166	33	199	507	81	588
1957	159	45	204	44	16	60	196	28	224	399	89	488

[1] No census.
[2] Incomplete census.

matures and adults in 1950 was followed by an increase in these combined age-classes in 1951 which was much greater than could be accounted for by cygnet production. It remains to be seen whether the same lack of agreement will occur between the 1957 census and that of 1958.[2] These census disparities apparently resulted from the movement of a substantial segment of the population out of the region censused (about 120 in 1950 and 100 in 1957).

The annual aerial census covers all possible trumpeter habitat in portions of three States, but not the many remote areas outside this region to which they conceivably might fly. Specific knowledge of any such outward migration is lacking at this time. Furthermore, no clue to their time of departure, return, or destination is now at hand. Their absence most likely began as a northward movement with the spring migration. After summering at a new location, rejoining the resident flocks on the traditional wintering grounds during the fall migration would be expected. But this is merely speculation.

Since banded trumpeters from northern flocks have never been found among the many handled in the United States during the summer molt, and United States-banded swans have not been recovered outside their expected range in this country, I assume that the

[2] A total of 703 trumpeters, 565 immatures and adults and 138 cygnets, was tallied in 1958.

Table 8.—Nonbreeding trumpeter swan populations at Upper Red Rock Lake, Lima Reservoir, and other important areas, 1939 to 1957

[Nonpaired (flocked) immatures and adults (cygnets excepted)]

Year	Upper Red Rock Lake	Lima Reservoir [1]	Island Park Reservoir, Sheridan Reservoir, and other waters	Malheur and Ruby Lake Refuges	Total
1939	11	—— [2]	20		31
1940	19	0	3		22
1941	18	10	17	3	49
1942	12	9	22		43
1943	42	10	12		64
1944	52	16	11		79
1945	66	15	8	18	107
1946	62	27	35	34	159
1947	51	26	32	27	136
1948	49	37	54	24	164
1949	50	74	26	27	177
1950	63	69	11	24	167
1951	99	83	39	17	239
1952	120	136	43	10	310
1953	135	112	10	8	266
1954	248	7	32	7	294
1955	150	11	87	1	249
1956	162	7	37	26	233
1957	77	35	39	40	181

[1] Lima Reservoir was dry during 1954–1956 inclusive. Most of the resident summer population on these waters apparently moved to Upper Red Rock Lake during this period as the latter area shows an abnormally large population during the summers of 1954–1956.
[2] No count was made in 1939.

missing birds moved out of the region before the annual census and then returned in time to be included in the following year's count.

Having mentioned the major departures from the otherwise fairly uniform population curves for the period 1931–57, let us look at the overall trend in the numbers of this species during this period. The main references for this discussion are tables 7 and 9. Disregarding the years 1935, 1942, 1943, and 1945 when complete counts were not secured in the Park, the two categories for which comparable information is available in table 7 are (1) total swan numbers and (2) cygnets. The data in table 9 are graphed in figure 44 to show the rates of change for certain segments of the population.

In figure 44, the total population curve shows a steady and rapid climb (about 10 percent annually) until 1954, when 642 swans were counted. This peak was followed by two slightly lower counts, in 1955 and 1956. The sharp decline in 1957 was explained earlier. The numbers of immatures and adults increased at a similar rate. Judging from these rates, mortality in the immature and adult age classes is low.

Surprisingly enough, the cygnet production rate has not kept pace with that of the mated pairs. The rising cygnet production curve mirrors some, but significantly not all, of the increases in breeding birds censused each year through 1951, when a population of approximately 90 mated pairs was reached. After 1951 the continued rise of breeders was followed by a decline in cygnet production when it

Table 9.—Trumpeter swan production data, 1931 to 1957 [1]

Year	Mated pairs censused	Cygnets censused	Cygnets per mated pair	Immatures and adults censused	Cygnets: immature-adult ratio
1931		15		20	0.75
1932		12		57	.21
1933		17		49	.35
1934		49		48	1.02
Mean		23.25		43.50	.58
1935		27		46	.59
1936		41		76	.54
1937		77		81	.95
1938		55		93	.59
Mean		50.00		74.00	.67
1939	46	76	1.65	123	.62
1940		68		123	.55
1941	47	69	1.47	143	.48
1942		53		98	.54
Mean	46.50	66.50	1.56	121.75	.55
1943		34		137	.25
1944	64	72	1.12	207	.35
1945		55		180	.31
1946	65	72	1.11	289	.25
Mean	64.50	58.25	1.12	203.25	.29
1947	78	60	.77	292	.21
1948	74	106	1.43	312	.34
1949	85	103	1.21	348	.30
1950	68	73	1.07	303	.24
Mean	76.25	85.50	1.12	313.75	.27
1951	89	118	1.33	417	.28
1952	84	93	1.11	478	.19
1953	106	99	.93	478	.21
1954	133	82	.62	560	.15
Mean	103.00	98.00	1.00	483.25	.21
1955	123	95	.77	495	.19
1956	137	81	.59	507	.16
1957	108	89	.82	399	.22
Mean	122.66	88.33	.73	467.00	.19

[1] Numbers of mated pairs approximate and not available for periods 1931–38, 1940, 1942–43, and 1945.

dropped from 118 young in 1951 to 93 in 1952, following which the annual production varied between about 80 and 100 cygnets.

Another characteristic shown in figure 44 is the much greater proportion of mated pairs which existed in relation to nonbreeders during the early years of the census for which data are available (1939–41). This is contrasted with the ratio which existed later during the general population rise 1950–54. This suggests to me that the greatly increased proportion of flocked nonbreeders which existed after 1950 apparently resulted from the incapability of mated pairs to reduce territorial claims within limited breeding habitats to the degree necessary to accommodate the rising numbers of potential nesters. Table 8 exhibits the growth of the two main flocks of nonbreeders which inhabit Upper Red Rock Lake and Lima Reservoir.

Because production is relatively stable and the period of immaturity comparatively long, it is difficult to trace with certainty, the impact of any year's production on later populations of the immature

FIGURE 44.—Trumpeter swan productivity rates, total population, 1931–57.[1]

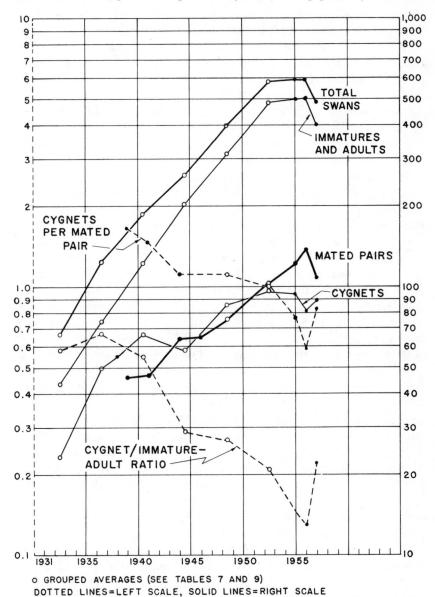

o GROUPED AVERAGES (SEE TABLES 7 AND 9)
DOTTED LINES=LEFT SCALE, SOLID LINES=RIGHT SCALE

[1] Complete data unavailable, 1931–38, 1940, 1942–43, and 1945; mated pair data 1931–57 approximate only.

and adult age classes. However, the near-peak production years of 1948, 1949, and 1951 apparently acted, possibly in concert with other factors, to cause the pronounced upward trend of nonbreeders in 1951, 1952, and 1954. This, in turn, appears to have resulted in the marked rise in numbers of mated pairs in 1953, 1954, and 1956. If cause and result relationships exist here, a 5-year breeding age is indicated, at least during periods of high breeding populations.

Although the *rate* of increase was previously higher, production reached a high plateau during the 1948–52 interval when a average of 80 pairs produced 99 cygnets annually by census time. This contrasts sharply with the 5-year period which followed, 1953–57, when an average of 121 pairs produced only 89 cygnets yearly. In this case an increase of 151 percent in breeders was followed by a cygnet production decrease of 10 percent. This hints that the higher populations of breeders may have depressed productivity.

When the related ratios are graphed, that is, cygnets to mated pairs and cygnets to immatures and adults, the apparent inverse relationship between the population level and productivity becomes clearer. The data for 1955, 1956, and 1957 are shown separately, to bring out the direct relationships suggested by the grouped averages, though, of course, there is much more possibility for the factor of chance to enter in these individual cases. The element of chance in the grouped average curves is, for all practical purposes, insignificant.

In figure 44, a number of other productivity relationships are also apparent. The grouped averages of immatures and adults combined are shown increasing at a constant rate from 1934 to 1954, after which a leveling off or decline is evident. The number of mated pairs censused increased at a rate comparable, but not equal to that of the immatures and adults. This suggests to me that a shortage of unclaimed breeding habitat may have caused potential mature breeders to remain in a flocked nonbreeding status somewhat longer, or to a somewhat greater degree, than would otherwise have been the case.

Data relating to the production dynamics of the two most apparent United States population segments are handled under separate categories: Red Rock Lakes Refuge populations and Yellowstone Park populations. (Due to a lack of comparable census data breakdowns for populations outside the Federal sanctuaries, it is not possible to study the dynamics of these populations.) It is realized that the activities of one population segment may affect the others, as shown by the following example, but it will also be demonstrated that the population mechanics of the Refuge and Park flocks manifest some characteristics separately.

A good example of the interaction existing between population segments is exhibited in figure 45. This shows that nonbreeding

FIGURE 45.—Nonbreeding trumpeter swans censused at Upper Red Rock Lake and Lima Reservoir,[1] 1940–57.

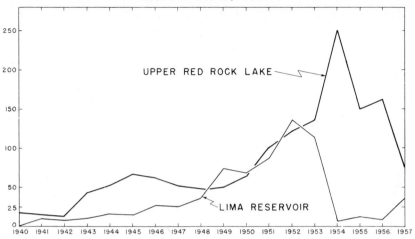

[1] Lima Reservoir practically dry 1954–56 summer season.

trumpeters which had habitually occupied the Lima Reservoir moved into Upper Red Rock Lake during the low water conditions in the Reservoir storage pool during 1954, 1955, and 1956. With the return of higher water conditions in the Reservoir in 1957, the census revealed an increased number of swans there.

RED ROCK LAKES REFUGE POPULATIONS

Since the breeding swans inhabiting the Red Rock Lakes Refuge play a major role in determining the status of the total population in the whole region, the census data for this area during the period 1932–57 were broken down insofar as possible, compiled in table 10, and shown graphically to arithmetic scale in figure 46. Semilog curves are shown in figure 47 for all cases where data breakdowns were possible.

Interestingly, the consistent inverse ratios expressed by breeder numbers in relation to production in the total population (figure 44) are shown to be even more pronounced for the Refuge population (figure 47).

It should be explained that while a certain proportion of paired swans inhabiting Refuge marshes each year apparently do not nest, the ratio of these pairs to known nesting birds is small. It is probably less than 10 percent for the whole marsh most years. Since so few nonnesting pairs were apparent in the initial phases of the study, their numbers were not recorded, but later, when the numbers of mated pairs were much higher, it is recalled that nonnesting pairs were more regularly observed. I therefore suspect that the numbers of nonnesting pairs may increase at a disproportionate rate during years of high breeding population. If true, this may significantly affect the rate of production which I attributed to mated pairs. However, the great majority of pairs on the Refuge nest and lay eggs, even in years of high population density, so the production rate decline so

FIGURE 46.—Trumpeter swan census, Red Rock Lakes Refuge, 1932–57.

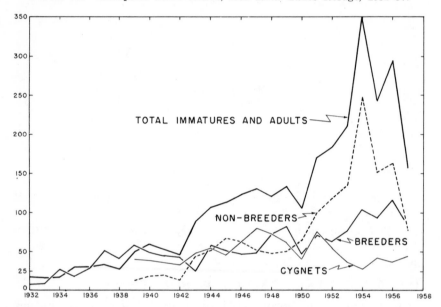

Table 10.—Trumpeter swan production data, Red Rock Lakes Refuge, 1936 to 1957 [1]

Year	Mated pairs censused	Broods censused	Cygnets censused	Broods per mated pairs	Cygnets per mated pair	Cygnets per brood
1936	14	9	26	0. 64	1. 86	2. 89
1937	14	12	51	. 86	3. 64	4. 25
1939	19	15	59	. 79	3. 11	3. 93
Mean	15. 66	12. 00	45. 33	. 76	2. 87	3. 69
1940	19	12	48	. 63	2. 53	4. 00
1942	16	13	43	. 81	2. 69	3. 31
Mean	17. 50	12. 50	45. 50	. 72	2. 61	3. 66
1951	31	20	76	. 65	2. 45	3. 80
1952	31	20	55	. 65	1. 77	2. 75
1953	34	14	38	. 41	1. 12	2. 71
1954	54	15	28	. 28	. 52	1. 87
Mean	37. 50	17. 25	49. 25	. 50	1. 47	2. 78
1955	44	12	41	. 27	. 93	3. 42
1956	63	16	39	. 25	. 62	2. 44
1957	36	17	45	. 47	1. 25	2. 65
Mean	47. 66	15. 00	41. 66	. 33	. 93	2. 84

[1] Data grouped to correspond with comparable information in table 12; unavailable prior to 1936 and for 1938, 1941, and 1943–50.

evident during the years of high populations is due principally to the failure of eggs to hatch and young to survive. Many possible theories for such failures could be advanced, but the underlying causes have not yet been systematically investigated.

FIGURE 47.—Trumpeter swan productivity rates, Red Rock Lake Refuge, 1936–57.[1]

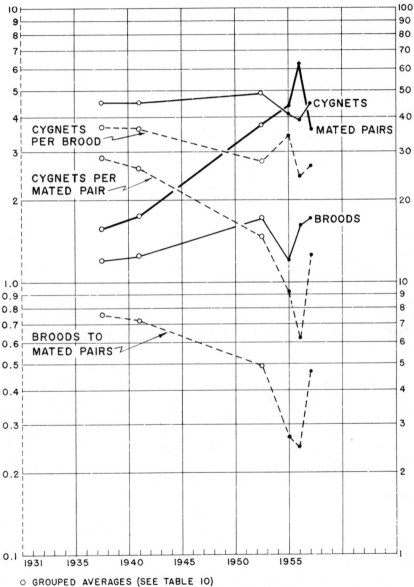

○ GROUPED AVERAGES (SEE TABLE 10)
DOTTED LINES = LEFT SCALE, SOLID LINES = RIGHT SCALE

[1] Data unavailable before 1936, and except for 1938, 1941, and 1943–50.

Table 11.—Variations in Refuge swan nesting density

Year [1]	Paired swans observed [2], [3]		
	Upper Lake; 2,880 acres	River Marsh; 8,000 acres	Swan Lake; 400 acres
1937	6 (9)	6 (13)	2 (8)
1939	8 (12)	12 (26)	6 (8)
1940	6 (10)	12 (18)	2 (0)
1941 [4]	(8)	10 (14)	2 (0)
Mean	6. 7 (9. 75)	10 (17. 75)	3 (4)
1954	16 (3)	56 (16)	14 (6)
1955	12 (14)	46 (14)	12 (0)
1956	12 (17)	54 (9)	18 (3)
1957	12 (6)	48 (27)	18 (6)
Mean	13 (10)	51 (16. 5)	15. 5 (3. 75)
Percent change	+94 (+2)	+410 (−7)	+416 (−6)

[1] Census data for 1938 not available in habitat breakdown form.
[2] Paired swans observed at census time (August) for the period 1937–41. Swans actually observed nesting (June) during the 1954–57 period, except for River Marsh data which are obtained from (aerial) census figures, as part of the marsh cannot be seen from lookout posts. Comparable data for Lower Red Rock Lake are not available because habitat boundary lines are not clear.
[3] Cygnets censused are shown in parentheses.
[4] Breakdown for Upper Lake population not available.

It will be noted from table 10 that the averages of pertinent cygnet production data between the two periods of 1936–42 and 1951–57 differ markedly. For instance, during the period of comparatively low breeding population (1936–42), 74 percent of the paired swans censused were seen with young, while broods averaged 3.7 cygnets each. During the 7-year period of comparatively high breeding population (1951–57) the percentage of paired swans censused with young dropped to 39 percent and the average brood declined 24 percent, from 3.7 to 2.8 cygnets per brood. Stated another way, a 250-percent increase in the average numbers of mated pairs censused on the Refuge between the periods 1936–42 and 1951–57 resulted in virtually no change in average annual cygnet production, being 45.4 cygnets during the 1936–42 period and 46.0 cygnets in 1951–57. Considering the percent of pairs with broods for the period 1936–42 versus 1951–57, there is a highly significant difference between the means, the odds being more than 2 million to 1 against a difference as great due to chance; the odds against a difference as great due to chance for the period 1957 versus 1951–56 are 2.6 to 1.

Table 11 shows the numbers of breeding swans which were attracted to each of the major habitat units when the total Refuge-paired swan population increased about 300 percent, from the 28–40 level to that of 86–104 magnitude. The numbers of mated swans are shown to have increased by different ratios on the two characteristic habitat units during the periods considered. On the shoreline of the Upper Lake, a large open-water body where nesting is restricted to the perimeter, the increase in breeding pairs averaged only 94 percent, while in the River Marsh and Swan Lake units, where potential nesting sites occur more frequently and uniformly, the increase was 410 percent and 416 percent, respectively. This points up the relative importance of habitat composition and arrangement to breeding swans when a high breeding population is present.

In figure 47, the numbers of mated pairs have shown an increasingly rapid rise from 1936 to 1956. The number of broods increased initially at a rate comparable to that of mated pairs, but this trend shows progressively greater signs of leveling off. The total number of cygnets produced annually rose only slightly from 1936 to 1954, but declined markedly during 1955 and 1956 when the numbers of mated pairs were highest.

The related productivity ratios, broods to mated pairs, cygnets to mated pairs, and cygnets to broods all declined at a similar rate, though in the opposite direction, from the increasing rate shown for mated pairs. When all curves are compared for 1955, 1956, and 1957, a strong inverse relationship between population density and productivity is apparent. Although the element of chance may enter to some degree in the case of the individual years, it is outside the realm of expected possibility in the cases of grouped averages.

YELLOWSTONE NATIONAL PARK POPULATIONS

As one might expect, a breakdown of Yellowstone Park's trumpeter census statistics over the 1931–57 period reveals that factors similar to those manifest in the Refuge also have influenced populations there. This is evident even though the breeding habitat in the Park is much more varied and discontinuous than in the Refuge.

As figure 48 shows, the Park's swan numbers during the past 27-year period have been characterized by several features. One has been the relatively constant population of paired swans supported prior to about 1949, considering the inadequacy of the very early census coverages. Another characteristic is the fairly constant rate at which cygnets have been produced during this long period. For most years since about 1949 the greater numbers of paired swans censused also coincided with a somewhat depressed productivity, though this relationship is not as strong as for the Refuge.

Figure 49, graphed from data compiled in table 12 in a form similar to the preceding Refuge population study, throws further light on these different expressions of population dynamics. From these statistics it is evident that the average number of paired swans censused in the Park during the periods of 1931–39 and 1940–50 rose only slightly, from 10.25 to 11.75, whereas from 1951 to 1957 the average rise was much more pronounced, to 15.9. This is an increase of about

FIGURE 48.—Trumpeter swan census, Yellowstone Park, 1931–57.

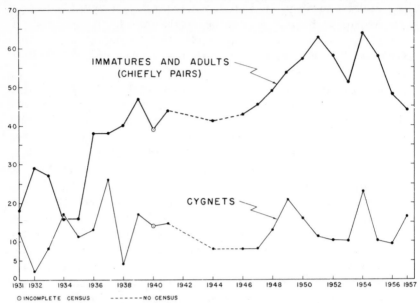

35 percent from the lowest pair population in the Park to the highest, compared with an increase of paired swans on the Refuge of over 250 percent from 1939 to 1957. It should be noted, however, that the average number of cygnets per brood censused in the Park also dropped, from 3.0 during the 1931–39 period to 2.5 during the 1951–57 interval, a decline of 17 percent. This is compared with a similar drop of 24 percent on the Refuge, from 3.6 to 2.8 cygnets per brood.

In figure 49, the decline in the number of cygnets per mated pair in the Park also closely parallels a downward trend of similar proportions which occurred substantially during the same period in the Refuge (figure 47). While table 12 shows the average number of cygnets per mated pair in the Park to have declined only slightly, from 1.20 to 1.10, between the periods 1931–39 and 1940–50, it dropped to 0.72 cygnet per brood during 1951 to 1957 when the number of mated pairs was highest. For the Refuge, table 10 lists 5 years' data collected from 1936 to 1942 showing an average of 2.77 cygnets for each pair, this average dropping to 1.24 for the period 1951–57.

Although the ratio of broods to mated pairs in the Park did vary for the periods 1931–39 versus 1940–50, there is no significant difference between the means. For the period 1940–50 versus 1951–56, however, the odds against a difference as great due to chance are 18 to 1; while for 1957 versus 1951–56, the odds are 13 to 1.

Unlike the situation at Red Rock Lakes, the decline in average number of cygnets per pair in the Park has been compensated for by a gradual rise in the average number of pairs having broods. These factors have almost exactly balanced, with the result that the average annual production of cygnets in the Park has remained practically

Figure 49.—Trumpeter swan productivity rates, Yellowstone Park, 1931–57.[1]

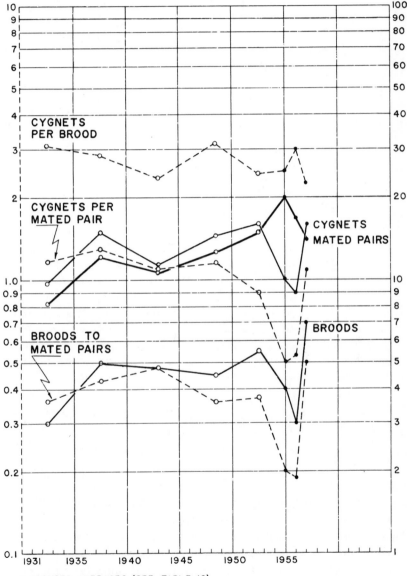

o GROUPED AVERAGES (SEE TABLE 12)
DOTTED LINES=LEFT SCALE, SOLID LINES=RIGHT SCALE

---

[1] Data unavailable for 1942–43, 1945; incomplete 1940; for mated pairs, 1931–57 approximate only.

Table 12.—Trumpeter swan production data, Yellowstone Park, 1931 to 1957 [1]

Year	Mated pairs censused [2]	Broods censused	Cygnets censused	Broods per mated pairs	Cygnets per mated pair	Cygnets per brood
1931	9	4	12	0. 44	1. 33	3. 00
1932	7	1	2	. 14	. 29	2. 00
1933	9	2	8	. 22	. 88	4. 00
1934	8	5	17	. 63	2. 13	3. 40
Mean	8. 25	3. 00	9. 75	. 36	1. 16	3. 10
1936	10	5	13	. 50	1. 30	2. 60
1937	10	6	26	. 60	2. 60	4. 33
1938	12	4	4	. 33	. 33	1. 00
1939	17	5	17	. 29	1. 00	3. 40
Mean	12. 25	5. 00	15. 00	. 43	1. 31	2. 83
1940	8	6	14	. 75	1. 75	2. 33
1941	10	6	15	. 60	1. 50	2. 50
1944	12	4	8	. 33	. 66	2. 00
1946	13	3	8	. 23	. 62	2. 66
Mean	10. 75	4. 75	11. 25	. 48	1. 13	2. 37
1947	14	3	8	. 21	. 57	2. 66
1948	10	4	13	. 40	1. 30	3. 25
1949	12	6	21	. 50	1. 75	3. 50
1950	15	5	16	. 33	1. 07	3. 20
Mean	12. 75	4. 50	14. 50	. 36	1. 17	3. 15
1951	13	5	11	. 38	. 84	2. 20
1952	10	6	10	. 33	. 55	1. 66
1953	18	4	10	. 40	1. 00	2. 50
1954	19	7	23	. 37	1. 21	3. 29
Mean	15. 00	5. 50	16. 00	. 37	. 90	2. 41
1955	20 (28)	4	10	. 20	. 50	2. 50
1956	17 (21)	3	9	. 18	. 53	3. 00
1957	14 (14)	7	16	. 50	1. 14	2. 29
Mean	17. 00	4. 66	11. 66	. 29	. 72	2. 60

[1] Data unavailable 1935, 1942–43, 1945; incomplete 1940.
[2] Approximate number 1931–57; exact data 1955–57 in parentheses.

constant over the 27-year period; namely 12.4 cygnets annually from 1931 to 1939, 12.9 cygnets annually from 1940 to 1950, and 12.7 young annually from 1951 to 1957.

Figures 47 and 49 allow close comparisons of Park and Refuge swan productivity characteristics. For instance, the numbers of mated pairs in the Park increased at a much lesser rate than in the Refuge until about 1946, after which they accelerated and then fell off to a degree comparable with that characterizing the Refuge population.

The total number of cygnets produced in the Park until 1954 increased at a slightly greater rate, though more irregularly, than on the Refuge, after which a similar leveling off is indicated in both environments. The number of broods censused in the Park decreased at only a slight rate until 1950, after which it dropped at a rate comparable to that shown for the Refuge.

As would be expected from the slower rate of increase of mated pairs in the Park, the productivity ratios of broods to mated pairs,

Table 13.—Characteristics of some Yellowstone Park lakes and their record of use by swans, 1931 to 1957 [1]

Lake	Acres	Remarks	Years of record [2]	Total number years occupied	Total number broods produced	Maximum number adults occupying lake during years of record
Tern	66	Adequate cover. Good food production.	24	24	13	4
Madison Junction	9	Cover rather poor. Food abundant.	18	18	10	2
Riddle	109	Ideal. Good food and cover	23	20	9	4
Trumpeter	20	Adequate cover. Abundance of food.	24	17	10	3
Geode	13	Poor cover but ample food	20	16	9	5
Grebe	90	Visited by too many fishermen.	19	15	9	4
White	439	Adequate cover. Good food production.	24	19	3	9
Shoshone	8,475	West end highly favorable for waterfowl.	24	18	4	4
Heart	2,730	Often disturbed by fishermen.	23	16	3	4
Beach Spring	29	Limited cover. Near highway. Good food supply.	22	14	5	2
Swan	19	Frequented by too many people.	22	13	4	2
Obsidian	14	Seems suitable. Water level low in Fall.	17	7	1	2
Lewis	2,926	Visited by too many fishermen.	20	3	2	2
Fern	97	Cover limited. Otherwise lake is fine.	23	19	0	7
Wolfe	20	Seems suitable for swans	13	10	0	6
Grizzly	232	Seems suitable. Cover limited.	18	12	0	4
Lily Pad	64	Large shallow areas dry up	17	11	0	4
Delusion	659	Limited feeding areas	18	9	0	6
Lake of the Woods	40	Seems suitable for swans	22	2	0	2

[1] Data obtained from Condon's (1941) MS plus annual Park and Refuge swan census reports since that time.
[2] Period 1931–57 except for 1942, 1943, and 1945.

cygnets to mated pairs, and cygnets to broods, held fairly constant from 1934 to 1950 with much lesser expression of definite trends than that exhibited by the Refuge population. After 1950, however, all of the Park's productivity indicators declined when mated pairs increased further, though this is shown not to have occurred as consistently or at as rapid a rate as in the Refuge.

A comparison of the Park and Refuge productivity data suggests to me that environment factors in the dissimilar habitat of the Park, other than population density, are more variable and influential in regulating annual production there.

In order to illustrate the variable capacity of the Park lake habitats to support swan broods, a sample of counts on breeding habitats was chosen from those areas on which swans have been censused for a period of 10 years or over. This information is shown in table 13. An examination of these data points up the limited capability of the lake habitat in the Park to support broods regularly, the upper limit actually being about 55 percent of the time over a long period (Madison Junction and Tern Lakes). On some other waters, in spite of regular records of swan occupancy, not a single brood has been produced. The brief "remarks" column does not entirely explain why breeding pairs select certain lakes and leave others unoccupied, nor why certain nesting waters are consistently more productive than others.

POPULATIONS OUTSIDE RED ROCK LAKES REFUGE AND YELLOWSTONE NATIONAL PARK

The annual swan tallies made over the years covering scattered areas contiguous to Yellowstone and Red Rock Lakes have not been quite as complete or consistent as on the federally administered areas. As a result, these data are not so reliable, especially before the aerial methods were employed in 1946, although they are believed to be highly representative. Furthermore, since census figures prior to the 1950's were generally "lumped," it is not possible to prepare a table or graph of productivity data as was done in the case of Red Rock Lakes and Yellowstone Park populations.

Figure 50 has been prepared from the most comprehensive information available in Park and Refuge files to show the increase in these "outside" populations. An especially rapid population rise is shown for the areas outside the Refuge and Park in 1946. This particular increase is believed to have been more apparent than real, reflecting the greater accuracy and coverage of the aerial census method which was employed for the first time. The apparent rise in population numbers was greater on the "outside" areas mainly because the large

FIGURE 50.—Trumpeter swan census outside Red Rock Lakes Refuge and Yellowstone Park, 1931–57.

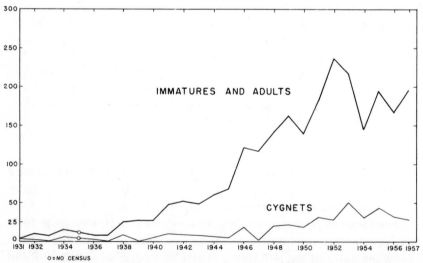

reservoirs outside the Park or Refuge boundaries were covered efficiently and completely for the first time.

The most significant feature of figure 50 is the tendency of areas outside the Park and Refuge not only to hold increasingly greater numbers of swans but at the same time to produce a generally rising number of cygnets as well. This is in contrast with the trend in Yellowstone Park and the Refuge where production recently declined. It is plain that habitat outside the two Federal sanctuaries is becoming increasingly important as the total number of swans in protected areas rises.

SUMMARY, POPULATION DYNAMICS

Total Population:

1. The population increased at a constant rate from about 1935 until 1954 (about 10 percent annually). Beginning in 1955 a definite leveling out became evident.
2. The rates of change for the total population reflected the survival rate of the immature-and-adult age class to a much greater extent than the progressively declining cygnet production rate. Population turnover (mortality) in the immature and adult age classes is thus shown to be low.
3. Mated pairs increased at a rate approaching, but not equal, that of the immature-and-adult age class. This suggests that a shortage of desirable unclaimed breeding territories may prolong the non-breeding status of potential nesters.
4. During periods of increasing populations at high levels, cygnets were produced at a rate progressively less than during periods of increasing populations at low levels.
5. During low levels, mated pairs comprised a much greater proportion of the total population than at high levels.
6. There is an indication that mated pairs initially occupied breeding territories as 5-year-olds, at least during periods of high population levels.
7. Cygnet production reached a plateau from 1948 to 1952.
8. An inverse relationship between population levels and productivity is shown.

Yellowstone Park Population:

1. Considering the inadequate coverage of the early years, the number of mated pairs remained nearly constant from 1931 to about 1952. A definite increase occurred beginning in 1953.
2. Broods were produced at a nearly constant rate from 1931 to 1957.
3. Cygnets were produced at a nearly constant rate from 1931 to 1953, and in ratio to the number of mated pairs present; after 1953 the

number of mated pairs increased and the production of cygnets declined.

4. The ratio of broods to mated pairs increased at a constant rate from 1931 to 1945 and then changed, but generally decreased at an irregular rate from 1946 to 1954. After 1954 the rate of decline accelerated, coincident with the further increase in mated pairs.

5. The rate at which cygnets were produced per brood remained nearly constant from 1931 to 1950; a decline occurred after 1950 with a further increase in mated pairs and the number of cygnets produced per brood remained low until 1957.

6. The rate at which cygnets per mated pair were produced was nearly constant from 1931 to 1950 and roughly proportional to the number of mated pairs present; after 1950 the cygnets per mated pair rate changed inversely with the change in number of mated pairs present.

7. Breeding habitats are "saturated" when occupied by about 15 pairs, greater breeding populations appear to depress productivity.

Red Rock Lakes Populations:

1. The number of mated pairs increased at a substantially constant rate during the 1936–57 period.

2. From 1936 to 1954, the increasing rate at which broods were being produced slightly outweighed the consistent declines in the ratios of cygnets to broods and broods to mated pairs. The result was a slight increase in the cygnet-production rate.

3. In 1955 and 1956, when populations of mated pairs were highest, cygnet production declined. The falling ratios of broods to pairs and/or cygnets to broods during this period resulted in the production drop. In 1957, when the number of mated pairs dropped, the production rate went up due to an increase in these same productivity factors. Thus, cygnet production is shown to be inversely related to the number of mated pairs when high populations are present.

4. Breeding habitats are "saturated" when occupied by about 40 pairs, greater breeding populations appear to depress productivity.

Population Outside Federal Sanctuaries:

1. The census data for this segment does not lend itself to the detailed analysis possible with other populations.

2. The total population, and cygnet production, show consistent through different growth rates.

Red Rock Lakes versus Yellowstone Park Populations:

1. The point of diminishing productivity was reached about the same time (1955) in both of these habitats. In view of the long period

when relatively constant numbers of mated pairs occurred in the Park, during which they increased about 300 percent on the Refuge, some interaction between these populations is suggested. It appears that at "supersaturated" levels, Refuge pairs may overflow to Park habitat, depressing the productivity rate there. The similar drop of mated pairs in the Refuge and Park between 1955 and 1957 leads to the same conclusion—that interaction may occur at high levels but not necessarily at low.

2. Where breeding territories are contiguous, as within the Refuge, increasing breeding populations at "saturation" levels or below exert a depressive effect on the potential production rate. This is apparently not true in isolated habitats, as in Yellowstone Park where the cygnet production rate tends to change directly with the number of mated pairs present, unless a "supersaturated" breeding population is sustained when the rate declines.

CONCLUSIONS

1. Trumpeter swans in the tristate region of Montana, Wyoming, and Idaho should no longer be considered an endangered species; this population has increased at a constant rate for 20 years, and it now exhibits signs of leveling off at the maximum level this environment will support.

2. The rate of population change in the total population varied inversely with changes in population density. This change occurred in two habitats of varying capacity, Red Rock Lakes and Yellowstone Park, and during periods of low and high populations, hence the phenomena is relative and probably occurs to some degree in all swan-occupied habitat.

3. The dynamics of the change in population are tied to the rate of productivity of mated pairs, which varied inversely with changes in population density.

4. The rate of increase approached zero about 1954 when the population peak was reached. After that, except for 1957 when an exodus apparently occurred, the population fluctuated around 590, apparently nearly the maximum population which can regularly be sustained. Continued population and production increases on areas outside Federal sanctuaries will raise this estimate if further expansion of their range occurs or more isolated breeding habitats within the existing environment are successfully occupied.

DISCUSSION

Howard and Fiske (1911) were the first to show that natural populations tend to vary inversely with population density, and Nicholson

(1933 : 132–178) and Smith (1935 : 873–898) also pointed out that the comparative stability of natural populations is controlled dynamically, meaning that the farther that numbers rise or fall, the stronger is the tendency to return to the previous level (Lack, 1954).

Lately Christian (1957 : 443–62) has shown that numerous field and laboratory studies involving mice support a theory that the growth of populations may be regulated and limited by sociopsychological factors, (social competition) through the production of stress in some proportion to population density. This possibility has not been as thoroughly studied in wild avian populations, presumably because of few hints in this direction and difficulties inherent in making accurate censuses of entire populations; nevertheless, there are clues to such a theorem. Working with great tits in Holland, Kluijver (1951) found that both the average clutch and the proportion of pairs raising second broods were lower at high than low population densities; but it was concluded by Lack (1954) that the difference was too small to have any important effect on subsequent numbers. Errington (1945), discovered that the summer gain in Wisconsin bobwhites (young and adults surviving autumn) varied inversely with the numbers present in April. The foregoing study, though concerned only with swan populations, parallels Errington's findings.

Since by far the great majority of paired swans on Refuge marshes complete nests and lay eggs, population density-dependent variations in the number of cygnets produced may be substantially attributed to the hatching and survival rate. Just how the number of cygnets raised may be regulated by the density of mated pairs is not understood, but it seems clear that the deterioration of habitat, usually associated with the population declines of some wildlife species, does not play a major role.

MANAGEMENT

PROTECTIVE LEGISLATION

The farsighted Congressional legislation which originally provided for the protection of wildlife in Yellowstone National Park, the Lacey Act of May 7, 1894, furnished essential protection for the ancestors of the few pairs of trumpeter swans which were discovered breeding in this famous Park in the summer of 1919. The early protective wildlife regulations which grew out of this initial National Park legislation were forerunners of continentwide laws which first applied specifically to waterfowl and later to waterfowl refuges. Each link of legislation which protected the trumpeter was forged as part of a greater plan to perpetuate portions of the representative native fauna in their natural environment.

Unfortunately, the passage of the second Lacey Act in 1900, the Weeks-McLean Law in 1913, and the Migratory Bird Treaty Act in 1918 arrived much too late to prevent the extirpation of the trumpeter over most of its United States breeding range. For two decades after 1900, a number of prominent American scientists interested in the problems of species survival commented on the fate of the trumpeter swan. William T. Hornaday (1913: 19) reported that in 1907 these swans were regarded as so nearly extinct that a doubting ornithological club of Boston refused to believe on hearsay evidence that the New York Zoological Park contained a pair of the living birds, and a committee was appointed to investigate in person and report. Edward Howe Forbush (1912: 475), an eminent ornithologist, lamented:

The trumpeter has succumbed to incessant persecution in all parts of its range, and its total extinction is now only a matter of years. . . . The large size of this bird and its conspicuousness have served, as in the case of the whooping crane, to make it a shining mark, and the trumpetings that were once heard over the breadth of a great continent, as the long converging lines drove on from zone to zone, will soon be heard no more.

Passage of the Migratory Bird Treaty Act 6 years later placed a closed season on both species of native swans for the first time when it became effective in 1918. This was the first aid to survival of the few trumpeters which still existed outside Yellowstone Park boundaries and which were to be so important in the eventual restoration of the species.

In 1929, the Migratory Bird Conservation Act authorizing the acquisition of land for waterfowl refuges was passed by Congress. When supported with funds in 1934, this basic waterfowl legislation was as important in providing for the future increase of the United States trumpeter flock as the Migratory Bird Treaty Act was in protecting the remnant populations.

Under the Migratory Bird Conservation Act, the Red Rock Lakes Migratory Waterfowl Refuge in southwestern Montana was established by Executive Order in 1935. This area, containing thousands of acres of historic trumpeter swan breeding habitat, was subsequently staffed by the Biological Survey, a predecessor of the United States Fish and Wildlife Service. . The 22,682-acre area originally set aside under this Order was enlarged in September of the same year, when about 18,000 additional acres were included in the Refuge in order to complete the breeding-ground acquisition and to bring under management certain warm spring-water areas important to the swans during the winter months. Although several management problems remained, the establishment of this Refuge provided the upward turning point for this species in the United States. While the status of the trumpeters in Yellowstone Park before the establishment of the Refuge was marginal, it was apparently improving slowly. But the existence of this species outside the Park was actually in jeopardy by the early 1930's.

Later, since it was discovered that irresponsible waterfowl hunters were killing swans under the claimed pretext of shooting snow geese, the hunting seasons on snow geese were closed in those States within the trumpeters' winter range. Service regulations, stemming from authority in the Migratory Bird Treaty Act, closed the snow-goose season first in the State of Idaho in 1941, and were modified about a decade later to exclude the counties where swan shooting was not a problem. In Montana the snow goose closure has been in continuous effect in Beaverhead, Gallatin, and Madison Counties from 1942 until the present. Similar Federal closures were initiated as a statewide measure in Wyoming in 1946 because of the threat posed to the newly established trumpeter flock introduced to the National Elk Refuge in Jackson Hole; however, these regulations were modified in 1955 to include only the pertinent areas of Teton and Lincoln Counties.

Unless these protective measures had been taken by the Federal Government, this large and conspicuous bird would surely have disappeared from its native breeding grounds in this country.

CAPTIVITY RECORD

The history of the trumpeter in captivity is long, varied, and interesting. It is valuable as avicultural history, for information on the traits this bird displayed in captivity, its breeding record, and the success which was attained by some of the various individuals or organizations which kept it in confinement.

Audubon (1838: 537, 541) has left us with an early note or two on the subject, writing:

I have traced the winter migrations of this species as far southward as the Texas . . . where I saw a pair of young ones in captivity, and quite domesticated, that had been procured in the winter of 1836.

    *   *   *   *   *   *   *

I kept a male [trumpeter] alive upwards of two years, while I was residing in Henderson in Kentucky. It had been slightly wounded in the tip of the wing, and was caught after a long pursuit in a pond from which it could not escape. . . . Although at first extremely shy, it gradually became accustomed to the servants, who fed it abundantly, and at length proved so gentle as to come to my wife's call, to receive bread from her hand. "Trumpeter" . . . now assumed a character which until then had been unexpected, and laying aside his timidity became so bold at times as to give chase to my favorite Wild Turkey Cock, my dogs, children and servants. Whenever the gates of our yard happened to be opened, he would at once make for the Ohio, and it was not without difficulty that he was driven home again. . . . in the course of a dark and rainy night, one of the servants having left the gate open, Trumpeter made his escape, and was never again heard of.

The next record of the trumpeter's history in captivity seems to be that left by Baird, Brewer, and Ridgeway (1884: 432), as they state:

A nest of this species was found by Mr. W. C. Rice at Oakland Valley, Ia., in the spring of 1871, and the Cygnets taken from it. Three of these were successfully raised, and were purchased for the Mount Auburn [Iowa] Cemetery, where they were received in December. They bore their transportation, in a week of unparalleled severity for the season, without injury, and were remarkably docile and tame. In the summer months when at large they would leave their pond and seek the companionship of their keeper, whose occupation as painter occasionally required his presence on the grounds near their place of abode. If permitted, they would spend the day in his company rather than remain in their pond. They were perfectly and completely domesticated and showed no fear of any person, feeding from the hands of any stranger. This swan has also been domesticated in the cemetery in Cincinnati, a pair of the progeny having been sent to the London Zoological Gardens, and another to Mount Auburn.

Jean Delacour (1954: 78, 79) provides a recent synopsis of both the foreign and domestic captivity record of this species. He begins with the arrival of the first specimens in Europe in 1866, which were apparently the progeny shipped from the Cincinnati cemetery just mentioned:

Trumpeter swans do very well in captivity. They soon become tame, prove completely hardy, easy to feed, and they breed readily. The first specimens to reach Europe arrived at the London Zoo in 1866, and the earliest breeding success in captivity took place there in 1870 when three cygnets hatched on July 6 and were reared on the Three-Islands Pond. Other successes followed. The species reached Paris, at the Jardin des Plantes, in 1873, but not until 1880 were eggs laid, and these proved infertile. In 1885, however, five eggs hatched and four cygnets were reared.

Later on, Trumpeters bred regularly in Europe, but since the beginning of this century, only the Duke of Bedford, in England, and F. Blaauw, in Holland, seemed to have possessed and raised any.

*   *   *   *   *   *   *

Blaauw reared Trumpeters at Gooilust almost every year until his death in 1936. There were then sixteen birds left, old and young, and they all went to Woburn Abbey, as they had been bequeathed to the Duke of Bedford, who still possessed four. Unfortunately, all these birds died through lack of food during the 1939–45 war. . . .

We kept only one pair at Cleres [France], in 1920 and 1921. They were two years old when they arrived from Gooilust, and they were placed on the lake. They swam and walked all over the park, at great speed. Very soon they became quarrelsome and attacked large birds, particularly white Rheas, which they pursued relentlessly over the hills. It became impossible to keep them at large, and as all suitable pens were already occupied, we sent them away to the London Zoo.

Trumpeters kept at liberty at Woburn did not molest other birds in the huge park. Each pair established a territory and nested, but the young were often lost. At Gooilust, each pair was kept on a comparatively small pond, and bred regularly.

As a result of the breaking up of F. E. Blaauw's waterfowl collection in Holland in 1936 after his death, the disastrous results of World War II upon the Woburn Abbey flock of trumpeters in England, and Delacour's earlier abandonment of his Cleres trumpeter raising efforts, it is doubtful whether any of these birds remain in Europe or England today, except of course for the trumpeters which were presented to the Queen of England by the Canadian Government.

Trumpeters were also apparently kept successfully in captivity in or near Washington, D. C., in the early days. The Patuxent Research Refuge records note that 5 sets of trumpeter eggs were in the collection of J. P. Norris, Jr., tagged "D. C. (captivity)" under the date of May 3, 1893. No other data are furnished except that this report was received from A. C. Bent.

The National Zoological Park in Washington, D. C., exhibited trumpeters for over 22 years, from May 24, 1900, until June 14, 1922, involving a total of 8 birds. The trumpeters at the Philadelphia Zoological Garden have been noted under "Longevity."

The New York Zoological Society kept trumpeters for over 20 years, commencing in 1899 and lasting until 1921 (W. G. Conway, correspondence). A total of 22 specimens were received as purchases, deposits, or exchanges during this time, having been obtained from such States as Idaho (3 in 1889), Utah (6 in 1901), and Maine (1 in 1901), as well as from the collections of L. C. Sanford of New Haven, Connecticut (4 in 1909), and F. E. Blaauw of Holland (4 in 1921). Apparently none of these trumpeters bred in New York.

H. K. Coale (1915: 89, 90) reported that, at the time of his writing, live Montana-originated trumpeters were in the collections of Dr. L. C. Sanford of New Haven, Connecticut, and Mr. John E. Thayer of Lancaster, Massachusetts; also that Judge R. M. Barnes of Lacon, Illinois, had written that he possessed 5 of the 10 trumpeters then known to be in captivity, though he had been unable to breed any. The origin of Judge Barnes's flock is unknown.

Before the days of the enforcement of the Migratory Bird Treaty Act in 1918, some traffic existed in live trumpeter swans between persons able to obtain them and those interested in their propagation or exhibition in captivity.

Dr. T. S. Roberts (1936: 206) stated that an old-time resident of Heron Lake, Minnesota, related that pre-flight cygnets were rounded up and captured there for shipment to the East, presumably sometime after the 1850's.

Mr. Cecil Wetmore, presently the proprietor of the Summit Hotel in Monida, Montana, and the oldest living pioneer of the Red Rock Lakes marshes, told me that about the turn of the century, when he was but a boy, his family captured young trumpeter cygnets for sale to zoos, municipal gardens, or interested individuals. The price, at least at one time during this period, was $50 a pair and all birds which remained unsold at the season's end were liberated in order to ensure ample breeding stock for future years. Mr. Wetmore recalled that several pairs were disposed of to the Columbia Gardens in Butte, Montana, but other purchasers had been forgotten and the pertinent records lost during the intervening years.

At least one other pioneer Valley resident, Mr. Fred Hanson, captured Red Rock Lakes swans for the live-bird trade during this period (Alta Hanson, correspondence). From the diary record of Lillian Culver it is clear that Mr. Hanson was active in supplying birds to the live-swan trade during the period 1896–1914, shipping them to various unnamed buyers located at unspecified destinations:

1896. August 20.   Fred has 15 swans and will ship tomorrow.
September 17.   Fred and Henry [Hackett, her brother] have gone after swan. They made $50 apiece clear on the last shipment.
September 21.   Henry left home with 12 swan this morning, he left 2.   He has 5 at Collins and will take them.
1897. September 12.   Fred and Henry have 35 swan now.   Fred expects to go with them soon now.
September 19.   Henry went Friday with 2 swan for King in Ohio.
September 24.   Well, Fred and Henry started at 2 p. m. with 32 swan in the hay rack.   I hope they will not have any trouble.
1898. August 29.   Fred has 17 swan.
November 10.   Fred left with six swan.
1899. July 25.   Fred went for swan.
1900. July 20.   Home about 4 p. m.   Fred and Emma gone after swan.
September 25.   Fred shipped 17 ducks.   He has only 8 swan left.
1901. October 31.   Been hunting Fred's swan all day.   They got out last nite.   One died and one flew away so he has only 6 left.
1902. October 5.   Fred is ready to take swan in the morning.
1906. October 15.   Fred went to Monida with the swan after dinner.
1908. October 20.   Matt [Reis] tore up boxes to make the swan crate and packed them over.   He will go with the swan Friday.
November 26.   The boys got their check for swan today, $66.00.
1911. August 31.   Henery came with 10 swan and put them in the stable.   We had dinner and I went to feed and water the swan when Fred came with one more.
1914. August 31.   Fred and Chester got 3 more swan.   5 new swan now.   [James F. Hanson, son of Fred Hanson, adds that these were the last swan taken.   Fred could not sell them and they stayed around Culver's pond for years.]

Apparently one of the early day "swan-brokers" who obtained some of the Red Rock trumpeters was Dr. Cecil French of Victoria, B. C., who wrote to the Kellogg Bird Sanctuary in 1934 (a copy was furnished by Dr. Pirnie), stating:

I have had quite a bit to do with native wild swans in my time.   Until the days of the War [WW I] I was located in Washington, D. C., and off and on for several years had been engaged in collecting various birds and animals for Zoological institutes throughout the world.   Until about the year 1913 I received annually, from a party in the State of Montana, from 2 to 6 young Trumpeter Swans, taken from the nests.   These went to a collector in Boston, Mass., to the Duke of Bedford in England, and to a Mr. Blaauw at Hilversum, Holland.

Patuxent Research Refuge records hold an entry that Dr. French reported in a letter of October 18, 1910, that trumpeter swans nested at Lakeview, Montana, the former postoffice address for residents of the Red Rock Lakes area.   So apparently at least some of the early-day Red Rock Lakes trumpeter population found its way via Dr. French to the East and thence abroad to foreign aviculturists.

FIGURE 51.—Trumpeter swan cygnets captured on the Red Rock Lakes by the Wetmore family for the live swan trade about 1900.

As any information regarding the whereabouts or availability of these rare fowl in the days before they were protected by the Migratory Bird Treaty Act could be turned to personal profit, such information was rarely published. No doubt the files of Dr. French and other early aviculturists such as F. E. Blaauw and the Duke of Bedford could reveal a wealth of information along these lines.

Dr. Miles D. Pirnie (correspondence) reported that the Kellogg Bird Sanctuary in Michigan, with which he was formerly associated, purchased 10 or more young trumpeters from F. E. Blaauw in Holland between 1927 and 1931 at a cost of about $500 apiece. According to Dr. Pirnie, copulation occurred seasonally among paired individuals but they made no attempts at nest building. The last pair was broken up when the male died about 1938. The surviving pen was then moved to the Chester K. Brooks estate near Cleveland where a cob trumpeter was available. This attempt at breeding trumpeters in captivity also ended in failure when the pen was killed by a dog. Dr. Pirnie indicated that extreme emaciation due to unknown causes resulted in the deaths of several trumpeters at the Kellogg Sanctuary. Human interference, intraspecific strife due to crowding, nest desertion, and malnutrition were believed to be principally responsible for low breeding success among the various other species of swans (whooper, whistling, and mute) which did breed on that sanctuary.

The following statement by Dr. J. M. Derscheid (1939: 94) has apparently led to some speculation in the past regarding the original source of the trumpeter swans in Yellowstone Park.

Mr. Blaauw told me then [upon the occasion of Derscheid's visit to Holland in 1924] that he was not only slowly but regularly increasing the strength of that [trumpeter swan] stock, but that he had had much satisfaction in sending some of the Trumpeter Swans bred at his place to the United States Federal Government, with the object of restocking some American National Parks with this species, formerly living there, but then practically extinct.

In spite of inquiries at the field headquarters of Yellowstone National Park, the likely recipient if any trumpeters had been sent, nothing could be learned which would verify this alleged transplanting. Regardless of Dr. Derscheid's statement, it is highly improbable that a Government project possessing so much inherent public interest was actually consummated at that early date without the usual publicity and deliberate recording of the facts involved. It is more likely that Blaauw's remark refers to the trumpeters which he shipped to the Kellogg Bird Sanctuary. Trumpeter swans (4) were noted in Yellowstone Park as early as 1915 (M. P. Skinner, 1925: 154), but the first breeding trumpeters were not reported until 1919, when 2 pairs were discovered. No special efforts to save them from extinction were made by the Park Service until a decade later.

C. G. Sibley (1938: 329) reported the hybridization of the trumpeter swan while confined in captivity with several other species of Anatidae. Drawing upon the testimony of other breeders as well as his own experience, Sibley lists hybrids of the trumpeter cross-breeding with the mute, whooper, and whistling swan and the Canada goose. What is perhaps of even greater significance is the indication that hybrids between the rather distantly related swans are sometimes fertile, this characteristic being noted in a whistling-mute cross (male). The young of a whistling-whooper hybrid were also said to be fertile.

NATIONAL PARK SERVICE INVESTIGATIONS

In 1929 the National Park Service launched a comprehensive series of biological studies which were needed to outline the most pressing wildlife problems which existed in the National Parks. Early attention was given to determining the status of the trumpeter in Yellowstone Park, with the aim of saving it from extinction. While M. P. Skinner (1925: 153–155) had outlined the precarious early status of the trumpeter in the Park during the period 1915–21, no special attempt had been made to assure its welfare since.

Dr. Joseph Dixon, then economic mammalogist at the University of California, served as the field observer during the initial phase of the new Park Service program and conducted the preliminary swan survey in Yellowstone Park during the fall of 1929. In the course of these investigations he learned that although a pair of trumpeters had nested every season since 1925 on a small lake near Junction Butte, known locally as Trumpeter Lake, they had never been known to raise their young to flight age. The need for study of egg loss and cygnet mortality was thus indicated and plans were made to do this the following season.

In the spring of 1930 Dr. Dixon returned to Yellowstone Park as planned, reinforced by National Park Service naturalists George Wright and Ben Thompson. Two nesting pairs of swans, one pair located at Trumpeter Lake and the other at Tern Lake, were placed under surveillance in order to determine the causes of egg loss and juvenile mortality, while a preliminary general survey of other swans in the Park was carried out as time and opportunity permitted.

At the end of the 1930 nesting season, only 3 cygnets were successfully raised from the total of 4 nesting pairs of trumpeters found in the Park that summer. The 6 cygnets which hatched at Trumpeter Lake were all lost, dropping out 'from unknown causes by ones and twos over the whole span of the breeding season in spite of several periods of dawn-to-dusk surveillance. The only cause of mortality actually observed all summer was a raven which was seen to pilfer the contents of a swan egg at the Tern Lake nest. Plainly, heavy losses of eggs and juveniles were holding the swan population in the Park at precariously low levels. Further investigations, coupled with localized predator control, were planned again for the following year.

About this time, the Park swan restoration program came to the attention of some of the local residents of the nearby Red Rock Lakes area, where these rare fowl were still commonly killed every year by hunters during the waterfowl season despite the Federal law. Letters from at least two ranchers in the Red Rock Lakes marshes, Mr. Clarence Hunt and Mr. A. Hayden, protested to Park authorities the unnecessary shooting and killing of swans in the vicinity of their marshland ranches. In one of these letters Mr. Hunt reported to Park Ranger Frank Anderson that 7 trumpeters were killed during the 1930 season alone. Mr. Hayden advised the Park that the numbers of swans were so reduced by hunters on the Red Rock and Henrys Lakes that their numbers probably totaled less than 15. Both ranchers made separate recommendations that something be done for the protection of these rare birds in the Red Rock Lakes area.

From 1931 until the Red Rock Lakes Refuge was established in 1935 the Park Service spared no labor in promoting the welfare of the trumpeter. To the everlasting credit of that Service this was true not only within the Park but in the important Red Rock Lakes area as well. During this critical period George Wright was placed in charge of the program, and he, together with his associates, Dr. Dixon and Ben Thompson, worked tirelessly with Park Superintendent Roger W. Toll on management measures designed to protect and increase the trumpeter population in the whole Yellowstone region.

When George Wright was specifically assigned to the trumpeter problem by the National Park Service in 1931, he accepted the challenge with characteristic enthusiasm and dedication. That summer he initiated the first annual swan census. The life history studies were also commenced at this time under his supervision. These led to such important discoveries as the recognition of the Red Rock Lakes area as a major breeding grounds of the species and the fact that the trumpeter wintered in Yellowstone Park, a fact apparently not recognized before 1932. Mr. Wright also wrote letters to officers of the various duck hunting clubs located about the Red Rock Lakes, stressing the lamentable status of the trumpeter and otherwise publicizing the problem locally. Acting in the light of Mr. Wright's publicity of the trumpeter's plight, the effort of Mr. Frank Conley of Deer Lodge, Montana, resulted in the Montana State Fish and Game Department's becoming interested in the swan killing problem, and in 1933 the Commission offered a $50 reward for information leading to the conviction of anyone found guilty of shooting a trumpeter in Montana.

Dr. Joseph Dixon also played a key role in the early restoration of the trumpeter. Besides his early survey work he later served as a consultant. It was Dr. Dixon who originally kindled public interest in this species by his now historic article which appeared in the August 1931 issue of *American Forests*. This not only authoritatively outlined the precarious position of the trumpeter during this period but did much to arouse public opinion in support of the progressive Park program, of which little was then known.

Ben Thompson served in the early swan restoration program chiefly by assisting George Wright and Dr. Dixon in the field, and later by outlining the trumpeter's survival problems at the first North American Wildlife Conference (1936: 639–41).

In Yellowstone Park, management measures were taken by Superintendent Roger Toll as a result of recommendations based on field investigations by Messrs. Wright, Dixon, and Thompson. Local predator control of coyotes and ravens was practiced, fishing waters were closed to prevent molestation of nesting swans, at least two small nesting islands were constructed to reduce the chances of predation, and the life history studies were continued. In one case Superintendent Toll decided to relocate a main Park road that was being constructed in order to furnish a space "buffer zone" to prevent undue disturbance of nesting swans by curious visitors.

The climax of Park Service efforts came when J. N. "Ding" Darling, then chief of the Biological Survey, impelled by the Park's swan restoration program and favorable reports, visited the Red Rock Lakes area in 1934 and subsequently recommended that these lakes and marshes be included within the Federal waterfowl refuge system which was then just getting underway. Twelve years previously, in the fall of 1922, Charles S. Sperry, a waterfowl food-habits biologist of the Biological Survey, had inspected the isolated Red Rock Lakes area and, though he reported these marshes a wonderful breeding ground for all kinds of wild fowl including the trumpeter, recommended against acquisition owing to opposition from hunting-club interests which had been entrenched in that area since the turn of the century. In 1934, following "Ding's" recommendations, these differences were resolved under the urgency of the swan restoration program, and in the following year Red Rock Lakes Migratory Waterfowl Refuge was created.

After the Refuge was established and management was undertaken in earnest by the Biological Survey, the Park Service did not consider the swan restoration program a finished matter. Wright, then Chief of the Wildlife Division of the National Park Service, and Superintendent Toll were both killed in a tragic automobile accident in 1936, but the new Superintendent, Edmund B. Rogers, established a firm liaison with the succeeding Red Rock Lakes Refuge managers. Rogers' interest led to a number of progressive swan projects during the next 20 years.

Several important studies of the trumpeter were made in Yellowstone Park during Rogers' tenure as Superintendent. In 1938 Frank Oberhansley, Assistant Park Naturalist, and Maynard Barrows, Assistant Chief Ranger, completed a season of important observations resulting in their 1939 manuscript. In 1941 David Condon, now Chief Naturalist of Yellowstone National Park, finished his manuscript on the trumpeters in the Park. Shortly afterwards Condon was in a position, along with refuge manager Dr. Ward M. Sharp, to stand in united opposition against the establishment of a U. S. Army mountain training and artillery center at Henrys Lake, Idaho. Construction of this base had actually begun before conservationists rallied behind recommendations made by Condon and Sharp in order to safeguard the breeding population of trumpeters at

Red Rock Lakes, which was only a few miles to the west of Henrys Lake, and almost within the proposed artillery-target sector.

The significant annual loss of swans to waterfowl hunters along Henrys Fork of the Snake River in Idaho was also brought to light for the first time as a result of Condon's investigations. To reduce this unnecessary mortality a cooperative educational project was organized in which the Park Service furnished film and information, and the Emergency Conservation Committee, headed by Rosalie Edge of New York City, supplied funds for an extended series of lectures throughout eastern Idaho. These were presented by George Marler, a seasonal Park Service naturalist. This 2-year series of lectures reached a total of 24,687 people, and its beneficial effects continued long after the project had ended.

Park Service cooperation continues to the present time. The annual swan census, now accomplished by aerial methods, is carried out with Park Service cooperation. Park Biologist Walter Kittams has served as an aerial observer on swan census flights over the Park in various U. S. Fish and Wildlife Service aircraft every year during the past decade. From a population standpoint this information has been most valuable in assessing current trends and as a guide to habitat evaluations.

SWAN MANAGEMENT ON THE RED ROCK LAKES REFUGE

GENERAL PRACTICES

When A. V. Hull assumed the initial managership of the Red Rock Lakes Refuge in 1935, an effective liaison was soon established with Park officials. Under the resulting association, ideas were exchanged on swan restoration measures, the annual swan census was coordinated, and both offices kept abreast of new developments. In addition, a number of projects designed to aid the swan program were placed in effect on the Refuge by Hull (1939: 378–382).

Most of these management measures were time-proved conventional wildlife restoration practices, and are continued where practical on the Refuge today. One of the most important was the elimination of human activity and trespass on or near the swan breeding waters. This was based on standard Service regulations, and in this case served especially well, since trumpeters are particularly sensitive to irregular human activity.

Marsh management was also begun at an early date on the Refuge. Grazing was limited to the conservative carrying capacity of the range, in order to help restore the marsh itself to a natural wilderness nesting environment. In more recent years the trumpeters' winter habitat has been improved through the development of two warm-water spring-fed ponds.

Muskrat trapping was also brought under direct regulation at an early date and, in fact, halted for a time. Hull found that muskrat houses furnished the main source of nesting sites, and overtrapping before establishment of the Refuge was apparently a major factor in reducing the population of these marsh rodents to a low level. Present management limits muskrat trapping to removal of only the animals surplus to the needs of a balanced marsh habitat, with the need for swan nesting sites being kept particularly in mind.

In order to supplement the few muskrat houses which were available as swan nesting sites immediately after the establishment of the Refuge, a number of floating artificial nesting platforms were constructed of wood on the ice, loaded with marsh hay to simulate muskrat lodges, and anchored over shallow marsh waters. The swans accepted these devices as nesting sites, but their construction was discontinued when the muskrat population again became sufficient to ensure a plentiful supply of natural sites.

Coyotes were very abundant on Refuge ranges for over a decade following establishment of this wildlife area. Since they were then believed to be one of the few natural limiting factors of the swan population, control by hunting, trapping, and poisoning was actively employed. In the fall of 1947, coyotes were brought under control on ranges surrounding the Refuge by the Branch of Predator and Rodent Control. Since their methods have proved very effective in suppressing the local coyote populations, no predator control measures have had to be carried out within the Refuge during the past 10 years. Subsequently, studies and observations have cast considerable doubt on the importance of the coyote as a factor limiting the trumpeter population.

Winter feeding of small grain to trumpeters was begun on the Refuge during the 1936–37 season and has been carried out every year since that time. This program began with a seasonal consumption of about 100 bushels by the swans and other waterfowl which frequented Culver's Pond, an artificial impoundment located at the east end of the Refuge and known colloquially as the Widow's Pool. Here 41° F. water gushing from the dual Picnic Springs keeps a few acres of shallow water open during even the coldest winter weather. The grain which is placed out for the swans in this shallow pond serves as a valuable supplement to natural foods, which are customarily greatly reduced by the swans and the seasonal waterfowl migrants even before winter sets in.

During recent years, with the increasing swan population, this amount has been increased to about 750 bushels. This is fed each season on a semiweekly schedule, with wheat and barley proving equally satisfactory. While seasonal feeding of wildlife is a questionable management practice under ordinary circumstances, it is felt that in this case it is necessary to carry the increasing numbers of the rare trumpeters safely through their most difficult season when natural food supplies are normally either greatly depleted or entirely exhausted. Otherwise, especially during severe winters, starvation would probably occur to some extent or the movement of swans to other areas outside Federal sanctuaries would result.

Present plans call for expanding the feeding program to include the recently created MacDonald Pond. While less water acreage is impounded here, the originating Elk Spring water is warmer (59° F.) and creates a larger open-water area during the winter. With the winter feeding areas at Culver and MacDonald Ponds in operation it is hoped that more swans can be held on the Refuge during the winter months, and thus reduce to some extent their dependence on waters outside federally protected areas during their critical season.

TRANSPLANTING PROGRAM

In view of the progress made in the swan restoration program by 1938 it was decided that the breeding range of the trumpeter should be extended. Accordingly, 4 cygnets were transferred from the Red Rock Lakes Refuge to the National Elk Refuge near Jackson, Wyoming. The following year this transplanting program was enlarged to include the vast marshes of the Malheur National Wildlife Refuge in southeastern Oregon. A decade later, in 1949, the high and isolated mountain valley marshes of the Ruby Lake National Wildlife Refuge in northeastern Nevada were included in the plan.

Table 14 documents the transfers of trumpeters from the Red Rock Lakes Refuge to the various areas selected for their introduction from 1938 through 1957. Twelve of the cygnets which were originally sent from the Red Rock Lakes Refuge to Malheur were retransferred to Ruby Lake in 1947. Thus the Ruby Lake Refuge has actually received a total of 12 more swans, and Malheur 12 less, than table 14 indicates.

Of the many introductions which were thus made over a period of 20 years, only the initial group transferred to the National Elk Refuge has bred successfully to date except for the hypothetical record at Ruby Lake cited previously.[1] Almer P. Nelson, formerly Refuge Manager at the Elk Refuge, sums up the history of these introductions on that area as follows (correspondence) :

---

[1] In 1958, a pair of trumpeters at Malheur and another at Ruby Lake Refuge nested successfully, bringing off 2 and 6 cygnets respectively.

FIGURE 52.—The U. S. Fish and Wildlife Service "snowplane" en route to the Culver Pond swan wintering grounds for semiweekly feeding of small grain. The Centennial Mountains in background form the Continental Divide along their 10,000-foot crest.

On October 24, 1938, four cygnets were transferred and liberated on this refuge. Following liberation, three of the birds were always seen together while the fourth did not associate with the other three, and in early December the lone cygnet disappeared from the area and was not seen again, while the other three remained.

On October 1, 1939, three additional cygnets were transferred in. These remained until the Flat Creek and marsh lands began to freeze in late November or early December when they also left the area and were not seen again.

On September 23, 1941, three more cygnets were transferred to the Elk Refuge. When these three birds were liberated, we clipped their wing tips and they were seen frequently on the area until late spring, when they too came up missing.

From then until 1944, the only swans seen on the area were the three adults that were transferred in 1938. In the case of these three they frequently left the refuge during the winter months and were known to be away for as long as two months. During their absence, they were at various times reported along the Snake River within the valley [Jackson Hole]. The three birds always returned to the refuge when the ice in the creek channel began to clear every spring and remained throughout the summer season. When these birds were 2 or 3 years old, two were frequently seen together while the third remained to itself. In 1944 the pair nested in the Flat Creek marsh.

Since 1944, nesting has occurred nearly every year on the Elk Refuge, with two nests established during the seasons of 1948, 1954, and 1955. The history of the Elk Refuge breedings follows in table 15.

Since clutch size, hatchability, and early cygnet mortality of the Elk Refuge breeders are largely unknown, an accurate comparison of these factors with similar data from the Red Rock Lakes area is not possible. What little data is available indicates that losses in both

Table 14.—Trumpeter swans transferred from the Red Rock Lakes Refuge, 1938 to 1957

Recipient area	Number	
	Cygnets	Adults
Elk Refuge:		
Oct. 24, 1938	4	
Oct. 1, 1939	3	
Sept. 23, 1941	3	
Total	10	
Malheur Refuge:		
Oct. 16, 1939	3	
Sept. 19, 1941	6	1
Sept. 4, 1944	20	
Sept. 4, 1945	22	
Sept. 12, 1948	19	
July 14, 1954	7	6 (3 pairs).
		1 (nonbreeder).
Sept. 27, 1955	17	
Aug. 11, 1956		11 (nonbreeders).
Sept. 25, 1957	20	
Total	114	19
Ruby Lake:		
Sept. 12, 1949	10	
July 28, 1954	1	6 (3 pairs).
Sept. 26, 1955	16	
Oct. 10, 1956	12	
Aug. 2, 1957		19 (nonbreeders).
Total	39	25
Delta Station:		
Aug. 7, 1956	3	3 (nonbreeders).
Total transferred	166	47

Table 15.—Trumpeter swan nesting data, National Elk Refuge, Wyoming, 1944 to 1957

Year	Pairs nested	Cygnets initially observed	Cygnets raised to flying age	Year	Pairs nested	Cygnets initially observed	Cygnets raised to flying age
1944	1	2	1	1952	1	3	3
1945	1	4	3	1953	1	2	2
1946	(1)	0	0	1954	2	2, 2	2, 1
1947	(1)	0	0	1955	2	3, 3	3, 3
1948	2	3, 5	1, 3	1956	(1)	0	0
1949	1	1	0	1957	1	1	0
1950	1	3	3				
1951	1	0	0	Total	14	34	25

[1] No nests observed.

the egg and preflight stages of existence are as serious as those observed in the Red Rock Lakes population.

The Malheur Refuge has received a total of 133 trumpeters transferred from the Red Rock Lakes Refuge during the period 1939–57. A variety of methods have been tried at Malheur during this period to establish a wild breeding population of these birds, but this goal has not yet been achieved. The chief factors contributing to failure in the early transplanting efforts were the practices of pinioning and confining the flock to a single large pool, where intra-specific strife and spatial competition not only created a situation which was unfavorable for breeding but led to significant losses from accidents and disease. Initial efforts to establish a breeding swan population by liberating the transplanted individuals directly into the marsh proper failed due to the dispersion and disappearance of the liberated birds.

As far as the Ruby Lake Refuge effort is concerned, with the exception of the hypothetical single breeding record noted near the Ruby Lake Refuge in 1953, the efforts to establish a wild breeding population of trumpeters at that location have been unsuccessful for many of the same reasons affecting the Malheur transplants.

In addition to the transplants involving only birds-of-the-year, a single attempt to achieve the desired goal at Ruby Lake and Malheur by transferring known breeding pairs from the Red Rock Lakes Refuge was attempted in 1954 when 3 pairs of mated trumpeters and their offspring were liberated in each marsh area. The adults apparently remained with their broods at their new locations for a time after regaining their flight feathers, but disappeared later. Perhaps these adults departed with their cygnets during the fall migration along with the whistling swans which pass through these areas during the autumn in considerable numbers. At any rate their fate remains unknown.

In 1957 a new transplanting program involving both the Ruby Lake and Malheur Refuges was begun. Specifically designed to avoid many of the shortcomings of the earlier attempts, the revised procedure employs a relatively short-term swan decoy flock, thereby minimizing the bad effects of the long periods of confinement for the entire group. This will be employed in connection with banding and dyeing techniques used on the liberated birds in order to trace dispersion.

In 1955, 6 trumpeters were transferred from the Red Rock Lakes Refuge to the Delta Waterfowl Research Station, Delta, Manitoba, Canada. These birds, 3 adults and 3 cygnets, supplemented the small group of Canadian trumpeters already at Delta and were transferred

Table 16.—Swans banded at the Red Rock Lakes Refuge, 1945 to 1957

Year	Number	Age class	Location released
1945	20	Cygnets	Red Rock Lakes Refuge.
1948	5	Cygnets	Red Rock Lakes Refuge.
1949	10	Cygnets	Red Rock Lakes Refuge.
	10	Cygnets	Ruby Lake Refuge.
	10	Non-breeders [1]	Red Rock Lakes Refuge.
1950	3	Non-breeders [1]	Red Rock Lakes Refuge.
	21	Cygnets	Red Rock Lakes Refuge.
1951	9	Cygnets	Red Rock Lakes Refuge.
1952	17	Non-breeders [1]	Red Rock Lakes Refuge.
1953	9	Non-breeders [1]	Red Rock Lakes Refuge.
1955	17	Cygnets	Malheur Refuge.
	16	Cygnets	Ruby Lake Refuge.
	9	Adults	Red Rock Lakes Refuge.
1956	10	Cygnets	Red Rock Lakes Refuge.
	5	Immatures	Red Rock Lakes Refuge.
	89	Adults	Red Rock Lakes Refuge.
	10	Adults	Malheur Refuge.
	1	Immature	Malheur Refuge.
	12	Cygnets	Ruby Lake Refuge.
1957	19	Non-breeders [1]	Ruby Lake Refuge.
	20	Cygnets	Malheur Refuge.
	2	Non-breeders [1]	National Zoological Park.
	45	Non-breeders [1]	Red Rock Lakes Refuge.
Total	369		

[1] Includes both adult and immature age-classes.

with the hope that breeding pairs could be established there, with methods which could eventually be applied to pertinent United States refuge areas. To date the transferred adults have not bred at Delta, though pairing has taken place. The cygnets transferred there are, of course, not yet sexually mature.

In 1957 a male and a female trumpeter from the Refuge's non-breeding flock were transferred to the National Zoological Park in Washington, D. C., for exhibition and research purposes.

BANDING

From 1945 to 1957, 261 swans of various age classes have been banded and released on the Red Rock Lakes Refuge alone. This was done to provide facts relating to local movement or longer migration, causes of mortality, longevity, etc. In addition, 107 swans banded at Red Rock Lakes have been released elsewhere, 48 on the Malheur and 57 on the Ruby Lake Refuges and the 2 transferred to the National Zoological Park. This information is shown in table 16.

A total of 369 swans have thus been banded and released. Only 16 recoveries have been reported as of February 14, 1957, 13 of these within the general Red Rock Lakes region, 2 on the Malheur Refuge, and 1 in the Ruby Lake marsh. There are no recoveries to reveal movement or migration outside their traditional known range or, in the case of the transferred individuals, outside the general area in which they were introduced.

A breakdown of the causes of death among the 16 recoveries shows that shooting was responsible in 5 instances. In the remaining 11 cases, information is not available, though it is probable that illegal shooting played a significant role here also.

A period of less than 2 years existed between the date of banding and that of band recovery in 10 of the 11 cases where pertinent recovery information was available. In the remaining example, a duration of slightly over 3 years occurred between banding and recovery dates.

In swan-banding operations on the Refuge, 27 returns of banded birds have been noted. The earliest return occurred when a fall-banded cygnet was captured again for banding in its initial post-juvenile molt the following summer, a period of 11 months. The maximum return period thus far was that of a male banded as a cygnet in the late summer of 1949 and recaptured in July 1957, a period of 7 years 11 months.

The standard U. S. F. W. S. size 9 aluminum bird band, the largest made, was first used in all Refuge trumpeter-swan banding operations, until it was discovered that this size was somewhat too small, and also that a significant proportion of banded captive trumpeters at the Malheur Refuge lost these aluminum bracelets from year to year. To avoid this difficulty a locking-type stainless-steel band was developed and placed in use in 1955. This steel lock-type band, carrying hand-stamped identification data, has been used exclusively since that time, except for 12 cygnets transferred to Ruby Lake in 1956 which were banded with standard aluminum bands when the supply of steel bands was temporarily exhausted.

A trumpeter-swan banding project has also been carried out by the Canadian Wildlife Service for a number of years, using the standard aluminum bands as well as colored plastic bands for sight record purposes. Except for those specific cases previously mentioned, the results of this work are not yet available.

MANAGEMENT RECOMMENDATIONS

As has been shown, the trumpeter-swan population in the United States has increased manyfold during the past 30 years and is apparently now being maintained near the highest level which its year-round environment will support. For all practical considerations it has been saved from any immediate threat of extinction in this country; hence the prime goal is to preserve the existing habitat necessary to hold the substantial population gains made in recent years and to increase their range by transplanting to new localities.

469660 O—60——13

FIGURE 53.—These trumpeters are only part of the flock of over 200 which pass the late winter months on the Refuge awaiting the spring breakup. The 94 trumpeters visible in this single photograph are more than existed in the entire United States 25 years ago.

Since by far the greatest proportion of breeding pairs is found within either the Red Rock Lakes Refuge or the National Parks of the area (Yellowstone and Grand Teton), the maintenance of the quality of the habitat should not require attention beyond that now being given. Little need is seen at present to develop the main swan breeding habitat already included within these Federal sanctuaries. Emphasis should rather be laid on preserving and maintaining a seasonally balanced habitat for all age classes.

The Red Rock Lakes Refuge marshes exist in practically a wilderness state, and as such, may be regarded as almost ideal breeding habitat. While a number of artificial nesting islands might be constructed on the open expanse of Upper Red Rock Lake, their occupation and defense by territorial nesting pairs would necessarily limit the use of these waters by large numbers of nonbreeders. Saving a

part of the limited federally protected habitat for the flocked, non-breeding segment of the population is important since the only other suitable waters are artificial impoundments subject to drawdown with the usual unfavorable results. Moreover, the mere accommodation of a few additional pairs of breeders on the Refuge probably would not increase the cygnet production if the experience to date has provided a true index.

If not filled in by sediments brought down by streams as a result of poor watershed practices, the Red Rock Lakes marsh system should continue to exist in virtually its present form for many years. Even if the threat of siltation becomes acute, the habitat could be saved by constructing a series of artificial pools within the Refuge along the main tributary streams. These could serve as silt-traps, and thus prevent the excessive deposition of alluvium in the already shallow lake beds.

Winter feeding of small grain on the Red Rock Lakes Refuge should be continued to the fullest extent practicable. In addition, the possibilities of initiating winter feeding wherever concentrations of the trumpeters exist during this season should be studied. Since artificial feeding during the winter apparently meets only a portion of the trumpeters' dietary requirements, ways of increasing the production or availability of the natural aquatic plants should be explored. This is especially applicable to the Island Park area in Fremont County, Idaho. In this region a comparatively few miles of the streambed along Henrys Fork of the Snake River and its tributaries form the most important single wintering grounds for this species on the continent. Winter use is especially concentrated on and in the vicinity of the Railroad Ranch.

Acquisition and management of an adequate portion of the swan wintering habitat along Henrys Fork and its tributaries would prevent development and hunting pressure which might adversely affect the trumpeters during their season of greatest vulnerability. Whether or not this is accomplished, special wildlife easements or regulations affecting these lands would assure additional protection and food for this rare species. A state wildlife sanctuary already exists on a portion of the Railroad Ranch wintering grounds. Specific recommendations should result from additional study of this problem in the field.

Investigations into various phases of the life history of the trumpeter should be continued both on the Red Rock Lakes Refuge and in Yellowstone Park, in fact wherever the time of qualified personnel and opportunity exist. Priority in these studies should be placed on the following subjects: banding for the purpose of revealing trumpeter distribution and mortality; causes of the low hatchability of trumpeter eggs; factors contributing to the high mortality of cygnets before flight age is reached; and relation between the density of trumpeters on the breeding grounds and production. Investigations of specific characteristics of trumpeters held in captivity might also be profitably given attention: territorialism, space requirements, breeding, and dietary considerations.

Outside their present Rocky Mountain environment, the emphasis should be placed on transplanting. In addition to introductions now being carried out at the Ruby Lake and Malheur Refuges, further efforts to establish a wild population should be extended to suitable areas within the former known breeding range of this species. Habitat in the Flathead Valley of Montana, the Minnesota-Iowa region, the Dakotas, and northwestern Nebraska may have areas suitable for future plantings.

Owing to the vulnerability of trumpeters to shooting, possibly the most important single requirement in transplanting, outside of favor-

FIGURE 54.—Trumpeters feed in Culver Pond with mallards, Barrows goldeneyes and common goldeneyes on grain placed out by Refuge personnel.

able habitat factors, is provision for sufficiently protected wintering waters, preferably in close proximity to managed breeding grounds. It is difficult to see how a wild population of these slow-maturing, conspicuous, low-flying birds could ever become established and thrive if they were compelled by the freezing of their breeding grounds to run the waterfowl hunter gauntlet each fall in moving to far distant wintering grounds.

The problems of successfully transplanting the trumpeter do not appear to be beyond solution if similar experience with the mute swan is comparable. In addition to the success of this exotic species in acclimating itself in both England and Denmark as a feral resident, during the past half century the mute swan has become firmly established in the thickly populated lower Hudson River Valley and vicinity. The mute has become established in Michigan, with a population wintering in Grand Traverse Bay and reportedly breeding on waters near East Jordan (correspondence). The numbers of these birds have increased steadily, about as follows: 1948 or 1949, 2; 1950, 5; 1951, 8; 1952, 11; 1953, 13; 1954, 17; 1955, 24; 1956, 41.

While the trumpeter usually lays a smaller clutch of eggs than the mute swan, and may be more vulnerable to shooting as well, there is no obvious reason why it should not respond to a sound program of transplanting and management if hunting losses can be eliminated or reduced to a low level.

As the trumpeter population becomes more widely distributed, the possibility of hybridization with the mute swan may become a threat. With feral mute swans spreading to new areas, and with the tendency for swan hybrids to be fertile, some interbreeding between the two species is possible. This could be serious when the small total population of trumpeters is considered. Such a possibility must be guarded against and controls be undertaken when and where the swan breeding populations begin to overlap.

Because of its rarity, beauty, and other intrinsic qualities, the trumpeter is greatly sought for display and breeding purposes, both by public and private institutions and individuals. A few are being kept in captivity for display and observation purposes, though at their present level of abundance none can be provided to aviculturists specifically for breeding purposes, nor would their release to breeders generally be in keeping with the responsibilities of the U. S. Fish and Wildlife Service as set forth in domestic regulations and international migratory bird treaty agreements. It is the objective of the Bureau to maintain the wild population of these rare fowl at an optimum level—the greatest number which can be consistently supported in their natural environment. Any swans which may be surplus to this responsibility should be included in the program to establish other wild breeding flocks, or loaned to qualified public zoological parks for display and breeding purposes. With continued diligent management and protection, the transplanting program should assure the continued growth in numbers and expansion of the range of the trumpeter swan in this country.

BIBLIOGRAPHY

Adams, Edward.
    1878. Notes on the birds of Michalaski, Norton Sound (Alaska). Ibis, vol. 2, No. 8, Fourth Series.

Allen, J. A.
    1878. A list of the birds of Massachusetts, with annotations. Bulletin of the Essex Institute, vol. 10. Salem, Mass.

American Ornithologists' Union.
    1957. Checklist of North American birds. Fifth Edition. Prepared by a committee of the A. O. U. 691 pp.

Anderson, R. M.
    1907. The birds of Iowa. Proceedings of the Davenport Academy of Science, Davenport, Iowa.

Armstrong, E. A.
    1947. Bird display and behavior. Oxford University Press, New York. 431 pp.

Audubon, John J.
    1838. Ornithological biography, vol. 4. Adam and Black, Edinburgh. 618 pp.

Bailey, Florence Merriam.
    1918. Wild animals of Glacier National Park; The birds. National Park Service, Washington.

Bailey, Vernon.
    1930. Animal life of Yellowstone National Park. C. C. Thomas, Springfield, Illinois. 241 pp.

Baird, Spencer F., Thomas M. Brewer, and Robert Ridgway.
    1884. The water birds of North America. Memoirs of the Museum of Comparative Zoology at Harvard College, vol. 12. Little, Brown and Co., Boston. 537 pp.

Baker, Frank C.
    1941. A study in ethnozoology of the prehistoric Indians of Illinois. Transactions American Philosophical Society, vol. 32, part 2.

Barnston, George.
    1862. Recollections of the swans and geese of Hudson's Bay. Zoologist, vol. 20.

Bates, J. M.
    1900. Additional notes and observations on the birds of northern Nebraska. Proceedings of the Nebraska Ornithologists' Union, First Annual Meeting 1899. (Published 1900.)

Beal, S. M.
    1949. Four cygnets disappear. Yellowstone Nature Notes, vol. 23, No. 1.

Beard, Daniel B., et al.
    1947. Fading trails, the story of endangered American wildlife. Macmillan. 279 pp.

Beebe, C. William.
    1906. The swans. Report of the New York Zoological Society, No. 10.

Belknap, Jeremy.
    1784. History of New Hampshire. 3 vols. Philadelphia; also 1791–92, Boston.

Bent, Arthur Cleveland.
  1925. Life histories of North American wild fowl (Order Anseres). U. S.
    National Museum Bulletin 130, vol. 2. 316 pp. Reprinted by Dover Pub-
    lications, 1951.
Blaauw, F. E.
  1904. On the breeding of some of the waterfowl at Gooilust in the year 1903.
    Ibis, vol. 4, No. 13. Eighth Series.
Blines, Jasper.
  1888. Letter to editor. Forest and Stream, vol. 31, No. 22.
Brooks, Allan.
  1926. The present status of the trumpeter swan. Condor, vol. 28, No. 3.
Brooks, Allan, and H. S. Swarth.
  1925. A distributional list of the birds of British Columbia. Contribution
    No. 423, Museum of Vertebrate Zoology, University of California. Cooper
    Ornithological Club, Pacific Coast Avifauna No. 17.
Brower, J. V.
  1897. The Missouri River and its utmost source. Pioneer Press, St. Paul,
    Minnesota.
Burnett, W. L.
  1916. Two trumpeter swan records for Colorado. Auk, vol. 33, No. 2.
Butler, A. W.
  1897. The birds of Indiana. 22d annual report, Indiana Department of
    Geology and Natural Resources. (W. S. Blatchley.)
Chaddock, T. T.
  1938. Laboratory report on whistler swan. Wisconsin Conservation Bulle-
    tin, vol. 3, No. 9.
Christian, J. J.
  1957. A review of the endocrine responses in rats and mice to increasing
    population size including delayed effects on offspring. Naval Medical
    Research Institute Lecture and Review Series No. 57-2.
Coale, H. K.
  1915. The present status of the trumpeter swan (*Olor buccinator*). Auk,
    vol. 32, No. 1.
Colwell, Gwen.
  1948. Trumpeters pay royal visit. Vancouver Province (magazine section)
    July 24, 1948. Vancouver, British Columbia.
Condon, David de Lancey.
  1950. An uncanny record in the snow. Yellowstone Nature Notes, vol. 24,
    No. 1.
Cooke, Wells W.
  1887. Bird migration in the Mississippi Valley in 1884 and 1885. Division
    of Economic Ornithology and Mammalogy, U. S. Department of Agri-
    culture, Bulletin No. 2.
Cooper, J. G.
  1869. The fauna of Montana Territory. The American Naturalist, vol. 3.
Coues, Elliott.
  1874. Birds of the northwest. Department of the Interior, U. S. Geological
    Survey of the Territories, Miscellaneous Publication 3. 791 pp.
  1893. The history of the expedition under the command of Lewis and
    Clark. Francis P. Harper. 4 vols.

Cowan, Ian McTaggert.
    1946. Death of a trumpeter swan from multiple parasitism. Auk, vol. 63, No. 2.

Dall, W. H., and H. M. Bannister.
    1869. List of the birds of Alaska, with biographical notes. Transactions of the Chicago Academy of Science, art. 9.

Day, Albert M.
    1949. North American waterfowl. Stackpole and Heck, Inc. 329 pp.

Delacour, Jean.
    1944. Government refuges are saving the trumpeter swan. Animal Kingdom, bulletin New York Zoological Society, vol. 47, No. 6.
    1954. The waterfowl of the world, vol. I. Country Life Limited, London, England. 284 pp.

Delacour, Jean, and Ernst Mayr.
    1945. The family Anatidae. Wilson Bulletin, vol. 57, No. 1.

Dementiev, Georges P., and N. A. Gladkov.
    1952. Die vogel der Sowjetunion, vol. 4. Moscow.

Derscheid, J. M.
    1939. The preservation of waterfowl and aviculture. Avicultural Magazine, vol. 4, No. 3.

Dewar, J. M.
    1936. Ménage à trois in the mute swan. British Birds, vol. 30, No. 6.

Dixon, Joseph.
    1931. Save the trumpeter swan. American Forests, vol. 37, No. 8.

Eklund, Carl R.
    1946. Mortality notes on the trumpeter swan. Auk, vol. 63, No. 1.

Ellis, John.
    1936. Ménage à trois in the mute swan (letter to the editors). British Birds, vol. 30, No. 7.

Errington, Paul L.
    1945. Some contributions of a fifteen-year local study of the northern bobwhite to a knowledge of population phenomena. Ecological Monographs, vol. 15, No. 1.

Evans, A. H.
    1903. Turner on birds. Cambridge University Press.

Featherstonhaugh, Duane.
    1948. Return of the trumpeter. Natural History, vol. 57, No. 8.

Fisher, James, and Peter Scott.
    1953. A thousand geese. London (Houghton Mifflin, Boston, 1954:)

Forbush, Edward Howe.
    1912. A history of the game birds, wild fowl, and shore birds of Massachusetts and adjacent States. Massachusetts State Board of Agriculture. 622 pp.
    1929. Birds of Massachusetts and other New England States. Part 1. Water birds, marsh birds and shore birds. Massachusetts Department of Agriculture. 3 vols.

Force's Historical Tract, vol. 2, tract 5.

Friedmann, Herbert.
    1935. Birds of Kodiak Island. Bulletin Chicago Academy of Science, vol. 5, No. 3.

Gabrielson, Ira N.
    1946. Trumpeter swans in Alaska. Auk, vol. 63, No. 1.

Gabrielson, Ira N., and S. G. Jewett.
    1940. Birds of Orégon. Oregon State College. 650 pp.
Grundtvig, F. L.
    1895. On the birds of Shiocton in Bovina, Outagamie County, Wisconsin,
        1881–83. Transactions of the Wisconsin Academy of Science, Arts, and
        Letters, vol. 9.
Haecker, F. W., R. A. Moser, and J. B. Swenk.
    1945. Check-list of the birds of Nebraska. Nebraska Ornithologists' Union,
        Nebraska Bird Review, vol. 13, No. 1.
Hart, R. O.
    1952. Trumpeter swan versus muskrat at Oxbow Lake. Yellowstone Nature
        Notes, vol. 26, No. 5.
Hearne, Samuel.
    1795. A journey from Prince of Wales Fort in Hudson's Bay to the North-
        ern Ocean, London. (Reprinted in The Publications of the Champlain
        Society, Toronto, Canada, 1911.)
Heerman, A. L.
    1859. Report upon birds collected on the survey. Pacific Railroad Survey
        Report, vol. 10. U. S. House of Representatives, 33d Congress, 2d Session,
        Ex. Doc. 91.
Heinroth, Oskar, and Magdalena Heinroth.
    1911. Beitrage zur Biologie, namenthlich Ethologie und Psychologie der
        Anatiden. Proceedings of the 5th International Ornithological Congress,
        Berlin.
    1928. Die Vogel Mitteleuropas, vol. 3. Hugo Bermühler, Berlin-
        Lichterfelde.
Hellmayr, Charles E., and Boardman Conover.
    1948. Catalogue of birds of the American Zoological Series, Field Museum
        of Natural History, vol. 13, part I, No. 2, Publication 615. 434 pp.
Hilden, O., and P. Linkola.
    1955. Suuri lintukirja (The big bird book), Helsinki. 750 pp.
Hilprecht, Alfred.
    1956. Hockerschwan, Singschwan, Zwergschwan. A. Ziemsen Verlag,
        Wittenberg Lutherstadt. 151 pp.
Hochbaum, H. Albert.
    1944. The canvasback on a prairie marsh. American Wildlife Institute.
        201 pp.
    1955. Travels and traditions of waterfowl. University of Minnesota.
        301 pp.
Holman, John P.
    1933. Sheep and bear trails. Frank Walters. 211 p.
    1950. Concentration of trumpeter swans, *Cygnus buccinator*, in British
        Columbia in winter. Auk, vol. 67, No. 3.
Hornaday, William T.
    1913. Our vanishing wildlife, its extermination and preservation. New
        York Zoological Society. 411 pp.
Howard, L. O., and W. F. Fiske.
    1911. The importation into the United States of the parasites of the gypsy
        moth and the brown-tail moth. U. S. Department of Agriculture En-
        tomology Bulletin, No. 91.
Hughes, J. C.
    1883. Letter to the editor, Forest and Stream, vol. 20, May 10.

Hull, A. V.
1939. Trumpeter swans, their management and preservation. Transactions of the Fourth North American Wildlife Conference, American Wildlife Institute.

James, Edwin.
1823. Account of an expedition from Pittsburgh to the Rocky Mountains, vol. 1. Philadelphia.

Jewett, S. G., W. P. Taylor, W. T. Shaw, and John W. Aldrich.
1953. Birds of Washington State. University of Washington Press. 767 pp.

Keating, William H.
1825. Narrative of an expedition to the sources of the St. Peter's River, Lake Winnepeek, Lake of the Woods, &c., performed in the year 1823, vol. 1. Geo. B. Whittaker, London.

Kluijver, H. N.
1951. The population ecology of the great tit, Parus m. major L. Ardea, vol. 39, Nos. 1–3.

Knight, W. C.
1902. The birds of Wyoming. Bulletin No. 55, Wyoming Experiment Station, University of Wyoming.

Kortright, F. H.
1943. The ducks, geese, and swans of North America. Wildlife Management Institute. 476 pp.

Kumlien, Ludwig, and N. Hollister.
1903. The birds of Wisconsin. Bulletin of the Wisconsin Natural History Society, Nos. 1, 2, and 3.

Lack, David.
1954. The natural regulation of animal numbers. Oxford University Press. 343 pp.

Lattin, Frank H.
1892. The Standard Catalogue of North American Birds Eggs. Third edition. Albion, New York. 53 pp.

Lawson, John.
1714. History of North Carolina. Reprinted by Observer Printing House, Charlotte, N. C., 1903. 171 pp.

Lister, R.
1951. Trumpeter swans breeding in the Cypress Hills of Alberta. Canadian Field Naturalist, vol. 65, No. 4.

Lorenz, Konrad.
1937. The companion in the bird's world. Auk, vol. 54, No. 3.

Low, G. C.
1935. (Edited paper by Marquess of Tavistock) The extent to which captivity modifies the habits of birds. Bulletin of the British Ornithologists Club, vol. 55, session 1934–35.

MacFarlane, Roderick.
1891. Notes on and list of birds and eggs collected in arctic America, 1861–66. Proceedings of the U. S. National Museum, vol. 14.
1905. Notes on mammals collected and observed in the northern Mackenzie River district, northwest territories of Canada, with remarks on explorers and explorations of the far north. Proceedings of the U. S. National Museum, vol. 28.

Mackay, R. H.
    1954. Trapping of the Queen's trumpeter swans in British Columbia. Sixth Annual Report of the Wildfowl Trust, 1952–53. London.
    1957. Movements of trumpeter swans shown by band returns and observations. Condor, vol. 59, No. 5.

Madsen, H.
    1945. On the different position of the legs of birds during flight and in cold weather. Dansk Ornithologisk Forenings Tidsskrift, vol. 39.

Mair, Charles, and Roderick MacFarlane.
    1908. Through the Mackenzie Basin (including notes on the mammals and birds of northern Canada). William Briggs, Toronto. 494 pp.

McDermott, John F.
    1942. Audubon's journey up the Mississippi. Journal of the Illinois State Historical Society, vol. 35, No. 2.

McLean, Donald D.
    1937. Some additional records of birds for northeastern California. Condor, vol. 39, No. 5.

Merriam, C. Hart.
    1877. A review of the birds of Connecticut, with remarks on their habits. Transactions of the Connecticut Academy of Arts and Sciences, vol. 4, part 1.
    1891. Birds of Idaho. North America Fauna No. 5, U. S. Biological Survey.

Merrill, D. E.
    1932. Trumpeter swan in New Mexico. Auk, vol. 54, No. 4.

Monson, Melvin A.
    1956. Nesting of trumpeter swan in the lower Copper River Basin, Alaska. Condor, vol. 58, No. 6.

Mosher, A. D.
    1882. The fauna of Spirit Lake. Forest and Stream, vol. 18, February 23.

Munro, J. A.
    1949. Conservation of the trumpeter swan in Canada. Proceedings of the 7th Pacific Science Congress, vol. 4.

Munro, J. A., and I. McT. Cowan.
    1947. A review of the bird fauna of British Columbia. British Columbia Provincial Museum, Department of Education. 285 pp.

Murie, Adolph.
    1940. Ecology of the coyote in the Yellowstone. Fauna of the National Parks of the United States, No. 4. National Park Service, U. S. Department of the Interior.

Nelson, E. W.
    1884. The arrow-head in the swan. Forest and Stream, vol. 22, May 8.
    1887. Report upon natural history collections made in Alaska between the years 1877 and 1881. Arctic series of publications issued in connection with the Signal Service, U. S. Army.

Newberry, J. S.
    1857. Report on the zoology of the route. Pacific Railroad Survey Report 1853–56, vol. 6. U. S. House of Representatives, 33d Cong., 2d Sess., Ex. Doc. 91.

Nice, Margaret Morse.
    1941. The role of territory in bird life. American Midland Naturalist, vol. 26, No. 3.

Nicholson, A. J.
   1933. The balance of animal populations. Journal of Animal Ecology, Vol. 2, No. 1.
Nute, Grace Lee.
   1945. Calendar of the American Fur Company's papers. Annual Report of the American Historical Association for the Year 1944. 3 vols.
Nuttall, Thomas.
   1834. A manual of the ornithology of the United States and Canada. Boston. 683 pp.
Orton, Alda.
   1951. Long necks. The Alaska Sportsman, vol. 17, No. 9.
Over, William H., and Craig S. Thoms.
   1920. Birds of South Dakota. Bulletin of the University of South Dakota, series 21, No. 9.
Paludan, Knud, and Jørgen Fog.
   1956. The Danish breeding population of wild living Cygnus olor in 1954. Danske Vildtundersøgelser, vol. 5.
Parmalee, Paul W.
   1958. Remains of rare and extinct birds from Illinois Indian sites. Auk, vol. 75, No. 2.
Patrick, R. W.
   1935. Mute swans attacking bullock. British Birds, vol. 29, No. 4.
Pilder, Hans.
   1914. Russisch-Amerikanische Handels-Companie bis 1825. Berlin. 174 pp. (Arctic Bibliography No. 25091.)
Poulsen, H.
   1949. Bidrag til Svanernes Ethologi. (Contribution to the Ethology of the Swans, English Summary.) Dansk Ornithologisk Forenings Tidsskrift, vol. 42, No. 4.
Roberts, Thomas S.
   1936. The birds of Minnesota. University of Minnesota Press. 2 vols.
Salter, R. J.
   1954. The trumpeter swan in Idaho. Proceedings Western Association Fish and Game Commissioners.
Saunders, Aretas A.
   1921. A distributional list of the birds of Montana. Pacific Coast Avifauna No. 14, Cooper Ornithological Club.
Scott, Peter, and James Fisher.
   1953. A thousand geese. London. (Houghton Mifflin, Boston, 1954.)
Sharp, Ward M.
   1951. Observations on predator-prey relations between wild ducks, trumpeter swans, and golden eagles. Journal of Wildlife Management, vol. 15, No. 2.
Sibley, Charles G.
   1938. Hybrids of and with North American Anatidae. 9th International Ornithological Congress, Rouen.
Silloway, P. M.
   1903. Birds of Fergus County, Montana. Bulletin No. 1, Fergus County Free High School, Lewistown. 77 pp.
Simon, James R.
   1952. First flight of trumpeter swans. Auk, vol. 69, No. 4.

Skinner, Milton P.
    1920. Trumpeter swan breeding in Yellowstone Park. Condor, vol. 22, No. 2.
    1925. The birds of Yellowstone National Park. Roosevelt Wildlife Bulletin. New York State College of Forestry at Syracuse University. Vol. 3, No. 1.
    1928. Yellowstone's winter birds. Condor, vol. 30, No. 4.
Smith, H. S.
    1935. The role of biotic factors in the determination of population densities. Journal of Economic Entomology, vol. 28, No. 6.
Smith, Stuart G., and Eric Hosking.
    1955. Birds fighting. Experimental studies of the aggressive displays of some birds. Faber and Faber, London. 125 pp.
Soper, J. D.
    1949. Birds observed in the Grande Prairie-Peace River Region of northwestern Alberta, Canada. Auk, vol. 66, No. 3.
Stejneger, Leonhard.
    1882. Outlines of a monograph of the Cygninae. Proceedings of the U. S. National Museum, vol. 5.
Stewart, Robert E., and Joseph H. Manning.
    1958. Distribution and ecology of whistling swans in the Chesapeake Bay region. Auk, vol. 75, No. 2.
Stowe, L.
    1957. The amazing Crusoes of Lonesome Lake. Reader's Digest, February.
Suckley, George.
    1859. Water birds. Pacific Railroad Survey Report, 1853–55. Vol. 12. U. S. House of Representatives, 36th Congress, 1st Session, Ex. Doc. 56.
Swainson, William, and John Richardson.
    1832. Fauna Boreali-Americana. Part 2, The Birds. London.
Swann, H. Kirke.
    1913. A dictionary of English and folknames of British birds. Witherby and Co., London. 266 pp.
Thompson, Ben H.
    1936. The problem of vanishing species—the trumpeter swan. Proceedings of the North American Wildlife Conference. Report of the Special Committee on Conservation of Wildlife Resources, 74th Congress, 2d Session, G. P. O. 675 pp.
Thwaites, R. G.
    1906. Early western travels (1748–1846). Arthur Clark Co., Cleveland. Vols. 21, 27, 29. (32 vols.)
Ticehurst, N. F.
    1921. A contribution to swan history. British Birds, vol 14, No. 8.
    1924. The early history of the mute swan in England. British Birds, vol. 18, No. 8.
    1926. An historical review of the laws, orders and customs anciently used for the preservation of swans in England. British Birds, vol. 19, No. 8.
    1926. On swan marks. British Birds, vol. 19, No. 11.
    1928. The office of Master of Swans. British Birds, vol. 22, No. 4.
    1930. Early records of the mute swan in Norfolk. British Birds, vol. 23, No. 11.
    1934. Letter to editors. British Birds, vol. 27, No. 9.
    1957. The mute-swan in England: its history and the ancient custom of swan-keeping. Cleaver-Hume Press Ltd., London, 136 pp.

Watson, W. Verde.
 1949. Trumpeter swan kills muskrat. Yellowstone Nature Notes, vol. 23, No. 5.
Watterson, W. H.
 1935. Notes on the nesting of captive mute swans.˙ The Wilson Bulletin, vol. 47, No. 3.
Weiser, C. S.
 1933. Flying with a flock of swans. Auk, vol. 50, No. 1.
Wetmore, Alexander.
 1931. The avifauna of the Pleistocene in Florida. Publication 3115, Smithsonian Institution.
 1935. A record of the trumpeter swan from the Late Pleistocene of Illinois. The Wilson Bulletin, vol. 47. No. 3.
 1951. Observations on the genera of the swans. Journal˙of the Washington Academy of Sciences, vol. 41, No. 10.
 1956. A check-list of the fossil and prehistoric birds of North America and the West Indies. Publication 4228, Smithsonian Institution.
Widmann, Otto.
 1907. A preliminary catalog of the birds of Missouri. St. Louis. 288 pp.
Wilke, Ford.
 1944. Auk, vol. 61, No. 655.
Witherby, H. F., F. C. R. Jourdain, Norman F. Ticehurst, and Bernard W. Tucker.
 1939. The handbook of British birds, vol. 3. H. F. and G. Witherby, London. 387 pp.
Wood, J. C.
 1908. Bird notes from southeastern Michigan. Auk, vol. 25, No. 3.
Wood, Norman A.
 1923. A preliminary survey of the bird life of North Dakota. University of Michigan Museum of Zoology. Miscellaneous Publication No. 10.
Wright, George M., and Ben H. Thompson.
 1935. Fauna of the National Parks of the United States; wildlife management in the National Parks. U. S. National Park Service, Fauna Series No. 2.
Yocom, C. F.
 1951. Waterfowl and their food plants in Washington. University of Washington Press. 272 pp.

Appendix 1. Excerpt from "Observations on the genera of the swans"

By Alexander Wetmore, Smithsonian Institution. From Journal of the Washington Academy of Sciences, vol. 41, No. 10, October 15, 1951.

Externally the species of white swans are so similar that the student of study skins has difficulty in separating them. The comparative anatomist, . . . working with skeletons, has no trouble whatever in dividing them into two principal groups on characters so evident that they cannot be disregarded. The differences are most apparent in the form of the trachea, sternum, and furculum. Following is a summary of these anatomical characters, with indication of the allocation of the species of the Northern Hemisphere and South America:

a. Trachea passing directly into thorax, not entering sternum; furculum simple; tail cuneate_____genus *Cygnus*
   Cygnus Bechstein, Orn. Taschenb., pt. 2, 1803:404.   Type, by monotypy, *Anas olor* Gmelin.
   Sthenelus Stejneger, Proc. U. S. Nat. Mus. 5:184, 185.   Aug. 5, 1882. Type, by monotypy, *Anas melancoripha* Molina.   (Not *Sthenelus* Marschall, 1873, emendation for *Sthelenus* Buquet, 1860, for a genus of Coleoptera.)
   Sthenelides Stejneger, Auk 1 (3):235.   July 1884.   Type, by monotypy, *Anas melancorphia* Molina.   New name for *Sthenelus* Stejneger (preoccupied).
   Euolor Mathews and Iredale, Austr. Avian Rec. 3 (5):117.   Dec. 28, 1917.   Type, by original designation, *Anas olor* Gmelin.
   Species included:
   Cygnus olor (Gmelin) (skeleton examined).
   Cygnus melancoriphus (Molina) (skeleton examined).
aa. Trachea making a loop that enters the sternum; furculum especially modified at symphysis to accommodate this loop; tail rounded_____genus *Olor*
   Olor Wagler, Isis, 1832:1234.   Type, by subsequent designation, *Cygnus musicus* Bechstein = *Anas cygnus* Linnaeus (Gray, 1840).
   Clangocycnus Oberholser, Emu 8 (pt. 1); 3.   July 1, 1908.   Type, by monotypy, *Cygnus buccinator* Richardson.
   b. Trachea entering anterior end of sternum smoothly, without a dorsal loop.
   subgenus *Olor*.
   Species included:
   Olor columbianus (Ord) (skeleton examined).
   Olor cygnus (Linnaeus) (skeleton examined).
   Olor bewickii Yarrell.
bb. Trachea making a dorsal loop as it enters sternum, protected by a bony case that projects into the anterior end of the body cavity
   subgenus *Clangocycnus*
   Species included:
   Olor buccinator (Richardson) (skeleton examined).
   The shape of the furculum and the looping of the trachea in the sternal keel are developed in the growing young, the loop lengthening and expanding to the end of the sternum as the individual becomes fully adult.   This change with age has led to misunderstanding of the characters by some not familiar with it.
   The arrangement of the genera above, it may be noted, is identical with that of Stejneger in his *Outlines of a monograph of the Cygninae*, published in 1882.

Appendix 2.—Status and Distribution of Trumpeter Swans in the United States, 1954

[Census, August 19–September 3]

Location	Groups [1]	Adult-cygnet ratio	Total swans
MONTANA			
Red Rock Lakes Refuge: [2]			
Lower Red Rock Lake_____	2–1, 2–0, 2–0, 2–0 2–0, 2–0, 2–0, 2–2.	16:3	19
Red Rock River, marsh and potholes__	2–0, 2–3, 2–0, 2–0, 2–0, 2–0, 2–1, 2–0, 2–0, 2–0, 1–0, 2–0, 2–0, 2–0, 2–4, 2–0, 2–0, 2–3, 2–0, 2–0, 2–0, 2–0, 2–0, 2–2, 2–0, 2–0, 2–3, 2–0, 2–0.	57:16	73
Upper Red Rock Lake and East Marsh.[3]	2–3, 2–0, 2–0, 199–0, 55–0.	260:3	263
Swan Lake and adjacent marsh potholes.	2–0, 2–3, 2–3, 2–0, 2–0, 2–0, 2–0, 2–0, 2–0.	18:6	24
Culver Pond_____	1–0_____	1:0	1
Total_____	_____	352:28	380
Centennial Valley (outside Refuge):			
Red Rock River, except Blake Slough_	1–0, 11–0_____	12:0	12
Blake Slough_____	2–8, 2–0_____	4:8	12
Jones Reservoirs_____	2–0_____	2:0	2
Passmore potholes_____	6–0_____	6:0	6
Stibal pothole_____	18–0_____	18:0	18
Lima Reservoir_____	7–0_____	7:0	7
Total_____	_____	49:8	57
Beaverhead National Forest:			
Elk Lake_____	2–2_____	2:2	4
Gallatin National Forest:			
Hebgen Reservoir_____	2–0, 2–1_____	4:1	5
Aldrich Lake_____	1–0_____	1:0	1
Total_____	_____	7:3	10
All other areas:			
Ennis Lake_____	2–0_____	2:0	2
Conklin Reservoir (Antelope Valley)__	2–1_____	2:1	3
Total_____	_____	4:1	5
Grand total (Montana)_____	_____	412:40	452
IDAHO			
Targhee National Forest:			
Beaver Lake_____	2–0_____	2:0	2
Pond, 1 mi. northwest of Steele Lake__	2–0_____	2:0	2
Steele Lake (Idaho and Wyoming)____	2–0_____	2:0	2
Pond, ½ mi. northeast of Goose Lake__	1–0_____	1:0	2
Goose Lake_____	2–0_____	2:0	1
"The Hole"_____	2–0_____	2:0	2
Total_____	_____	11:0	11

See footnotes at end of table.

Location	Groups[1]	Adult-cygnet ratio	Total swans
Island Park Area:			
Henrys Lake	2–0, 2–2	4:2	6
Island Park Reservoir	2–0	2:0	2
Gold Lake	2–4	2:4	6
Silver Lake	2–1, 6–0, 2–0, 9–0	19:1	20
Total		27:7	34
Grand total (Idaho)		38:7	45
WYOMING			
Yellowstone Park:			
Pond, south of Bunsen Peak	2–0	2:0	2
Geode Lake	2–4	2:4	6
Trumpeter Lake	3–2	3:2	5
Fern Lake	6–0	6:0	6
Tern Lake	2–1	2:1	3
White Lake outlet	2–0	2:0	2
Solfatara Lake	1–0	1:0	1
Grebe Lake	2–0	2:0	2
Madison Junction Lake	2–4	2:4	6
Mouth of Alum Creek	2–0	2:0	2
Mouth of Pelican Creek	1–0	1:0	1
Beach Springs	2–0	2:0	2
Mouth of Trail Creek	2–0	2:0	2
Upper Yellowstone River	2–0	2:0	2
Mouth of Chipmunk Creek	2–0	2:0	2
Yellowstone Lake near Delusion Lake	2–0	2:0	2
Delusion Lake	2–0	2:0	2
Ponds between Delusion Lake and Flat Mountain Arm.	4–0	4:0	4
Riddle Lake	2–3	2:3	5
Shoshone Lake	2–0	2:0	2
Heart Lake	2–0	2:0	2
Pond, 1 mi. west of Beula Lake	2–0	2:0	2
Pond, 2 mi. west of Boundary Creek patrol cabin.	1–0	1:0	1
Pond, 2 mi. north of Bechler River Ranger Station.	4–3	4:3	7
Robinson Lake	2–6	2:6	8
Lilypad Lake	3–0	3:0	3
Phone Line Lake	2–0	2:0	2
Pond, south of mouth of Mountain Ash Creek.	3–0	3:0	3
Total		64:23	87
Grand Teton National Park:			
Pond, 3 mi. northwest of Moran	2–4	2:4	6
Emma Matilda Lake	2–0	2:0	2
Two Ocean Lake	4–0	4:0	4
Total		8:4	12
Grand Total (National Parks)		72:27	99
National Elk Refuge	2–0, 2–3, 2–0, 4–0	10:3	13
Teton National Forest:			
Bridger Lake	2–0	2:0	2
Snake River	2–0	2:0	2
Total		4:0	4

See footnotes at end of table.

Location	Groups [1]	Adult-cygnet ratio	Total swans
Targhee National Forest:			
Pond, 3 mi. west of Fish Lake	2–0	2:0	2
Pond, 4 mi. west of Fish Lake	1–0	1:0	1
Pond, 1 mi. southwest of Winegar Lake.	3–0	3:0	3
Loon Lake	2–0	2:0	2
Indian Lake	2–2	2:2	4
Reservoir 1 mi. southwest of Indian Lake.	2–0	2:0	2
Total		16:2	18
Grand total (Wyoming)		98:32	130
NEVADA			
Ruby Lake Refuge [4]	7–0	7:0	7
OREGON			
Malheur Refuge [4]	5–3	5:3	8
Total for all areas		560:82	642

[1] First number in combination denotes adults, second cygnets.
[2] Does not include 21 swans (13 adults and 8 cygnets) transferred to Malheur and Ruby Lake Refuges earlier in the year.
[3] East marsh includes only those potholes draining into the Upper Lake.
[4] Transplanted swans.

Appendix 3.—Measurements of Trumpeter Swan Eggs

The following measurements of the eggs of trumpeter swans were recorded in 1955 on Red Rock Lakes marshes from a random sample of 21 nests which contained normal clutches. Measurements were made accurately to the nearest half-millimeter at the points of greatest length and girth. These measurements are believed to be representative of this species in its United States breeding habitat.

	Length	Width		Length	Width
	Mm.	Mm.		Mm.	Mm.
Clutch No. 1:			Clutch No. 3:		
Egg 1	116	72.5	Egg 1	119.5	75
Egg 2	111.5	69.5	Egg 2	118.5	74
Egg 3	118	75	Egg 3	118.5	74.5
Egg 4	119	74	Egg 4	121	76
Egg 5	117.5	74	Egg 5	123	74
Clutch No. 2:			Clutch No. 4:		
Egg 1	106	70.5	Egg 1	112	73.5
Egg 2	105.5	71	Egg 2	112.5	74
Egg 3	106	71	Egg 3	113	73
Egg 4	106	68	Egg 4	112	72.5
Egg 5	110	71	Egg 5	114.5	72.5
Egg 6	111.5	70			
Egg 7	109.5	70			
Egg 8	108	70			

	Length	Width		Length	Width
	Mm.	*Mm.*		*Mm.*	*Mm.*
Clutch No. 5:			Clutch No. 13:		
Egg 1	108.5	71	Egg 1	120	76
Egg 2	111	70.5	Egg 2	116.5	74
Egg 3	113.5	69	Egg 3	114	74
Egg 4	113	68	Egg 4	117	72
Egg 5	108	71	Clutch No. 14:		
Egg 6	111	71	Egg 1	113.5	76.5
Clutch No. 6:			Egg 2	113.5	75
Egg 1	109	71	Egg 3	111	74.5
Egg 2	109.5	73	Egg 4	108	74
Egg 3	110.5	72.5	Egg 5	109	77.5
Egg 4	107.5	72	Egg 6	110	74
Egg 5	108	71.5	Clutch No. 15:		
Clutch No. 7:			Egg 1	114.5	74.5
Egg 1	108	72	Egg 2	115.5	72
Egg 2	107	72	Egg 3	114	73
Egg 3	108	72	Egg 4	111.5	73
Egg 4	109	71.5	Egg 5	113.5	71.5
Egg 5	110	73	Egg 6	113	74
Clutch No. 8:			Clutch No. 16:		
Egg 1	112	72.5	Egg 1	116	73
Egg 2	105.5	71.5	Egg 2	121.5	73
Egg 3	109	72	Egg 3	114	74
Egg 4	106	71	Egg 4	117	74
Egg 5	110.5	72.5	Clutch No. 17:		
Egg 6	106.5	72	Egg 1	109	71
Clutch No. 9:			Egg 2	107.5	69.5
Egg 1	106	75	Egg 3	105.5	67.5
Egg 2	113	75	Egg 4	105.5	69
Egg 3	110	74	Egg 5	108.5	69.5
Egg 4	110	73	Egg 6	109	70.5
Egg 5	109	75	Clutch No. 18:		
Egg 6	109	75	Egg 1	110	71.5
Clutch No. 10:			Egg 2	111.5	72
Egg 1	118	76.5	Egg 3	106	72
Egg 2	117	75	Egg 4	112	72
Egg 3	114	75.5	Egg 5	108	73
Egg 4	117	74.5	Clutch No. 19:		
Egg 5	117	77	Egg 1	107	72
Clutch No. 11:			Egg 2	106.5	74
Egg 1	104.5	72	Egg 3	104.5	74
Egg 2	104	70.5	Egg 4	111.5	73
Egg 3	106	71	Clutch No. 20:		
Egg 4	107	71.5	Egg 1	109	72
Egg 5	108	72.5	Egg 2	108	72
Clutch No. 12:			Egg 3	104	70.5
Egg 1	104	69	Egg 4	109	71
Egg 2	106	72	Clutch No. 21:		
Egg 3	105	72	Egg 1	115	69
Egg 4	105	72	Egg 2	114	71
Egg 5	105	70.5	Egg 3	112	69
Egg 6	104	71			

Appendix 4.—Food Analysis

The following detailed data were obtained by stomach or scat analysis.

Stomach contents of predator-killed cygnet, estimated age 4 weeks, in Yellowstone Park, found and examined by Condon:

Freshwater fairy shrimp (*Eubranchipus* sp.)—three complete specimens plus several fragments

Carex sp.—shoot fragments

Chara sp.—small piece

Quartz sand grit—considerable quantity

Stomach contents of 6 cygnets, estimated ages 3–4 weeks, found dead, 5 on loafing ground and 1 at nesting site, at Red Rock Lakes Refuge (Montana) on July 12, 1951, by Banko (analysis by Charles C. Sperry, Section of Food Habits, U.S. Fish and Wildlife Service, March 19–20, 1952):

209941 **(RR 1)** female.

Percentage of animal matter—0; of vegetable—100; of gravel—40.

Contents: Leaf and stem fragments of aquatic plants—98 percent. Seeds: 34 *Carex* (plus fragments of a few more)—2 percent; 1 *Eleocharis*, 1 *Hippuris*, and 2 *Myriophyllum*—trace.

209942 (RR 2) sex (?):

Percentage of animal matter—trace; of vegetable—100; of gravel—25.

Contents: Leaf and stem fragments of aquatic plants—95 percent. Seeds: 126 *Carex* (and fragments of a few more)—5 percent; 5 *Eleocharis*, 1 *Galium*, and 2 *Myriophyllum*—trace.

209943 **(RR 3)** female, weight 449.5 gms.

Percentage of animal matter—0; of vegetable—100; of gravel—18.

Contents: Leaf and stem fragments of aquatic plants—80 percent. Seeds: 208 *Carex* (plus many fragments)—20 percent; 2 *Eleocharis*, 1 *Galium*, 2 *Hippuris*, 2 *Myriophyllum*, 2 *Potamogeton*, and 5 *Scirpus*—trace.

209944 (RR 4) male.

Percentage of animal matter—0; of vegetable—100; of gravel—75.

Contents: Leaf and stem fragments of aquatic plants—100 percent.

209945 **(RR 5)** male, weight 381 gms.

Percentage of animal matter—0; of vegetable—100; of gravel—20.

Contents: Leaf and stem fragments of aquatic plants—90 percent. Seeds: 86 *Carex* (and fragments of about as many more)—10 percent; 4 *Eleocharis*, 1 *Myriophyllum*, and 11 *Scirpus*—trace.

209946 (RR 6) sex (?), weight 447 gms.

Percentage of animal matter—0; of vegetable—100; of gravel—25.

Contents: Leaf and stem fragments of aquatic plants—90 percent. Seeds: 51 *Carex* (and fragments of about as many more)—10 percent; 2 *Eleocharis* and 1 *Scirpus*—trace.

Analysis of 17 samples of droppings from Grebe Lake, Yellowstone Park. Collected September 2, 1943, by O. J. Murie:

Algae—About ⅓ of the droppings are hard or very hard and these almost invariably consist largely of filamentous green algae intermingled with much fine quartz grit.

Carex—Four of the 17 envelopes contained droppings that consisted largely of remains of *Carex* spikes (the perigynia, achenes, scales and rachis).

Potamogeton—Seeds of a *Potamogeton* resembling *P. pusillus* were found in one sample. It is suspected that the unidentified herbaceous vegetation found in 6 samples (of the 17) may be largely *Potamogeton*.

Nuphar polysepala—In a sample consisting largely of *Carex* but also containing considerable algae, fragments of the seed wall of *Nuphar polysepala* were present to the extent of 10–20 percent of the whole.

Sagittaria—Shredded tissues in one sample are suggestive of *Sagittaria* but definite identification could not be made.

State of plant material—Most, possibly all, of the plant material seems to have been in a living state when eaten though in some cases the color of the substance does not seem to support this.

Insect—Animal material was almost negligible in the dropping samples. However, in the one sample containing seed fragments of *Nuphar* together with *Carex*, there were numerous specimens of caddis fly larvae (*Trichoptera*) totaling possibly 5 percent of the whole.

Report on the examination of 2 stomachs collected on the Red Rock Lakes Refuge, Montana, by A. V. Hull.   Analysis by Sperry :

206172, female, killed by flying into a fence.   December (early) 1938.

Stomach—full ; gullet—full.

Percentage of animal matter—trace ; vegetable—100 ; sand and gravel, etc.—10.

Contents: *Potamogeton pectinatus*, 443 tubers (largest being ½ x ⅞ inch) and fragments of rootstock—100 percent ; 1 caddis larvae case—trace ; fragments of 2 gastropods—trace, and possibly taken as "gravel", which was 70 percent fine sand.   Weight of food : gullet—4 oz. ; gizzard—3½ oz.   Weight of gravel : 2 oz. (in gizzard).

206190, sex (?).   June 10, 1939.

Stomach—full ; gullet—full.

Percentage of animal matter—trace ; vegetable—100 ; of sand and gravel, etc.—15.

Contents : *Potamogeton pectinatus*, 597 tubers (largest being ¾ x ⅝ x ½ inch), rootstock fragments and parts of leafy plant—96 percent (leafy part about 6) ; other leaf and stem material : *Ranunculus aquatilis*—3 percent ; *Ceratophyllum*—trace ; also algae (fine stringy type)—1 percent.   Seeds : 29 *Carex*, 1 *Hippuris vulgaris*, 3 *Scripus acutus*, 84 *Potamogeton*, 1 *Sparganium*, and 1 *Zannichellia*—trace ; 2 caddis larvae cases—trace.   Notes on weights : food (wet)—11½ oz. ; sand and gravel—2 oz. ; stomach and gullet tissue (wet)—6 oz.

Stomach examinations of trumpeters found at Picnic Springs, Red Rock Lakes Refuge, Montana, by A. V. Hull.   Report by E. R. Kalmbach, in charge, Denver Laboratory, U.S. Fish and Wildlife Service :

212892, adult.   Examined by F. M. Uhler, April 2–7, 1937.

Percentage of animal matter—0 : vegetable—100 percent ; 3 lead shot, gravel, etc.—30 percent.

Contents : leaves and stems of white water buttercup (*Ranunculus* sp.—probably *R. trichophyllus*)—70 percent ; aquatic mosses (*Amblystegium* sp.—30 percent and *Fissidens* sp.—trace).

212893, juvenile.   Examined by C. Cottam, April 2–7, 1937.

Percentage of animal matter—0 ; vegetable—100 percent ; 17 lead shot, gravel, etc.

Contents : 1 seed of *Potamogeton perfoliatus* ; moss plant fiber ; undetermined plant fiber.   (The stomach was too nearly empty to give percentages.)

212894, juvenile.   Examined by C. Cottam, April 2–7, 1937.

Percentage of animal matter—1 percent ; vegetable—99 percent ; 11 lead shot, tooth of *Thomomys* sp., gravel, etc.—33 percent.

Contents : plant fiber of white water buttercup, *Ranunculus* (*Batrachium*), probably *trichophyllus*—63 percent ; moss, *Fissidens*, probably *grandifrons*—30 percent ; moss, *Calliergon* sp.—3 percent ; moss, *Amblystegium* sp.—1 percent ; buds and leaves of *Potamogeton panormitanus*—1 percent ; 3 seeds of *Potamogeton perfoliatus*—tr. ; 7 seeds (2 species of *Carex* sp.—tr. ; undetermined plant fiber—1 percent ; 3 larvae of caddis fly of 3 species, one of which appeared to be a *Hydropsychidae*—1 percent ; fragments of larvae of *Dytiscidae*—tr. mollusk shell fragment—tr.   (Feather fragments—2 percent).

On the basis of the material available I should say that each bird had succumbed to lead poisoning.   The stomach of the adult male contained three pellets of lead, weighing 0.248 gram. The juvenile female had eleven pellets of lead, weighing 0.498 gram, and the juvenile male, seventeen pellets, weighing 0.857 gram.

In each instance there was a pronounced greenish discoloration of the contents, and a hardening of the gizzard pads.

Appendix 5.—Supplementary Data, Annual Swan Census

Period	Coverage; Agency	Remarks	References
Fall 1929	Yellowstone Park (NPS)	Survey only, complete census not attempted; 1 nesting pair located (Trumpeter Lake).	Joseph Lixon, 1931: 452. Wright and Thompson, 1935: 104.
Summer 1930	Yellowstone Park, Jackson Lake Swamp (NPS).	Survey expanded; 1 nesting pair—Trumpeter Lake, Tern Lake, Jackson Lake swamps.	Wright and Thompson, 1935: 104. E. L. Arnold, ltr., August 1930.
Summer 1931	Expanded coverage in Yellowstone Park (NPS).	Initial complete census attempted: nesting pairs —Yellowstone Park (4), Jackson Lake swamps (1).	G. W. Wright, ltr., May 2, 1934. G. W. Wright, ltr., May 2, 1934.
Summer 1932	Further expanded coverage in Yellowstone Park, also including Red Rock Lakes area (NPS).	Nesting pairs—Yellowstone Park (4) Red Rock Lakes (5), Hebgen Reservoir (1).	Do.
Summer 1933	Coverage similar to 1932 (NPS).	Nesting pairs—Yellowstone Park (3), Red Rock Lakes (7) (aerial census recommended for 1934).	Do.
Summer 1934	_____do_____	Nesting pairs—Yellowstone Park (6), Red Rock Lakes (7), Henrys Lake (3), Rock Lake, Wyo. (1).	F. W. Childs, ltr., Oct. 20, 1934.
Summer 1935	_____do_____	Detailed data missing_____	Unsigned report (NPS files).
Summer 1936	Yellowstone Park plus adjacent areas (NPS). R.R.L. Refuge and adjacent areas (FWS).	Bridger Lake and Squirrel Meadows included. Henrys Lake, Elk Lake, Blake Slough included.	E. B. Rogers, ltr., Aug. 19, 1936. A.V. Hull, ltr., July 28, 1936.
Summer 1937	Coverage similar to 1936 (NPS and FWS).	Coverage probably not quite as complete as 1936.	E. B. Rogers, ltr., July 24, 1937. A. V. Hull, ltr., Aug. 5, 1937.
Aug. 4–7, 1938	_____do_____	Winegar area adjacent Yellowstone Park included; both Park and Refuge counts conducted Aug. 4–7.	E. B. Rogers, ltr., Aug. 15, 1938. A. V. Hull, ltr., Sept. 8, 1938.
Aug. 15–16, 1939	Coverage similar to 1938 (NPS and FWS).	Coverage probably equal to or slightly greater than in 1938.	E. B. Rogers, ltr., Aug. 23, 1939. A. V. Hull, ltr., Aug. 19, 1939.
Aug. 16–17, 1940	Yellowstone Park only partially covered (NPS). Refuge census expanded to include many contiguous areas (FWS).	Park areas missed in 1940 held 10 swans in 1939. Malheur and Elk Refuges included for first time.	E. B. Rogers, ltr., Sept. 24, 1940. A. V. Hull, ltr., Oct. 31, 1940.
Aug. 15–16, 1941	Yellowstone Park only covered (NPS). FWS coverage expanded.	Areas adjacent Yellowstone Park not included. Ennis and Elk Lakes included.	E. B. Rogers, ltr., Aug. 19, 1941. A.V. Hull, ltr., Aug. 20, 1941.
Aug. 20–22, 1942	No census in Yellowstone Park. FWS coverage same as 1941.	No census personnel for park due to World War II and bad fire season.	E. B. Rogers, ltr., Aug. 18, 1942. A. V. Hull, ltr., Sept. 11, 1942.
Aug. 26–28, 1943	No census in Yellowstone Park. FWS coverage similar to 1942.	No census personnel for park—World War II.	E. B. Rogers, ltr., Oct. 8, 1943. W. M. Sharp, ltr., Sept. 2, 1943.
Aug. 12–18, 1944	Yellowstone Park and adjacent areas (NPS). R.R.L. Refuge and adjacent areas (FWS).	Including Indian, Loon, Puddle, Chain Lakes. Sheridan Reservoir, Wade, and Conklin Lakes.	E. B. Rogers, ltr., Sept. 1, 1944. W. M. Sharp, undated ltr., 1944.

Appendix 5.—Supplementary Data, Annual Swan Census—Con.

Period	Coverage; Agency	Remarks	References
Aug. 16–31, 1945_____	No census in Yellowstone Park (NPS). R.R.L. Refuge and adjacent areas (FWS).	No census personnel World War II. Coverage similar to 1944___	E. B. Rogers, ltr., Aug. 13, 1945. Refuge Narrative Report, May–August 1945. MacDonald, ltr., Oct. 1, 1945.
Aug. 11–17, 1946_____	Yellowstone Park, greatest coverage to date (NPS). R.R.L. Refuge and adjacent areas (FWS).	Ground count swans on 21 of 68 lakes checked. Aerial coverage for 1st time.	E. B. Rogers, ltr., Aug. 27, 1946. Refuge Narrative Report, May–August 1946. W. M. Sharp, undated report, 1946.
Aug. 10–16, 1947_____	Yellowstone Park, coverage similar to 1946 (NPS). Refuge and adjacent area coverage similar to 1946 (FWS).	Ground and aerial counts in park. Aerial counts in refuge and vicinity.	E. B. Rogers, ltr., Sept. 10, 1947. Refuge Narrative Report, May–August 1947. W. N. Anderson, ltr., Sept. 19, 1947.
Aug. 16–20, 1948_____	Yellowstone Park and adjacent areas (NPS). FWS coverage of refuge and adjacent areas similar to 1947.	Park, refuge, and adjacent areas covered aerially; similar to 1947, Ruby Lake Refuge included.	E. B. Rogers, ltrs., Aug. 24 and Sept. 1, 1948. W. N. Anderson, ltr., Sept. 22, 1948.
Aug. 3–5, 1949_ ____	Coverage similar to 1948 (NPS and FWS).	Aerial counts all areas; Railroad Ranch area added.	E. B. Rogers, ltr., Aug. 9, 1949. Refuge Narrative Report, May–August 1949.
Aug. 1–4, 1950_____	Coverage similar to 1949 (NPS and FWS).	Aerial counts, all areas____	E. B. Rogers, ltr., Aug. 11, 1950. Refuge Narrative Report, May–August 1950.
July 31–Aug. 3, 1951_	Coverage comparable to 1950 (NPS and FWS).	_____do_____	E. B. Rogers, ltr., Aug. 6, 1951. Refuge Narrative Report, May–August 1951.
July 16–21, 1952_____	Aerial coverage, similar to 1951 (NPS and FWS).	Bridger Lake and waters north of Moran, Wyo., added.	E. B. Rogers, ltrs., July 22, 1952. Refuge Narrative Report, May–August 1952.
Aug. 3–6, 1953_____	Aerial coverage, similar to 1952 (NPS and FWS).	Upper Jackson Hole areas included for first time.	NPS Circular 12, Aug. 14, 1953. Refuge Narrative Report, May–August 1953.
Aug. 31–Sept. 3, 1954_	Aerial coverage, similar to 1953 (NPS and FWS).	Teton National Park ˝ added.	NPS Circular 7, Sept. 8, 1954. Refuge Narrative Report, May–August 1954.
Aug. 29–31, 1955_____	Aerial coverage, similar to 1954 (NPS and FWS).	Does not include 6 swans transferred from Red Rock Lakes to Delta, Manitoba, before census.	NPS Circular 11, Sept. 8, 1955. Refuge Narrative Report, May–August 1955.
Aug. 27–31, 1956_____	Aerial coverage, similar to 1955 (NPS and FWS).	Same NPS and FWS observers conducted census 1950–1956.	NPS Circular 15, Sept. 7, 1956. Refuge Narrative Report, May–August 1956.
Aug. 20–23, 1957_____	Aerial coverage, similar to 1956 (NPS and FWS).	Pair-family-group status tabulated for 3d year.	NPS Circular 15, Aug. 21, 1957. Refuge Narrative Report, May–August 1957.

INDEX